Ready
for the Classroom?

Preparing Reading Teachers
With Authentic Assessments

Mary A. Avalos • Ana Maria Pazos-Rego
Peggy D. Cuevas • Susan R. Massey • Jeanne Shay Schumm

INTERNATIONAL
Reading Association
800 BARKSDALE ROAD, PO BOX 8139
NEWARK, DE 19714-8139, USA
www.reading.org

Executive Editor, Books   Corinne M. Mooney
Developmental Editor   Charlene M. Nichols
Developmental Editor   Tori Mello Bachman
Developmental Editor   Stacey L. Reid
Editorial Production Manager   Shannon T. Fortner
Design and Composition Manager   Anette Schuetz

Project Editors   Charlene M. Nichols and Christina Lambert

Cover   Design, Linda Steere; Photographs, Shutterstock.com

Library of Congress Cataloging-in-Publication Data

Ready for the classroom? : preparing reading teachers with authentic assessments / by Mary A. Avalos ... [et al.].
     p. cm.
 Includes bibliographical references and index.
 ISBN 978-0-87207-468-2
 1. Reading (Elementary)--Evaluation. 2. Education--Standards. I. Avalos, Mary A., 1964- II. International Reading Association.
 LB1573.R296 2008
 378.48--dc22

2008038385

In loving memory of Bobby Avalos, whose courage inspires us
and reminds us of what is truly important in life.
Heaven gained, but we lost an angel.

CONTENTS

ABOUT THE AUTHORS

 **Mary A. Avalos, PhD**, is an assistant research professor at the University of Miami in Coral Gables, Florida, USA. Her research interests involve teacher education, language and literacy learning, and professional development for practicing teachers. Publications of note include *Modified Guided Reading: Gateway to English as a Second Language and Literacy Learning* and "No Two Learners Are Alike: Readers With Linguistic and Cultural Differences" in *Reading Assessment and Instruction for All Learners: A Comprehensive Guide for Classroom and Resource Settings*. She can be reached at mavalos@miami.edu.

 **Ana Maria Pazos-Rego, PhD**, is an assistant professor at St. Thomas University, Miami, Florida. Her primary area of study is learning disabilities and reading with an emphasis on English-language learners. She has designed and directed a model family literacy clinic, which serves as a practicum for graduate and undergraduate students in reading and exceptional student education. She can be reached at apazos@stu.edu.

 **Peggy D. Cuevas, PhD**, is a former visiting assistant professor at the University of Miami. Her research focuses on language and literacy issues that affect the learning and assessment of mathematics in grades K–12. Peggy has published in journals such as the *Journal for Research in Science Education* and the *Journal of Reading Education*. Her most recent work includes a text on the integration of literacy strategies in the secondary mathematics classroom. Peggy presently teaches mathematics in the Hays County Independent School District in Kyle, Texas, USA. She can be reached at peggyd@gate.net.

Susan R. Massey, PhD, is a research associate at the University of Miami. She recently completed her doctorate in the field of learning disabilities and reading at the University of Miami. Susan has worked as a research assistant on an Institute of Educational Sciences grant for the evaluation of curricular interventions for bilingual students. Her research interests include fluency and reading processes. Susan can be reached at smassey@miami.edu.

Jeanne Shay Schumm, PhD, is a professor of reading at the University of Miami, where she teaches courses in reading and in inclusion of students with exceptionalities in the general education classroom. She serves as professor in residence at Henry S. West Laboratory School. Her research interests include teacher education and differentiated instruction in elementary classrooms. She can be reached at schumm4841@aol.com.

ACKNOWLEDGMENTS

The authors are deeply indebted to Charlene Nichols and the books and editorial production staff at the International Reading Association. Their patience and help were invaluable. We also acknowledge our students for their contributions to our work and continued learning. Finally, we thank our families for their support throughout this lengthy publishing process—from prospectus to finished product!

INTRODUCTION

Many institutions of higher education (IHEs) face the challenge of meeting state and national teacher performance standards in a manner that demonstrates applied professional growth on the part of their students (hereafter referred to as *candidates*) and increased reading achievement among the K–12 students they are (or will soon be) charged to teach (Blackwell & Diez, 1998; Diez & Blackwell, 2001; Elliott, 2003). Since September 2001 when the National Council for Accreditation of Teacher Education (NCATE) shifted the emphasis of accreditation criteria from what the IHEs offer to what the candidates learn and are able to do, the burden of proof has rested on the IHEs to demonstrate that their candidates have the knowledge and skills necessary to teach effectively, the dispositions to teach, and the ability to apply these qualities so that all students learn (Elliott, 2003). Other accrediting organizations (e.g., the Teacher Education Accreditation Council [TEAC] and regional or state offices of education) follow similar criteria, requiring evidence of successful candidate performance before granting accreditation or program approval to institutions under review.

Additionally, NCATE calls for assessments of these teacher qualities to be aligned with state and content standards, to contain multiple measures, and to evaluate a wide range of knowledge, skills, and dispositions. Unfortunately, assessment practice at the postsecondary level generally leaves much to be desired. IHEs have customarily evaluated candidates by measuring discrete learning outcomes and disintegrated learning skills using traditional or standardized testing models (Diez & Blackwell, 2001). Traditional assessment has required no experiential basis on the part of the learner for successful outcomes, and most questions have been those that have one "correct" answer (Liebars, 1999; Meadows, Dyal, & Wright, 1998; Tellez, 1996). According to McLaughlin and Vogt (1997), there are many problematic issues related to using traditional or standardized testing models for preschool–12th-grade (P–12) students:

> 1) They are based on an outdated model of literacy; 2) they frequently promote achievement, but exclude development; 3) they lack coordination with instructional goals and are easily misinterpreted and misused; 4) they prohibit the use of learning strategies; 5) they serve as poor predictors of individual performance; and 6) they categorize and label students. (p. 9)

These types of measures are also based on the assumption that all learners learn at the same pace and in the same way, although researchers of human development agree that this is not the case (Neill & Medina, 1989). The same limitations can be applied to assessment in higher education contexts, contributing to short-term learning (i.e., for testing purposes only) rather than promoting and monitoring growth and development over time.

Such inauthentic assessment of candidates does not provide a complete picture of their ability to perform as educators (Nicholson, 2000). Test preparation consists of memorizing facts and formulas that have little relation to the world of teaching. Because such tests often dictate the curriculum (Herman, 1997; Neill & Medina, 1989), candidates will learn for the test and not for the purpose of implementing the concepts. Additionally, traditional measures may also contain inherent biases, such as timed formats and insensitivity toward culturally and linguistically diverse groups (Neill & Medina, 1989).

Authentic assessment has been defined as immersing candidates in tasks that are grounded in instruction, personally meaningful, and provided within real-world contexts (McLaughlin & Kennedy, 1993). Moreover, authentic assessment allows the student to have a voice in how he or she will be assessed (McLaughlin & Vogt, 1997; Tellez, 1996). Portfolio assessment meets the criteria of authentic assessment and is increasingly cited as a feasible alternative to testing (Flood & Lapp, 1989; Heibert & Calfee, 1989; Jongsma, 1989; Katz, 1988; Shepard, 1989; Valencia, 1990; Wiggins, 1989; Wolf, 1989). There are those, however, who view the use of teaching portfolios with uncertainty (Fallon & Watts, 2001). Inconsistency exists in the way portfolios are defined, how they are implemented (Sparapani, Abel, Edwards, Herbster, & Easton, 1997), and the extent of their perceived benefit (Barton & Collins, 1993; McLaughlin & Vogt, 1997). Additionally, there has been a call for more consistency in the grading of portfolios through a clearer framework and specific guidelines (Klenowski, 2000) to address questions of validity (Maclellan, 2004) and reliability (Baume, Yorke, & Coffey, 2004).

In sum, with regard to assessment, traditional pen and paper tests create an unrealistic teaching scenario, misrepresenting the integration of multiple skills and knowledge (Darling-Hammond & Snyder, 2000). Even though it is true that preparing teacher candidates for classrooms involves more than testing, many (if not most) teacher educators require exams of some sort to pass their classes. "The experience of taking a written test is quite different from that of teaching a class, preparing a lesson, or most other aspects of the teacher's craft" (Shulman, 1988, p. 38); therefore, the use of portfolios as a means of authentic assessment and evaluation has become increasingly popular and common in teacher education programs (Tellez, 1996). Portfolios in IHEs allow teacher educators to "practice what they preach" concerning authentic assessment; however, there are still areas of concern within the literature, such as standardization or guidelines and extent of actual benefits for candidates. More work needs to be done in making authentic assessment a viable approach to measuring candidates' knowledge and application of skills. Using Wiggins's (1998) framework for educative assessment, this book highlights one component of a comprehensive portfolio assessment system (Avalos, Pazos-Rego, Cuevas, & Massey, 2006) to assess candidates' knowledge of professional teaching standards in reading and intends to provide possible solutions to issues of reliability and validity in using portfolios in teacher preparation.

Theoretical Framework

According to Wiggins (1998), educative assessment is "anchored in authentic tasks" and "provides feedback and opportunities" to revise and improve performance on these tasks (p. xi). It should not only measure performance but also be designed to teach and provide input that will, if necessary, steer the candidate in the right direction. In other words, educative assessment should improve performance. Wiggins outlines key elements that form the characteristics of this approach to assessment:

1. Student and teacher's performances should be improved by using an educative assessment system to evoke exemplary pedagogy. What we ask candidates to do should be realistic, credible, engaging, and built on meaning-based tasks. The system should also:

   a. Be open—the tasks, criteria, and standards should be known to teachers instead of obscure or too broad;

   b. Model exemplary instruction to encourage rather than undermine desirable teaching practice;

   c. Use grades that are clear, stable, valid, and linked to state or national standards;

   d. Student performance should improve measurably over time so that standards once thought to be out of reach are reachable by all.

2. Useful feedback must be provided to students, teachers, administrators, and policymakers that includes

   a. Data and commentary that do not center on blame or praise; rather, feedback should enable candidates to accurately self-assess and self-correct their performance over time;

   b. Many opportunities for timely and ongoing feedback should be given, implying a longitudinal assessment system that frequently alerts all involved to exit-level standards, thus permitting intervention, when needed, before it is too late. (pp. 14–15)

This learning-centered approach to assessment is not always uncommon among teacher educators; however, what is unusual is a comprehensive system of assessment over time that provides reliable and valid measures from one assessment to the next or from one instructor to the next. As educators, we believe that case studies fit Wiggins's assessment criteria when used with high-quality, standards-based rubrics and, along with other data (e.g., course assignments, contributions to the field), provide a discrete window of what candidates are learning and internalizing throughout their reading courses. This approach to assessment not only allows for effective candidate demonstrations of how well the standards are understood, it also provides feedback to instructors about their teaching, enabling improvement of instructor and candidate performance as well as entire reading education programs (Avalos et al., 2006).

Cases (i.e., hypothetical situations) and case methods (i.e., the approach used to instruct with cases, such as discussions) have been used for decades with success in many professions, including the education, human relations, medical, and agricultural fields (Andrews, 1953; Barrows & Tamblyn, 1980; Silverman & Welty, 1994; Stanford, Crookston, Davis, &

Simmons, 1992). More specifically, cases in education have had multiple purposes, including demonstrating exemplars of practice, providing opportunities to practice analysis, internalizing different perspectives and articulating action plans, and working as stimulants for personal reflection (Shulman, 1992). Case methods have also been used as a bridge between K–12 performance standards and classroom practice (Shulman, 2000). We propose that, with the proper rubrics and procedures to score written case responses, cases can and should also be seen as evaluation tools, allowing faculty to see not only how candidates apply what they did learn during their course work but also what they did not learn. In other words, cases supply hypothetical yet realistic situations, and candidates' responses to the cases offer a glimpse into the candidates' thinking and application processes—whether complete or not.

When using cases as evaluation tools, the rubrics for scoring responses become critically important in the overall assessment process. Rubrics have been known to be problematic because of subjectivity and vague language (Popham, 1997); therefore, strong, descriptive rubrics are essential to successfully using cases as assessment tools because language that is vague or unclear creates discrepancies, questioning validity and reliability. Clear, purposeful language and quantitative indicators assist both the assessors and those being assessed to define and uphold expectations.

Rubrics generally have three essential components: evaluative criteria, quality definitions, and a scoring strategy (Popham, 1997). The evaluative criteria denotes acceptable from unacceptable responses with either equal or differentiated weight given to the different criterion. This book focuses on rubrics that use the *Standards for Reading Professionals—Revised 2003* (International Reading Association [IRA], 2004) as its evaluative criteria (hereafter referred to as *Standards 2003*). Each of the elements that make up the standards was placed upon a continuum with quantitative indicators to foster a strong inter-rater reliability.

Quality definitions are descriptors that illustrate the qualitative differences in students' responses. Each qualitative level should have a separate description with different expectations clearly stated in order for the response to fall into one of the qualitative categories. The rubrics in this book use two different qualitative categories—one for the rationale provided for each response (i.e., Distinguished, Proficient, Sufficient, Novice, and Unacceptable) and the other for the content of the response, indicated by numbers 0 (lowest possible score) and up.

The scoring strategy used by these rubrics is both analytic and holistic. An analytic rubric requires the assessor to determine a score for each criterion. This is done for every element that the case response measures. For example, if a response is provided for Standard 2, Element 3 (2.3), the assessor analyzes the response against the element's criteria. A holistic scoring strategy takes all of the evaluative criteria into consideration for a single, overall quality judgment. When assessing a candidate's rationale for case study responses, a holistic scoring strategy is used because a single score is given, taking into consideration the overall rationale for each response.

The rubrics should be viewed as professional development tools for IHE faculty and candidates to grow and expand their understanding of the standards and authentic assessment at the postsecondary level. Popham (1997) posits that rubrics should assist instruction. Integrating the standards within the rubrics facilitates the use of standards during instruction as well as the use of authentic assessment when instruction is aligned with assessment.

This system should also be viewed as a valid tool for program evaluation because using rubrics allows for identification of limitations with regard to faculty knowledge or instructional gaps within reading programs. These identified gaps can be targeted for future faculty professional development. Case study responses, when scored using well-articulated rubrics with clear and purposeful language, can serve as decision-making tools for program evaluation. In using case responses to evaluate our programs, we have found that certain areas are weak across candidates' responses. For example, when asked to respond to cases addressing technology in reading instruction, few, if any, responses adequately addressed this area. Such a blatant lack of adequate responses speaks to the instruction and content of the reading courses within the reading education program itself. In our positions as teacher educators, although there were objectives within our courses that focused on technology in reading instruction, we determined technology to be an area of need with regard to faculty professional development after discussing possible reasons behind the lack of appropriate responses.

Purpose of This Book

The goals in writing this book include sharing what we have learned about case studies and rubrics as a means to do the following:

- Foster the use of higher level, critical-thinking skills among candidates as they go from theory to practice and practice to theory by providing rationales for each response or suggestion made—in other words, the candidates not only have to suggest what should be done for each case, they also have to state why their suggestion is feasible, grounding their response in theory, experience, or research

- Assess candidates' understandings and applications of material taught throughout their course work

- Assist IHEs in demonstrating how teaching and K–12 performance standards are met, going beyond term papers and fabricated unit or lesson plans to real-life applications

- Grow professionally as faculty and to better understand *Standards 2003*

In the next section, we provide an overview of how the rubrics were developed and how to use them as well as an outline of suggested procedures to follow in administering and scoring the cases. In the event there are candidates who do not make progress responding to the cases as expected, alternative activities are proposed as well as possible sources for literacy cases.

Standards-Based Rubrics: An Overview

Standards 2003 provides criteria for developing and evaluating practitioner reading programs by establishing guidelines as to what professionals should know and be able to do. Those who need to know and understand the standards include candidates at all levels: paraprofessionals, classroom teachers, reading specialists/literacy coaches, administrators, personnel of accrediting agencies and state departments of education, and IHE faculty or adjunct faculty. The focus of these standards is on candidates' performance with an emphasis on their knowledge and skills as they complete their teacher education curricula (IRA, 2004); therefore, a highly qualified reading professional must exhibit specified indicators at the appropriate level of expertise in order meet the standards. Different professional categories (i.e., paraprofessional, classroom teacher, reading specialist/literacy coach, and so forth) define the criteria for what is expected at each level. These categories build on each other. In other words, a teacher-educator candidate must meet the criteria defined for that category, plus the previous three category levels (paraprofessional, classroom teacher, and reading specialist/literacy coach).

The five core areas of *Standards 2003* pertaining to reading instruction are as follows:

1. Foundational Knowledge

2. Instructional Strategies and Curriculum Materials

3. Assessment, Diagnosis, and Evaluation

4. Creating a Literate Environment

5. Professional Development

Each standard consists of three to four elements that address aspects of the particular standard's area. Every element details understanding and proficiency related to the standard at varying levels of expertise (see Table 1).

Developing and Using the Standards-Based Rubrics

As explained earlier, this book focuses on standards-based rubrics as a means of educative assessment (Wiggins, 1998). Cases, or hypothetical situations mirroring classroom challenges and contexts, were administered to candidates in an IHE graduate reading education program. We developed the rubrics to assess case responses as one means of determining candidates' progress in meeting *Standards 2003* at the reading specialist level. For example, a portion of the rubric pertaining to Standard 2 is shown in Table 2 (see Appendix for complete rubric). The top portion of the rubric is used to score the rationale for each response (Novice to Distinguished), whereas the bottom portion is used to score content of responses according to the element being assessed (the higher the number, the higher the score). Within the rubric, each element has a different possible scale of scores; the scales differ with regard to the highest possible score because some elements have more quantifiable criteria than others. Standard 2, Element 2 (2.2) includes accounting for

TABLE 1. IRA's Standards for Reading Professionals

Standard 1: Candidates have knowledge of the foundations of reading and writing processes and instruction. As a result, candidates:

1.1 Demonstrate knowledge of psychological, sociological, and linguistic foundations of reading and writing processes and instruction.

1.2 Demonstrate knowledge of reading research and histories of reading.

1.3 Demonstrate knowledge of language development and reading acquisition and the variations related to cultural and linguistic diversity.

1.4 Demonstrate knowledge of the major components of reading (phonemic awareness, word identification and phonics, vocabulary and background knowledge, fluency, comprehension strategies, and motivation) and how they are integrated in fluent reading.

Standard 2: Candidates use a wide range of instructional practices, approaches, methods, and curriculum materials to support reading and writing instruction. As a result, candidates:

2.1 Use instructional grouping options (individual, small-group, whole-class, and computer-based) as appropriate for accomplishing given purposes.

2.2 Use a wide range of instructional practices, approaches, and methods, including technology-based practices, for learners at differing stages of development and from differing cultural and linguistic backgrounds.

2.3 Use a wide range of curriculum materials in effective reading instruction for learners at different stages of reading and writing development and from different cultural and linguistic backgrounds.

Standard 3: Candidates use a variety of assessment tools and practices to plan and evaluate effective reading instruction. As a result, candidates:

3.1 Use a wide range of assessment tools and practices that range from individual and group standardized tests to individuals and group informal classroom assessment strategies, including technology-based assessment tools.

3.2 Place students along a developmental continuum and identify students' proficiencies and difficulties.

3.3 Use assessment information to plan, evaluate, and revise effective instruction that meets the needs of all students, including those at different developmental stages and those from different cultural and linguistic backgrounds.

3.4 Communicate results of assessments to specific individuals (student, parents, caregivers, colleagues, administrators, policymakers, policy officials, community, etc.).

Standard 4: Candidates create a literate environment that fosters reading and writing by integrating foundational knowledge, use of instructional practices, approaches and methods, curriculum materials, and the appropriate use of assessments. As a result, candidates:

4.1 Use students' interests, reading abilities, and backgrounds as foundations for the reading and writing program.

4.2 Use a large supply of books, technology-based information, and nonprint materials representing multiple levels, broad interests, and cultural and linguistic backgrounds.

4.3 Model reading and writing enthusiastically as valued lifelong activities.

4.4 Motivate learners to be lifelong readers.

Standard 5: Candidates view professional development as a career-long effort and responsibility. As a result, candidates:

5.1 Display positive dispositions related to reading and the teaching of reading.

5.2 Continue to pursue the development of professional knowledge and dispositions.

5.3 Work with colleagues to observe, evaluate, and provide feedback on each other's practice.

5.4 Participate in, initiate, implement, and evaluate professional development programs.

TABLE 2. Standard 2 Rubric: Instructional Strategies and Curriculum Materials

Candidates use a wide range of instructional practices, approaches, methods, and curriculum materials to support reading and writing instruction. As a result, they:

Element	Distinguished	Proficient	Sufficient	Novice
Use this row to score rationale.	Rationale is expanded—Uses explicit, in-depth statements referring to case study information, as well as other sources (i.e., theory, research, experience, etc.) *throughout* the response. A deep conceptual understanding is evident.	Rationale is focused—Uses explicit statements referring to case study information and is clearly written. A good conceptual understanding is evident.	Rationale is adequate—Uses more specific statements referring to case study, but reader must infer at times while reading. An emergent conceptual understanding is evident.	Rationale is limited—Uses broad, general statements (i.e., "to improve reading…") or generic statements that could apply to almost any reader. There is little evidence of conceptual understanding.
2.1 Use instructional grouping options (individual, small-group, whole-class, and computer-based) as appropriate for accomplishing given purposes. **Use this row to score content.**	8 = Identifies four or more instructional grouping options appropriate for the purpose.	7 = Identifies three instructional grouping options appropriate for the purpose. 6 = Identifies two instructional grouping options appropriate for the purpose.	5= Identifies one valid instructional grouping option appropriate for the purpose. 4 = Identifies two or more valid instructional grouping options *along with* invalid options.	3 = Identifies one valid instructional grouping option *with* invalid grouping options. 2 = Identifies invalid grouping options only and includes other information that does not qualify as a grouping option (i.e., provides strategy suggestions). 1 = No instructional grouping suggestions identified. 0 = Response did not address standard element or question from case study.

Element	Distinguished	Proficient	Sufficient	Novice
2.2 Use a wide range of instructional practices, approaches, and methods, including technology-based practices for learners at differing stages of development and from differing cultural and linguistic backgrounds.	9 = Identifies three or more instructional practices, approaches, or methods addressing two or more of the element's variables, *along with* other valid instructional approaches that may or may not address these variables.	8 = Identifies two instructional practices, approaches, or methods addressing two of the element's variables, *along with* other valid instructional approaches that may or may not address these variables. 7 = Identifies one instructional practice, approach, or method addressing two of the element's variables, *along with* other valid instructional approaches that may or may not address these variables.	6 = Identifies three or more instructional practices, approaches, or methods addressing one of the element's variables, *along with* other valid instructional approaches that may or may not address these variables. 5 = Identifies two instructional practices, approaches, or methods addressing one of the element's variables, *along with* other valid instructional approaches that may or may not address these variables. 4 = Identifies one instructional practice, approach, or method addressing one of the element's variables, *along with* other valid instructional approaches that may or may not address these variables.	3 = Identifies one or more valid instructional practice, approach, or method, but does not address the bolded variables in this element. 2 = Identifies invalid or inappropriate instructional practices, approaches, or methods only and includes information that does not address instruction (i.e., provides generic grouping suggestion such as "cooperative learning" without instructional approach). 1 = Invalid or inappropriate instructional practices, approaches, or methods suggested. 0 = Response did not address standard element or question from case study.
Use this row to score content.				

use of technology, learners at differing levels of development, and cultural and linguistic differences when carrying out instruction, thus there are more possible criteria to meet when writing a case response to Element 2.2 as compared with Standard 4, Element 4 (4.4) that calls for teachers to motivate students to be lifelong readers. (Scoring will be discussed at greater length later in other chapters.) We also developed the rubrics to fill a need for an authentic yet standard means to assess candidates' mastery of reading standards. Evolving over three years, the rubrics were developed as we worked together to refine and establish inter-rater reliability. We administered approximately 10 cases covering multiple standards to our graduate candidates and scored all responses in groups of two. After scoring in our groups, we came together and articulated our scores, coming to consensus when we didn't have agreement and making any revisions needed to the rubrics.

Initially, the case responses were administered as "in-class" assessments, requiring individual candidates to write timed responses during class. During this time, we collected data to compare responses between and among cohorts so it was important that conditions for all candidates were equal. Most recently, however, the candidates have been able to complete the case responses online (using an Internet-based course management or portfolio system), during class, or at home—without time and other related pressures. To follow Wiggins's (1998) educative assessment principles, we felt the candidates needed to have fewer restrictions to bring about a more authentic assessment context. In reality, if challenged with a student or classroom situation, teachers would and should use resources (written or verbal) to overcome the issues facing them. In comparing the case responses using more restrictions (timed periods, no notes, texts, Internet, or collaboration) and fewer restrictions (more time allowed, notes, texts, Internet, and oral discussions with others in class), the responses elicited from the administrations with fewer restrictions were more comprehensive, and we feel more of a learning experience for the candidates. The next section includes procedures followed during both types of administrations. It is important to note that prior to administering the cases, two or three faculty who will score responses still meet to predetermine possible content they feel would indicate a quality response. This helps to establish inter-rater reliability and avoid a quantity-over-quality emphasis when using the rubrics.

Administering Cases

There is not one right way to administer cases. Each instructor or program director must decide the purpose, goals, and objectives for candidates in using cases. What is written here is an example of how the administration of cases has evolved over a period of three years to measure individual student growth over time and to compare responses holistically. To review responses systematically, a standardized administration process with greater restrictions should be in place. Outlined are procedures currently used that best fit the needs of our reading education program and other purposes (i.e., accreditation data, standards-based curricula). Possible sources for cases are provided in Table 3. We have used self-created cases in the past but found the cases from CaseNEX, an online database founded at University of Virginia's Curry School of Education, to be of high quality and to mirror

TABLE 3.　Possible Sources for Cases

CaseNEX (www.casenex.com)

> Founded at the University of Virginia's Curry School of Education, CaseNEX supports educators through an online, case-based approach. Multimedia cases, or "slices of life," form a realistic connection between professional learning and the complex school environment. The CaseNEX problem-solving model is engaging, collaborative, and effective. School district and university partners across the U.S. integrate the CaseNEX learning model and access the library of case studies to enhance, enliven, and extend their existing programs.

Falk-Ross, F.C. (2001). *Classroom-based language and literacy intervention: A programs and case studies approach.* Boston: Allyn & Bacon.

> Written from a sociocultural perspective, this text discusses the many roles of a reading specialist, from diagnostician to action researcher, and can be used as professional development to prepare those who must evaluate, coordinate, and implement reading/language arts programs.

Richards, J.C., & Gipe, J.P. (2000). *Elementary literacy lessons: Cases and commentaries from the field.* Mahwah, NJ: Erlbaum.

> Written with preservice teachers as the primary audience, this book supplies cases of literacy teaching and sample responses.

Rossi, J., & Schipper, B. (2003). *Case studies in preparation for the California reading competency test* (2nd ed.). Boston: Allyn & Bacon.

> Cases included in this book provide a wide overview of student profiles and grade levels, providing real-life scenarios of diverse literacy learning situations. Although written to prepare teachers for the California Reading Competency Test, the cases are appropriate for reading methods, diagnosis, and intervention courses.

Zarrillo, J. (2007). *Are you prepared to teach reading? A practical tool for self-assessment.* Upper Saddle River, NJ: Pearson/Merrill PrenticeHall.

> The majority of this text presents multiple-choice questions to prepare candidates for a reading certification exam; however, there are some cases included that are excellent scenarios for the purpose of using the *Standards 2003* rubrics presented in this book.

Although there are not many resources available at this time, research on the use of cases is in progress and could lead to more sources (see, for example, the work of Charles Kinzer, Linda Labbo, Donald Leu, and William Teale [ctell.uconn.edu/home .htm] or the work of Michael W. Kibby and Logan Scott, University of Buffalo, SUNY [www.readingonline.org/articles/art_index .asp?HREF = /articles/kibby]).

Standards 2003 requirements, as well as include diverse populations, which is important to our local public schools' teaching context. Also, CaseNEX incorporates multimedia, videos, and student work samples within their cases, providing more authentic information for the candidates when writing their responses.

More Restrictions. First, the case materials (scenario and other documents) were read aloud either by the instructor as the candidates followed along with their own copies of the case materials, or silently by all. When using video cases, the videos were accessed online and viewed via projector or computer during class. The instructor then addressed questions and a planning period of 10 minutes was provided for candidates to make notes, create an outline, and get organized and ready to write. After the initial 10 minutes for planning, candidates were given a time limit of 45 minutes to complete their responses. If too much time was given, responses were wordy and would wander, but if not enough time was given, responses were disorganized and sparse. Forty-five minutes appeared to be a good amount of time for the case administrations (see subsequent chapters for examples). It is important that each instructor or program determine the right amount of time so that responses can be elaborated upon, yet not so much time that extraneous information is included.

Fewer Restrictions. Cases were posted online or provided as handouts in class to be due at a later time. With an online course management system, it was possible to give the candidates a certain time frame to view the cases and complete their responses. In this way time was still managed to a certain extent, but notes, resources, and peer discussions or chats regarding the cases were possible. Collaboration among candidates and use of notes or texts and the Internet were encouraged as resources in developing responses. Defining *collaboration* was important so that parameters were clear. Collaboration for this purpose meant candidates were able to discuss the case situation but were not allowed to write or send resources to each other; collaboration was oral discussion only. If the goal is to exclude collaboration completely to ensure candidates are able to complete responses appropriately without peer support, honor statements can be signed (e.g., "On my honor I have neither received nor provided assistance with this assessment.") and policies strictly enforced.

Scoring Responses

Cases were scored simultaneously by at least two instructors using the rubric corresponding to the questions for the case. Prior to administering the case, the instructors came to agreement on content they hoped would appear within the responses based on course or program objectives and readings. This prevented a focus on quantity over quality when using the rubrics and provided a framework for scoring. If, however, a response included content not on the agreed-upon list, it was accepted with a rationale that substantiated its use and could earn a high score. Once cases were scored and results logged in, responses were analyzed for strengths and weaknesses as a whole to inform program-related curricular decisions. Responses for each candidate were also analyzed to gauge student progress and growth over time.

The following chapters include sample cases and anchor responses to assist those who wish to begin using cases to document their candidates' knowledge of standards in realistic situations. Scoring cases is discussed in greater detail as the sample responses are presented along with the rubrics. This approach allows for a multitude of "correct" and valid possible responses. This is evident as you review the sample responses in the following chapters. Examples of solid responses using different perspectives are included, making them very different from each other but just as viable within the case context.

Alternative Activities

Typically candidates are able to respond appropriately and score well using these assessments; however, that isn't always the case. Weak or unrefined writing skills may be problematic when using this type of assessment because expressing oneself in written form is how knowledge is primarily demonstrated. Many of our graduate candidates are practicing teachers who learned English as a second language, coming to the United States as adults. Most, if not all, of their formal education was completed using a language other than English. In this situation, candidates were asked to take their responses to the campus writing center to receive assistance with form and organization. Once revised, the case response was scored again, but original scores were also kept on file to demonstrate candidates' growth over time.

Responses that were weak in content were dealt with differently. The instructor met with the candidate individually to explain how the response was scored. A brainstorming session followed with the instructor eliciting other or additional possible solutions to the case situation. By brainstorming, the instructor determined if the candidate lacked the knowledge base to give an appropriate response, or if there was another reason for the low score. After writing notes on what the candidate brainstormed, along with rationale statements, the instructor asked the candidate to rewrite the response based on the notes taken during the brainstorming session. This approach was also effective for candidates who needed assistance with planning and organizing their responses.

When candidates lacked the knowledge base to reply satisfactorily to the case questions, extra assignments were given (e.g., article summaries, annotated bibliographies) to build the knowledge base in the specific area or standard assessed. Thereafter, the candidate met with the instructor a second time to discuss and turn in the extra assignments and brainstorm once more. In a situation like this, the instructor establishes that the candidate is ready, and the case study response is rewritten using a different case pertaining to the same standard's element. Generally this procedure is effective in building the knowledge base for the element, and high scores follow when subsequent, relevant cases are administered. Original scores are always kept to demonstrate growth over time in the program.

Organization of Chapters

Chapters 1 to 5 focus on the five standards outlined in *Standards 2003* and the elements that make up those standards. Each chapter begins with a brief literature review focusing on what teacher educators should know concerning these standards. The information provided within these reviews varies in length due to factors such as the newness of the area (e.g., technology), amount of research, and established foundations for each area. Given that the audience for this book is teacher educators, this literature review is not intended to be exhaustive; prior knowledge and access to professional resources are assumed. Moreover, the goal is not to mandate a curriculum. The professional belief systems of individual teacher educators combined with institutional and state and local contexts can and must define curriculum. The standards offer that flexibility. Rather, we present an overview of related literature that guided our thinking in the development of rubrics and in competencies we want our students to demonstrate. Although IHE faculty with literacy expertise may know and understand the standards, faculty with other areas of expertise (e.g., teaching of English to speakers of other languages, exceptional student education) will benefit from a brief description of the standards and their foci. Sources for further reading pertaining to each standard are provided at the end of the literature review. These references can serve as course readings or additional reading for faculty professional development. A sample case study and question for response follows, with details concerning how each case was administered, sample responses, and explanations as to how responses were scored (anchor responses). The corresponding rubrics are located in the Appendix.

This book was written to assist other literacy teacher educators in implementing an authentic, standards-based assessment system. We share our work as a starting point for you to begin a similar system, making modifications as needed to make this system your own and customize the rubrics to the needs of your candidates, programs, and institutions.

CHAPTER 1

Learning About and Assessing Standard 1—Foundational Knowledge

Standard 1 of *Standards 2003* (IRA, 2004) embodies the theoretical, empirical, and historical underpinnings of reading and writing processes, principles of first and second language and literacy acquisition, and basic components of reading instruction. Standard 1 specifically recommends that "candidates have knowledge of the foundations of reading and writing processes and instruction" (p. 8). This standard serves as an anchor for reading professionals as they develop ongoing expertise in the remaining standards.

Bond and Dykstra's (1967/1997) oft-cited studies of first-grade reading instruction found greater variation of student reading achievement *within* methods (programmed instruction, initial teaching alphabet, basal readers) than *among* methods. Bond and Dykstra conclude that teachers are the most important variable for learning in classrooms. Even when the reading curriculum is highly prescribed, reading teachers and reading specialists make daily decisions about individuals and groups of students. The decisions are often based on their belief system about the teaching of reading.

Decisions are also based on teachers' belief systems about the children they teach. As classroom populations become more culturally, linguistically, and academically diverse due, in part, to immigration and inclusion of students with disabilities in the general education classroom, issues related to first- and second-language acquisition, culturally responsive instruction, and meeting individual needs of students must be addressed as they pertain to literacy education.

Consequently, it is vital that teacher preparation programs provide a forum for preservice and inservice teachers to explore their beliefs based on personal and professional experience. It is also important to provide opportunities to understand the vast array of professional knowledge that has evolved in the field of reading (Vacca et al., 2005). As Braunger and Lewis (2006) state,

> Without a solid knowledge base about the nature of reading and how it develops, teachers may function more as program deliverers than as thoughtful providers of instruction based on their knowledge of literacy and learning and informed daily by professional assessment of the young readers in their charge. (p. ix)

In addition, when practitioners are armed with strong foundational knowledge, they can serve as advocates for their students and colleagues in shaping public policy. In writing about teachers on the frontline, Lewis, Jongsma, and Berger (2005) assert,

> Every educator must advocate for policies and actions that facilitate best practices in instruction and assessment. Policymakers and members of the community at large need to hear our voices when we have concerns about schools and how schools are not working for the students they are intended to serve. (p. 4)

Clearly, any professional charged with the teaching of our youth should have grounding in the "why" of what they are teaching. Nonetheless, incorporating theoretical foundations in the curriculum can be challenging for teacher educators. Theoretical models are often dense, complex, and (particularly for undergraduate students) difficult to sift through. In the National Academy of Education report *Knowledge to Support the Teaching of Reading*, Snow, Griffin, and Burns (2005) encourage teacher educators to focus on "usable knowledge." They write,

> There are years' worth of fascinating things one could learn about the cognitive psychology of learning, about linguistics, about social and motivational development, and about other topics relevant to children to read.... The challenge of sifting the usable from the merely interesting is huge and constitutes one of the reasons that teacher education is hard to do well. (p. 11)

It is the responsibility of teacher educators to assist teacher candidates in their journey toward linking theory and research to practice. Classroom and online conversations as well as activities such as case study analysis can foster this type of thinking.

Teacher education should include a focus on the elements that are described in Standard 1 (IRA, 2004), which comprises the following:

- Knowledge of psychological, sociological, and linguistic foundations
- Knowledge of reading research and histories of reading
- Knowledge of language development and reading related to cultural and linguistic diversity
- Knowledge of the major components of reading

Element 1.1

Demonstrate knowledge of psychological, sociological, and linguistic foundations of reading and writing processes and instruction.

In the Foreword to *Theoretical Models and Processes of Reading* (Singer & Ruddell, 1985) Ralph Staiger (1985) writes,

> It is significant in that, in the complex area of reading, no single best method can be espoused, by the thoughtful teacher, for all individuals and class groups. Instead, differing situations, diverse students, and varied available materials enter into decision which must be made every

day in the classroom...without an understanding of the theoretical bases for reading, teaching can become tedious and diffuse, waste much student and teacher energy, and discourage the spirit of learning and enjoyment which should be the ultimate purpose of reading. (p. vi)

Element 1.1 addresses the importance for reading professionals to have working knowledge of the major theories that undergird reading research and instruction. Classroom teachers should have a growing awareness of literacy theory and how that theory relates to classroom practice. Reading specialists and coaches should have a facile understanding of the theories and how they engage in such activities as curriculum development, selection of instructional materials, and professional development of colleagues. In thinking about our teacher candidates' knowledge of reading theory, three major themes emerged: (1) reading theory has evolved from multiple disciplines, (2) reading theory can be linked to instruction through an understanding of theoretical models of the reading process, (3) the reflective educator should use reading theory to inform instructional decisions.

Reading Theory Has Evolved From Multiple Disciplines

Reading research and theory find their roots in the psychological laboratories of Europe in the late 1800s (Venezky, 1984). This early work was summarized in Edmund Burke Huey's *Psychology and Pedagogy of Reading* (1908). Since that time, scholars representing a wide variety of professional fields have influenced our understanding of how individuals learn to read. Walsh, Glaser, and Dunne Wilcox (2006) report that for more than half a century many disciplines, including psychology, linguistics, pediatrics, education, and neurobiology, have studied the reading process. Through the reading of primary and secondary sources, teacher candidates can develop an awareness of the contributions of various disciplines to where we are in the field today—and where we yet need to explore. As a starting point, *Standards 2003* recommends that reading professionals have an understanding of "psychological, sociological, and linguistic foundations of reading and writing instruction" (p. 10).

Psychological Foundations. Educational psychologists "study what people think and do as they teach and learn a particular curriculum in a particular environment where education and training are intended to take place" (Berliner, 1992, p.145) with the intent of affecting changes in practice. For the first half of the 20th century, psychologists were associated with educational development, such that educational psychology was considered "a guiding science of the school" (Cubberley, 1919, p. 755). Three major theories in psychology of reading acquisition present important pedagogical implications for understanding reading research and reading instruction; they include (1) developmental psychology, (2) behavioral psychology, and (3) cognitive psychology.

First, developmental psychology, or human development, is the study of social, emotional, and cognitive changes that occur in human beings as they age. A fundamental premise of developmental psychology is the sequential advancement of skills based on a child's maturation status at preset rates of growth (Bender, 1957). Various researchers have purported assorted models of maturational stages of cognitive development (see Fischer, 1980; Fischer & Knight, 1990; Havighurst, 1952; Piaget, 1969). They all contend that when teachers understand every level of cognitive development and students' thinking, teachers' instruction and remedial strategies can be matched to ability levels.

Second, behavioral psychology has molded major applications and practices for promoting learning beginning with the work of Watson (1913), who claimed that psychology is concerned with objectively observable and quantifiable events and behavior based on reflexes and conditioning. Cohen (1987) writes,

> The central tenet of behaviorism is that thoughts, feelings, and intentions, mental processes, all do not determine what we do. Our behavior is the product of our conditioning. We are biological machines and do not consciously act; rather we react to stimuli. (p. 71)

According to behaviorists, students learn through classical and operant conditioning. Classical conditioning was demonstrated through Pavlov's (1928) landmark experiment with dogs involving two stimuli. Operant conditioning occurs as a result of a relationship between a behavior and a consequence. By 1952, behaviorism dominated the scientific foundation of American pedagogy, influencing textbook content and classroom curricula, but its prevalence diminished with the introduction of cognitive psychology in the mid-1900s. With the publication of Skinner's (1976) seminal work, *About Behaviorism*, however, behavioral psychology quickly penetrated educational research and continued to be an anchor in determining how educators understood that behavior was learned.

The role of the teacher, for example, is to provide the student with appropriate behavioral responses to specific stimuli, reinforced through an effective reinforcement schedule (Skinner, 1976). Instructional practices include direct or explicit teaching of skill and drill exercises wherein the material is broken down into small tasks and presented sequentially, such as direct teaching of phonics with a focus on texts and decoding. Motivation grows out of a desire to procure positive reinforcement such as verbal praise, good grades, and tokens. The theory of behaviorism loses efficacy in the teaching of skills that demand analytical abilities and higher order skills such as reading comprehension and composition writing.

Third, in the 1940s and the 1950s cognitive psychologists pioneered the theory that focuses on the human processes of learning, thinking and knowing (i.e., Chomsky, 1968; Miller, 1956; Piaget, 1969; Skinner, 1957). Cognitive psychologists' goal is to understand human thinking; their approach to research on reading is different than that of behaviorists. Cognivitists embrace the concept that learning becomes meaningful when new knowledge can be connected to existing knowledge through elaborations. According to Rayner and Pollatsek (1989), psychologists' interest in reading emanated because of the inability of behaviorism to account for language processing. Information processing models (LaBerge & Samuels, 1974), schema theory (Anderson, Reynolds, Schallert, & Goetz, 1977; Bransford & Johnson, 1972), metacognitive theory (Brown, 1985), and transactional theory (Rosenblatt, 1969) emanate from cognitive psychology.

Linguistic Foundations. Linguists first adopted the field of reading in the early 1960s, identifying reading as a language process strongly associated with the other language processes of writing, speaking, and listening (Pearson & Stephens, 1994). Linguistic models encompass the study of the nature of language, including aspects of vocabulary, grammar, and syntax. Because reading is a linguistic skill, it necessitates that the reader must attain proficiency in oral language, which in turn demands that the educator have a fundamental knowledge of language structure at all levels.

Prior to the introduction of a linguistic perspective in the 1960s, the teaching of beginning reading involved task-related activities to assist students to translate the written symbols into an oral code. Therefore, instruction centered on phonics and disparate skills on whole-word activities targeting techniques to drill acquisition of letter–sound correspondence. With the publication of *Linguistics and Reading* by Charles Fries in 1963 and publications from other scholars (see Wardhaugh, 1969), it became evident that teaching reading from a linguistic perspective would demand adopting different models and methods. Furthermore, with the publication of Chomsky's two books *Syntactic Structures* (1957) and *Aspects of the Theory of Syntax* (1965), the prevailing behavioristic views of teaching reading were being questioned. Linguists, therefore, introduced new approaches that arose with the way psychologists approached the study of language comprehension and acquisition processes.

Psycholinguistics emerged from descriptive linguistics and the generative-transformational linguistics introduced by Chomsky's work (Phillips & Walker, 1987) to determine if the views that Chomsky had promoted could be used as psychological models of language performance by studying language comprehension or language acquisition (Pearson & Stephens, 1994). Psycholinguistics is the study of relationships between linguistics and psychological behavior. It is concerned with how information to be conveyed is transferred from a mental process to the actual sounds, encompassing how readers subconsciously interpret visual signals and apply syntax to gain meaning from text.

The study of reading instruction was highly influenced by the work of two psycholinguists, Goodman (1965) and Smith (1971) who maintained that the object of learning to read is not to recognize words but to make sense out of the written text. Since Goodman (1965, 1967) coined the term *miscues* (i.e., unexpected responses derived from oral reading), both researchers and practitioners have been using syntactic (sentence structure), semantic (word meaning), and graphophonemic (sound–symbol relationship) miscues to determine how a child's linguistic knowledge influences comprehension processes. Goodman demonstrated that the errors students were making in reading indicated that there was a genuine effort to make sense out of what was being read. Goodman also acknowledged that even though the teacher is responsible for providing suitable instructional materials for motivating learning and to monitor learning activities, it is ultimately the learner who extracts the information that is personally relevant and meaningful.

According to Pearson and Stephens (1994), the psycholinguistic perspective highly influenced reading instruction. The classroom skill and drill worksheets of the late 1960s and early 1970s to assist students in making the letter–sound connection were no longer considered a valuable technique because the focus was on making meaning from literacy experiences. Texts for emergent and beginning readers were now scrutinized and value was placed on those texts allowing a reader to use their knowledge of language to make predictions for word identification and word meanings. There was a greater understanding of the reading process and an appreciation of the efforts put forth by children as they were reading. Errors in reading were now used as a means to give insight into readers' strategies. Furthermore, the introduction of miscue analysis and the insight that reading is a constructive process altered the theory that the acquisition of literacy was a natural process to a theory of reading as language-based process. Views of teaching and learning to read were dramatically altered. Teachers began to ask, "What can I do to help this child as a reader?" as opposed to "What can I teach this child so that she will eventually become a reader?" (p. 29).

Sociological Foundations. Two theories that are influential in understanding the sociological foundations of reading are sociocognitive theory and sociolinguistic theory. Sociocognitive theory maintains that literacy is culturally based and is learned through children's interaction with family, community, and schools. Langer (1991) purports that "literacy can be viewed in a broader and educationally more productive way, as the ability to think and reason like a literate person, *within a particular society*" (p. 11). The sociocognitive perspective of reading comprehension adopts a constructivist view that argues that interaction of the social and cognitive spheres between the reader, the text, and the teacher leads to reading for meaning and involves higher level cognitive processes, leading a student from the present knowledge in their world to the external world (Langer, 2002). Also,

> the role of the classroom's social context and influence of the teacher on the reader's meaning negotiation and construction are central to this model as it explores the notion that participants in literacy events form and reform meanings in a hermeneutic circle. (Ruddell, Ruddell, & Singer, 1994, p. 813)

This would imply that there needs to be a simultaneous scrutiny of the interaction between the social processes within the classroom and the individual development of the student (Applebee, Langer, Nysstrand, & Gamoran, 2003).

In the sociocognitive theory, literacy learning is developed in social groups and interaction between purposeful, authentic text at the zone of proximal development (Vygotsky, 1978). Instruction extends to skills and strategies that connect with a child's experiences, prior knowledge, and text through student conversations, rather than focusing on discrete skills (Langer, 2002). The teacher is a powerful instrument in effectively guiding discussions, scaffolding children's support for literacy development (Heath, 1993; Martinez & Teale, 1993).

Sociolinguistics is the field associated with the study of language as a social and cultural phenomenon and involves studying the relationship between the use of language and factors that affect language such as social class, ethnic group, age, and sex (Bloome & Green,

1984). The sociolinguistic view challenged the independence of language to encompass social and cultural context such that language has been contextualized (Phillips & Walker 1987). Unlike psycholinguistics, which is concerned with the intrapersonal context, the background knowledge, and the unique skills an individual reader brings to the comprehension process, sociolinguistics is concerned with the interpersonal context. In other words, the sociolinguistic perspective is concerned with the study of language in its social setting as part of a larger communicative system. The premise of this theory is that language cannot be separated from its context so the reader personally interacts with the text through background knowledge and skills as well as the individual differences in knowledge and skills that the reader brings to the context (Phillips & Walker, 1987). Reading and writing are not only cognitive processes, but social and linguistic processes as well.

Views of reading and reading instruction from a sociolinguistic perspective are rooted in the fields of anthropology, linguistics, and literacy analysis (Bloome & Green, 1984). In the early 1980s anthropologists aligned reading to culture (see Heath, 1982; Scribner & Cole, 1978), which influenced reading research to examine both the interpersonal and intrapersonal nature of reading. Sociolinguists extended the linguistic view of language from analysis in isolation to examining language as it is used naturally, in daily situations for social functions.

Reading Theory and Theoretical Models of the Reading Process

Ruddell and Unrau (2004) explain how models assist educators to acquire a deeper understanding of the reading processes. A model incorporates our present knowledge and integrates this with current research to create a visual illustration as it presents an explanation of how a reader learns to read. Because of the ability of models to create a visualization of the process, we can see where the comprehension processes break down. This knowledge leads to an understanding of the areas of particular difficulty that a struggling reader is experiencing. Also, using a model that is grounded in research can guide the implementation of appropriate instructional interventions. Whereas a number of models of the reading process exist, three general models are typically used to contrast dominant points of view: bottom-up, top-down, and interactive.

Bottom-up (or data-driven) models are based on information processing theory that equate human learning to the functions of a computer (Gough, 1972; LaBerge & Samuels, 1974). Instruction begins with an introduction to letter names (graphemes) and their accompanying sounds (phonemes). The next progressive phase is to introduce entire words, and then sentences, with lengthier and more complex texts presented as the reader becomes more proficient and automatic with decoding. These models have been recommended as the basis for instructing students struggling with decoding issues because the bottom-up approach to reading instruction hypothesizes that learning to read begins with knowledge of word parts (letters) to gaining meaning from the text (Adams, 1990; Ehri, 1994). Advocates of bottom-up models identify rapid, context-free word recognition as the hallmark of the proficient reader. A basal reading approach is often aligned with bottom-up models.

On the other hand, the top-down or meaning-driven model of reading instruction emphasizes readers' linguistic competency, prior knowledge, and experiences in creating meaning from the text. The top-down model of reading processes evolved from psycholinguistic theory, which maintains that reading is not simply the deciphering of symbols on a page, but that reading is mainly a meaning-construction process (Goodman, 1985; Smith, 1971, 1994). Proponents of this theory contend that an extensive oral language vocabulary is the bridge to interpreting print as learning to read occurs from processing the whole to the parts. Instructional focus is on the reading of sentences, paragraphs, and entire passages rather than the decoding of letters and words. Top-down aficionados see facile use of language and context as the hallmark of a proficient reader. Whole language approaches are most closely associated with top-down approaches.

Interactive models offer a third alternative. Cognitive-based models such as the interactive (Rumelhart, 1985) and interactive-compensatory model (Stanovich, 1980) incorporate both bottom-up and top-down reading approaches that take into account both the readers' decoding acumen and prior knowledge to make meaning from texts. Such models recognize that the hallmark of a good reader is not only rapid, context-free word recognition, but also the ability to tap other cue systems in a facile, interactive manner. Poor readers, on the other hand, have a tendency to overuse a single cue system (typically context) and do so inefficiently. Balanced literacy and differentiated instructional programs are typically associated with interactive models.

Why is an understanding of these models important? Take the case of Tanya. Tanya is a preservice teacher enrolled in her first reading class. Tanya has been somewhat baffled about what she has heard in class and what she sees in her elementary school field placement. Now a 19 year old, Tanya was taught in a whole language classroom. She has fond memories of reading a wide range of trade books and sitting in the "author's chair" to read aloud and share her own creative pieces to others in the classroom. She never saw or heard of a basal reader before this semester and now will be expected to use a basal reader as her primary tool for teaching reading while being involved in field experience and ultimately in the classroom where she plans to teach.

As a novice to the profession, Tanya is becoming oriented to not only what to teach but also why she is teaching in that way. Understanding the different models as well as associated instructional approaches is vital to her professional development—her knowledge of her profession. Several instruments have been developed to help practitioners explore their beliefs about reading instruction and to align their personal beliefs with extant models of the reading process (DeFord, 1985; Leu & Kinzer, 1991; Vacca et al., 2005). Use of these instruments can trigger discussion about the pros and cons of theoretical models and how they relate to classroom instructional practices.

Using Reading Theory to Inform Practice

Teacher candidates need ample opportunities to develop the language of their profession as well as the theoretical concepts that are the basis of reading instruction. Moreover, they need ample opportunities to articulate how reading theory and instructional practices are linked. Teale, Leu, Labbo, and Kinzer (2002) propose a case approach to prepare literacy teachers to function in complex environments where they are forced to make instant and thoughtful decisions. The authors report on Case Technologies for Early Literacy Learning (CTELL) and document that recent research has adopted the case method approach for preservice teachers using multimedia, case-based instruction (Greenleaf & Schoenbach, 2001; Kinzer & Risko, 1998; Kinzer, Singer Gabella, & Rieth, 1994). The CTELL study uses cases that consist of print as well as video interviews, excerpts, and reading performances of students. Furthermore, the Internet provides the virtual access for preservice and inservice teachers to real classroom contexts. Digital video cases enable teacher candidates to study a variety of literacy practices in ideal (and less ideal) classroom environments. Students actively engage in reflection, analytical analysis, and decision making via cases, affording them the opportunity to think like an expert with practice that is grounded in theory and research.

Element 1.2

Demonstrate knowledge of reading research and histories of reading.

Since the advent of No Child Left Behind (NCLB) in 2001, school administrators, reading specialists, and classroom teachers have been mandated to implement evidence-based instructional practices (Pressley, 2003; Slavin, 2002). In an attempt to ensure high-quality instruction for all students, federal and state governments have legislated policies that require a research base for materials and methods used in public education. This movement toward evidence-based practice was fueled, in part, by a well-recognized gulf between research and practice (Gersten & Dimino, 2001; Gersten, Vaughn, Deshler, & Schiller, 1997). As Stanovich and Stanovich (2003) put it, "A vast literature has been generated on best practices that foster children's reading acquisition.... Yet much of this literature remains unknown to many teachers...." (p. 8).

Element 1.2 recommends that classroom teacher candidates should be able to "articulate how their teaching practices relate to reading research" (IRA, 2004, p. 10) and that reading specialist/literacy coach candidates should also be able to "summarize seminal reading studies and articulate how these studies impacted reading instruction" (p. 10).

Similarly, the teaching of reading has a rich history that is well documented in the literature (Fresch, 2008; Smith, 1934/2002), but that has not typically been incorporated in teacher education at all levels. Monaghan (1989) observes, "virtually all academic disciplines incorporate a look at the past into their coursework. The assumption has been that it is intrinsically valuable to know something about those who have trodden a particular path before" (p. 6). Element 1.2 recommends that candidates "recognize historical antecedents to contemporary reading methods and materials" (IRA, 2004, p. 10) and in addition that reading specialist/literacy coach candidates "recount historical developments in the history of reading" (p. 10). In an age of accountability and emphasis on educational reform, an understanding and knowledge of the history of reading research and instruction are vital to understand the context of current issues and events encompassing reading instruction (Alexander & Fox, 2004).

Knowledge of reading research and the histories of reading can broaden the reading professional's belief system about the reading and writing processes and instruction. Teacher education programs can provide candidates with opportunities to develop the knowledge, skills, and confidence they need to be critical consumers of reading research and histories and to bridge the gulf between professional literature and classroom practice.

Knowledge of Reading Research

The professional and public discussion about implementing evidence-based practices has fueled a debate about what constitutes "evidence" (Allington, 2006; Krashen, 2001, 2002; Shanahan, 2003). Whereas some advocate randomized experimental group designs as the gold standard for educational research (NCLB, 2001), others recognize that different research questions warrant different methodologies—both qualitative and quantitative (Klingner & Edwards, 2006; Shavelson & Towne, 2002). IRA has leaned more toward the latter point of view. In 2002, the IRA issued a position statement titled, *What Is Evidence-Based Reading Instruction?* Key to this position statement is the notion that evidence to support a program or practice should be "reliable, trustworthy, and valid" (IRA, 2002c, n.p.). As Farstrup (2004) wrote,

> At the end of the day our common goal, as researchers and teachers, is to make instructional choices and decisions that give all our students, no matter their circumstances, the best possible chance of reaching a high level of reading achievement. To do this we need to pay attention to multiple sources of valid and reliable research paradigms. (p. 8)

Although classroom teachers and reading specialists may or may not become engaged in formal research, there are at least three areas where teacher education programs can provide support in developing appropriate professional expertise in research. First, teachers should be able to articulate how their classroom practice relates to best practices in the field to a variety of key stakeholder audiences: administrators, colleagues, parents, and students (when appropriate). Second, Rosemary, Roskos, and Landreth (2007) recommend, "They [teachers] should be familiar with the work of leading researchers and practitioners in the field, as well as being alert and critical consumers of information about the teaching of reading and writing" (p. 26). As previously stated, IRA recommends that reading specialists should be able to summarize seminal works of reading research. This skill is particularly important for reading specialists who are engaged in the professional development of classroom teachers and teacher aides. Third, Stanovich and Stanovich (2003) point out the importance of teachers' awareness of the basic principles of the scientific method and becoming reflective practitioners who "inquire into their own practice and who examine their own classrooms to find out what works best" (p. 4). High quality professional development is the key to bridging the research/practice gap (Boardman, Arguelles, Vaughn, Hughes, & Klingner, 2005; Gersten & Dimino, 2001). Gersten and Woodward (1992) maintain that for teachers to become less skeptical of research, professional development must seek an explicit link between research and their own teaching—a concept they refer to as the reality principle.

Regarding the depth and breadth of research in reading, Robinson (2005) writes, "Any attempt to be cognizant of all of the available research and writing on even a small aspect of literacy education is virtually impossible when faced with the large number of possible studies to be considered" (p. 2). Moreover, literacy research (both historical and contemporary) stems from a variety of disciplines (e.g., psychology, sociology, linguistics, special education, teaching English as a second language). Fortunately, there are tools available to make research both accessible and comprehensible to the practitioner.

First, there is a series of articles that summarize findings from classic studies that made an impact on research and practice (*Reading Research That Makes a Difference* [Russell, 1961], *Research That Should Have Made a Difference* [Singer, 1970], *Research in Reading That Should Make a Difference in the Classroom* [Singer, 1978], *Literacy Research That Makes a Difference* [Shanahan and Neuman, 1997]). Second, research handbooks provide in-depth reviews of literature in a wide range of topics in reading. This includes the three volumes of the *Handbook of Reading Research* (Barr, Kamil, Mosenthal, & Pearson, 1991; Kamil, Mosenthal, Pearson, & Barr, 2000; Pearson, Barr, Kamil, & Mosenthal, 1984) as well as the *Handbook of Research on Teaching the English Language Arts* (Flood, Lapp, Squire, & Jensen, 2002). Third, research syntheses (e.g., Adams, 1990; Chall, 1967; National Institute of Child Health and Human Development [NICHD], 2000) provide systematic, replicable, and integrated examinations of investigations in reading (Shanahan, 2000). An understanding of the differences between literature reviews and research syntheses as well as their pros and cons, strengths and limitations, is important as teachers attempt to make sense of research and how it affects educational policy and classroom practice (Shanahan, 2003). Finally, candidates should be familiar with the range of print and online peer-reviewed resources available through professional organizations such as International Reading Association, College Reading Association, National Reading Conference, and National Council of Teachers of Reading.

If we think about the teaching of reading as a craft rather than an art, making connections between the existing science of what frames our profession and classroom practice seems more tenable (Vaughn & Dammann, 2001). As Stanovich and Stanovich (2003) explain,

> One could argue that in this age of education reform and accountability, educators are being asked to demonstrate that their craft has been integrated with science—that instructional models, methods, and materials can be likened to the evidence a physician should be able to produce showing that a specific treatment will be effective. As with medicine, constructing teaching practice on a firm scientific foundation does not mean denying the craft aspects of teaching. (p. 3)

The teaching of reading is an enormously complex process and for decades the professional development needed for individuals to become excellent teachers of reading has been seriously underestimated (Moats, 1999). A working knowledge of the research foundations of our craft is vital in the ongoing quest to provide high quality reading instruction for all students.

Knowledge of Histories of Reading

Cranney (1989) cites a number of reasons why a focus on the history of reading instruction is important. Certainly historical study can identify the roots, controversies, and variations of reading methods. Standard 1.2 requires that candidates "recognize historical antecedents to contemporary reading methods and materials" (p. 12). Putnam and Reutzel's comments (1997) illustrate the importance of this standard:

> If you think reading with phonics is new, it isn't. In 1612 Brinsley [minister and schoolmaster]... changed the method from learning the sounds of the whole alphabet at once to combining initial sounds with short vowels.... If you think teaching by the sight word method is new, it isn't. Comenius [scientist and writer] recommended it in 1500. (p. 52)

To provide the profession with the sometimes long and sometimes controversial history of how reading is taught, Fresch's (2008) *An Essential History of Current Reading Practices* includes chapters documenting the history of key components of reading instruction. Certainly, a look to our professional historical journey can inform the future of our professional practice.

A study of history also can shed light on the people who shaped reading instruction. Those interested in biographical studies can learn about "the values and personalities of the people who made reading history" (Cranney, 1989, p. 5). Hearing their voices through the reading of primary sources can help educators better understand those who went before and learn valuable lessons to inform their own beliefs and professional practice. Oral histories serve as one way to chronicle reading history (Stahl, King, Dillon, & Walker, 1994). In addition to reading oral histories, professionals can create oral histories from a wide range of individuals including local reading leaders, former teachers at their own school, family members, students, and so forth.

An additional reason that a study of the history of reading instruction is vital is related to equity and access. Reading instruction in the United States has not always been fair and equitable to women and minorities (Huerta, 2009). Issues about equity and access persist today with minorities, immigrant populations, and English-language learners (Au, 2000; Edelsky, 2006; Harry & Klingner, 2005). An understanding of historical and current inequities is imperative as we continue to pursue educational opportunities for all learners. As Monaghan and Hartman (2000) point out, a look to the past may not prevent mistakes in the future, but it does provide us "with possible rather than probable understandings, and the ability to take precautions rather than control possible futures" (p. 109).

Finally, when teachers understand local, state, and federal educational policy from the past, they are better equipped to deal with current educational policy. Public policy in education has consequences. Federal legislation over the past decade has greatly affected how reading is taught in elementary and secondary classrooms as well as the content of assessments and commercial reading programs. Such public policies didn't just happen. It is important that candidates know how policies have an impact on their own professional lives as well as the lives of students they teach evolved.

Element 1.3

Demonstrate knowledge of language development and reading acquisition and the variations related to cultural and linguistic diversity.

Element 1.3 requires classroom teacher candidates to demonstrate the following competencies:

- Articulate developmental aspects of oral language and its relationship to reading and writing.
- Summarize the developmental progression of reading acquisition and the variations related to cultural and linguistic diversity.
- Describe when students are meeting developmental benchmarks.
- Know when to consult other professionals for guidance.

In addition, the element further requires reading specialists to be able to "Identify, explain, compare and contrast the theories and research in the areas of language development and learning to read" (IRA, 2004, p. 10).

Moats (1994, 1999) emphasizes the importance for reading professionals to be cognizant of the structure of the English language and how it relates to reading. She states that it is essential that teachers understand

> how children develop reading skill, how good readers differ from poor readers, how the English language is structured in spoken and written form, and the validated principles of effective reading instruction. The ability to design and deliver lessons to academically diverse learners, to select validated instructional methods and materials and use assessments to tailor instruction are all central to effective teaching. (1999, p. 13)

The literature review for Element 1.3 provides an overview of topics related to language development, developmental progression of reading and writing acquisition, and variations related to cultural and linguistic diversity.

Language Development

Language has been defined as a form of communication using complex rules to form and manipulate symbols (e.g., words or gestures) to generate an infinite number of messages (Plotnik, 1999). Oral language incorporates receptive and expressive skills. For the past 50 years, there has been considerable research to investigate how children acquire language with most theories based on the doctrines of behaviorism and nativism. Behaviorist theory poses that knowledge arises from the interaction with the environment (Skinner, 1957). Language learning is broken down into simpler parts and acquired through the power of consequences and reinforcements. A second theory, nativism, maintains that human beings are predisposed with an innate ability to generate sentences. Chomsky (1968) purports that humans have a genetic mechanism for the acquisition of language. He identifies this as a Language Acquisition Device. More recently, interactionist theory, which supports the interaction between environmental influences and innate abilities, has dominated work in language acquisition (Bruner, 1986; McCormick & Schiefelbusch, 1984).

Braunger and Lewis (2006) contend that most models of language acquisition are based on foundational theories of Piaget (1969) and Vygotsky (1978) wherein language is learned through meaningful social interactions within a child's environment. Also, there is a growing body of research in the literature that supports the theory that children are active participants and theory builders who constantly test their hypotheses in the construction and acquisition of oral language (Chomsky, 1959, 1967; Clark & Clark, 1977; Clay, 1991; Morrow, 1993; Ruddell & Haggard, 1985; Ruddell & Unrau, 1994). Ruddell and Ruddell (1994) contend that the required competencies for the process of constructing oral language demand that children become increasingly more proficient in language phonology, morphology, syntax, grammar, and lexicon.

An understanding of theories of language acquisition as well as the stages of language development can help practitioners implement developmentally appropriate oral language activities in the classroom as well as help students make the link between the oral and written word in meaningful and motivational ways (Glazer, 1989). This understanding can also help reading professionals to recognize when developmental, cultural, or linguistic differences seem to have an impact on the reading process and when consultation with colleagues in related professions (e.g., speech pathology, school psychologists, teachers of English as a second language) might be warranted.

Developmental Progression of Reading Acquisition

Language development is a complex process that is inextricably intertwined with reading processes. Research has shown that proficiency in reading is related to language proficiency. Skill in auditory discrimination, blending, vocabulary knowledge, syntactic competence, and phonological awareness are predictors of early reading achievement (Sawyer, 1992). According to Cambourne (1988), children progress through developmental cognitive phases in the process of reading, writing, speaking, and listening similar to those of oral language development.

Indeed, a number of experts in the field of reading have offered explanations of reading development beginning with Jeanne Chall's *Stages of Reading Development* (1983). These developmental progressions are represented in the work of Ehri (1997), Frith (1985), Juel (1991), Spear-Swerling and Sternberg (1997), and Bear, Invernizzi, Templeton, and Johnston (1996). In comparing these developmental progressions from novice to expert reading, Bear and colleagues (1996) note the similarities in the different descriptions and also note that developmental models are evolving to represent the integrated nature of reading, writing, and spelling development.

Element 1.3 requires not only that teacher candidates become familiar with developmental stages of reading, writing, and spelling, but that they identify key benchmarks for the stages. This requires a great deal of expertise in ongoing assessment and in instructional interventions, topics covered in subsequent standards.

Variations Related to Cultural Diversity

Numerous demographic reports have documented the growing diversity among school populations in the United States (see Garcia & Cuellar, 2006, for a discussion). It is important to acknowledge that students enter the mainstream classroom bringing not only their language, but their culture as well. Culture has been defined as the shared beliefs, values, and patterns of behavior of a group (Saville-Troike, 1978). Spradley (1980) extends this definition further by stating that culture is acquired knowledge people use to interpret experiences and generate behavior. Defined in this way, culture is the roots of understanding and interpreting texts. Teachers should appreciate, value, and affirm cultural identities by acknowledging that there is more than one way to interpret or comprehend texts. Understandings and interpretations are, in large part, determined by the cultural backgrounds of the students we serve.

In discussing culturally responsive literacy instruction, Klingner and Edwards (2006) write, "culturally responsive teachers make connections with their students as individuals while understanding the sociocultural-historical contexts that influence their interactions" (p. 109). When a mismatch between the culture of home and the culture of school exists, literacy learning—indeed all learning—can be impeded (Au, 2000). Au's (1995) review of the research in this area indicated that there is much classroom teachers can do to bridge the home–school differences, including using multicultural literature, providing opportunities for genuine learning tasks, and developing a better understanding of the communities in which they teach. Most significantly, recognizing and celebrating the "funds of knowledge" that students bring to the classroom (Moll & Gonzalez, 1994) creates a climate of acceptance that is vital for student learning.

Variations Related to Linguistic Diversity

Because of the effects of globalization and hardships found in many areas of the world, there has been an influx of immigrants who bring their cultures and languages with them to their new homeland (Garcia & Cuellar, 2006). Research in the last two decades has demonstrated that being bilingual could be an asset to acquisition of knowledge (August & Hakuta, 1997; Hakuta, 1997) although there exists a significant achievement gap between English-language learners (ELLs) and the native English speaking population in U.S. public schools. Furthermore, ELLs have experienced greater retention rates (U.S. Department of Education, 2000), higher dropout rates (Kauffman & Alt, 2004), and an overrepresentation in special education categories (Donovan & Cross, 2002; Harry & Klingner, 2005).

Weber (2000) creates an awareness of the obstacles that exist when learning more than one language:

> The psychological intricacies of becoming literate multiply across languages, whether children are taught in the language they are only learning to speak, whether they are taught in the language they already speak as a foundation for reading in a second language, or whether they are taught to read in two languages at the same time. (p. 100)

She further contends that complications occur as a result of how the language is valued and the number of opportunities that are presented to apply the language in spoken and written form. In "Linguistic Diversity and Reading in American Society," Weber characterizes the history and research of learning to read and write in a second language from emergent readers to older readers to that of English language acquisition, "but subject to differences in linguistic structure, differently organized similarities in structure, differential knowledge of the language and ability to process it, as well as cultural disparities in content and use for print" (p. 115). She discusses learning to read across languages and presents a fundamental critique of the different types of programs that have been implemented to deal with second-language reading. Also, Weber notes that the research focusing on second-language learning is mainly dedicated to the comprehension processes.

Because students learning a second language must simultaneously learn language orally as well as printed text, it requires great efficiency, not only on the part of the student, but the teacher as well. Lesaux and Geva (2006) argue that it is imperative for candidates to understand not only the fundamentals of ELLs' literacy development, including developmental trajectories similar to those of native English students, but also unique developmental trajectories. For example, very little emphasis is placed on instruction for the development of oral language ability for monolinguals as this skill begins to develop prior to a child entering school. August and Shanahan (2006) substantiate this in a report on language minority students. They found that reading and writing instruction targeting the five major components identified by the National Reading Panel (NRP; NICHD, 2000) to be incomplete without oral language proficiency. Even though lower level decoding skills are adequate, in that language-minority students attain the same proficiency as native English speakers, there is a disparity between text level skills of reading comprehension and writing, with language-minority students falling well below their native-speaking peers. The proficiency level of language-minority students signifies that present classroom instructional techniques targeting higher level reading skills and reading processes are not appropriate for language minority students, and the need to further support ELLs as they become more proficient in the second language is evident. Furthermore, a study of Spanish-speaking ELLs found that "given adequate L2 decoding ability, L2 vocabulary knowledge is crucial for improved English reading comprehension outcomes for Spanish-speaking ELLs" (Proctor, Carlo, August, & Snow, 2005, p. 246).

To make accurate decisions regarding placement of language-minority students as well as develop individual instructional programs, understanding the strengths and weaknesses of each student is necessary. This is accomplished through assessment. However, the present assessments to predict language-minority students' performance over time on reading or content area assessments in English are inadequate (August & Shanahan, 2006). The use of teacher judgment, presently playing a predominant role in the teaching of language-minority students, to determine if a student needs intensive reading instruction or is at risk of failing school has also been called into question by August and Shanahan. They recommend that teachers address specific criteria rather than spontaneously expressing their opinions.

Even though the nucleus of current research on language diversity focuses on issues faced by practitioners, there are many areas with unresolved and unexamined issues (Artiles & Klingner, 2006). Lesaux and Geva (2006) argue that more research needs to be conducted to add to the knowledge base about the development of ELLs' literacy skills as well as to understand the root of their reading difficulties because there is a high proportion of this population that are failing in school (National Center for Education Statistics, 2003). Grant and Wong (2003) contend that the problem is a result of the inadequacy of higher institutions to adequately train reading specialists to work with language-minority students. To compound this problem, there exists a limited amount of meaningful research on second-language reading (Bernhardt, 2000; Garcia, 2000). Grant and Wong offer seven recommendations that institutions of higher learner can incorporate into research, teacher preparation, and practice to develop equality in the education arena for ELLs in the United States. Among these is "provid[ing] clinical experiences for reading specialists that involve English language learners" (p. 392) and "work[ing] to change tests and testing practices that disadvantage children from nonnative English speaking backgrounds" (p. 392).

Element 1.4

Demonstrate knowledge of major components of reading (phonemic awareness, word identification and phonics, vocabulary and background knowledge, fluency, comprehension strategies, and motivation) and how they are integrated in fluent reading.

The first three elements of Standard 1 address theoretical, empirical, and historical topics about models of the reading process and individual differences in reading acquisition. These elements help teachers form foundational knowledge about *why* we teach the way we do and, more important, *whom* we teach. The fourth element deals with *what* we teach—the knowledge of the elements of content that form reading curriculum. Whereas subsequent Standards 2 through 4 focus more on the *how* of assessment and instruction, Element 1.4 emphasizes that classroom teachers become aware of the building blocks of the reading curriculum, understand their evidence base, and recognize their own students' strengths and challenges in mastering the various elements. Reading specialists are further required to demonstrate the capacity to detect how students integrate these components as they progress in becoming fluent, proficient readers.

Element 1.4 defines the major components of reading as phonemic awareness, word identification and phonics, vocabulary and background knowledge, fluency, comprehension strategies, and motivation. Most of these components were encompassed in the *Report of the National Reading Panel* (NICHD, 2000). As mentioned previously, in 1997 the U.S. Congress appointed the NICHD to construct a committee to investigate reading research. The committee's charge was to assess "the status of research-based knowledge, including the effectiveness of various approaches to teaching children to read" and "if appropriate, a strategy for rapidly disseminating this information to facilitate effective instruction in the schools" (p. 1). The NRP highlighted five important components required for reading performance, the same elements that the No Child Left Behind Act mandates as policies for teachers to adopt and implement within their core literacy instruction. This includes phonemic awareness, phonics, fluency, comprehension, and vocabulary. Indeed, IRA (2004) cites the 2000 NRP report as part of the evidence base for the development of the professional standards.

Because the NRP has been highly visible and has had an extraordinary effect on both state reading standards as well as commercial curriculum development, it is imperative that practitioners understand the findings of NRP and their impact. For example, prior to NRP, fluency instruction was largely ignored in both research and practice (Padak & Rasinski, 2008). Now, fluency instruction is a key component of the reading curriculum in many parts of the United States. Some areas of impact have been positive; others questionable. For instance, Braunger and Lewis (2006) argue that focus on the "Big Five" fragments both research and practice and ignores the interactive nature of these components in real reading.

Practitioners should understand the controversy surrounding the panel's report (Allington, 2002b; Krashen, 2001, 2002). The report has been criticized on a number of counts, including a narrow focus of topics, exclusion of qualitative research findings, lack of attention to the impact of wide reading on reaching achievement, and omission of investigations related to students with disabilities and students who are ELLs (Allington, 2006; Braunger & Lewis, 2006; Edelsky, 2006). An understanding of the promise and perils of the report is vital as teachers talk with parents, administrators, and other key stakeholders (Shanahan, 2003).

Missing from NRP's meta-analysis was research related to motivation in reading. IRA has included motivation as a key component of professional standards. Given the sometimes stressful climate high-stakes testing creates, the challenge of how to keep students positive about themselves as readers and writers and engaged in the act of genuine reading and writing is one that practitioners face on a daily basis (Fink & Samuels, 2008).

In taking a look at reading education textbooks over the past 50 years, we see the components incorporated in Element 1.4 have been traditional bedrocks of teacher preparation in reading. Whereas there is little controversy about what the components are, opinions differ (depending on one's theoretical orientation to the teaching of reading) about how much these components should be emphasized in the curriculum and how they should be taught. As previously stated, since the publication of Bond and Dykstra's (1967/1997) first-grade reading studies, IRA has emphasized the importance of a well-prepared teacher as key to quality reading instruction as opposed to the importance of a particular program or curriculum. Knowledge of the key components of the reading curriculum is a starting place; an overview follows.

Phonemic Awareness

Phonemic awareness is the ability to hear, identify, and manipulate the individual sounds (or phonemes) in spoken words (Liberman, Shankweiler, Fischer, & Carter, 1974) and is a key element in beginning reading achievement (NICHD, 2000; Snow, Burns, & Griffin, 1998). Phonemic awareness is a prereading skill that is also known to be the most sophisticated level of phonological awareness. Both phonological and phonemic awareness are aural skills; however, phonological awareness is a broader term that depicts understanding the different ways that oral language can be divided into smaller components and manipulated.

An awareness of phonemes is essential to understand the alphabetic principle that underlies our system of written language. Research has established the significance of alphabetic awareness to determine future success in reading acquisition (Johnston, 1985; Stanovich, 1986). Because of the complexity of the English writing system, it is essential to train children in the alphabetic principle to promote acquisition of phonemic segmentation, letter–sound correspondences, and spelling patterns (Ehri, 2004). The role that reading experience brings to the development of phonemic knowledge is evidenced in studies of illiterate adults, longitudinal studies of first graders, and studies investigating Chinese readers (Rayner, Foorman, Perfetti, Pesetsky, & Seidenberg, 2001).

The strong positive relationship between phonological awareness and learning to read has been shown by numerous studies (Perfetti, Beck, Bell, & Hughes, 1987; Snow et al., 1998; Stanovich, 1986). Also, knowledge of phonological awareness in kindergarten is a strong predictor of later reading success (Calfee, Lindamood, & Lindamood, 1973; Ehri & Wilce, 1980, 1985; Liberman et al., 1974; Perfetti et al., 1987). Furthermore, the results of a study conducted by Share, Jorm, Maclean, and Matthews (1984) found phonemic awareness and letter knowledge to be the two best predictors of school achievement during grades 1 and 2.

The NRP's meta-analysis of phonemic awareness instruction found that phonemic awareness can be taught and learned and is most effective with pre-K and kindergarten children, as well as children who are at risk of reading failure or children from low socioeconomic backgrounds. They also reported that coding letters in combination with phonemes was more effective than phonemic awareness taught without letters. Since the publication of the 2000 NRP report, IRA has highlighted many articles acknowledging the importance of teaching phonemic awareness and guiding teachers through confusing definitions to specific classroom activities.

Word Identification and Phonics

Phonics is the method of instruction that teaches there is a relationship between phonemes, the sounds of spoken language, and graphemes, the letters and spelling that represent those sounds in written language. The role of phonics instruction has been part of a pendulum swing in the history of reading instruction in the United States. Phonics instructional methods became popular in the 1600s with the publication of the *New English Primer*, which had a strong phonics base. In the mid-1800s when the focus was on the education of the large populace, emphasis on comprehension through whole-word approach was adopted and became the preferred method until the 1920s. During the late 1920s to the 1940s, Gray advocated for whole-word approach and developed the *Dick and Jane* reading series with Scott Foresman and Company (Blevins, 1998), making the look-say and its emphasis on analytic phonics very popular.

From the 1950s to the early 1970s, the focus on early reading instruction targeted skills such as visual and aural discrimination, word recognition, and phonics sound–symbol relationship because of the publication of Flesch's (1955) *Why Johnny Can't Read*. He attributed low reading ability to the look-say approach and campaigned for educational reform to return to the synthetic phonics approach. According to Turbill (2002), reading, writing, and spelling were thought of as unrelated skills during this time period. It was believed that comprehension was a byproduct of rapid and accurate decoding. Reading lessons were composed of disparate skills and isolated lessons, including phonics, word drills, comprehension, and supplementary reading. This began the era known as the "reading wars."

Jeanne Chall's (1967) review of the literature in phonics instruction, *Learning to Read: The Great Debate*, underscored the importance of systematic phonics instruction as part of a comprehensive reading program. Anderson, Hiebert, Scott, and Wilkinson (1985) and Adams (1990) substantiated Chall's findings and further identified a balanced approach to teaching reading that did not support a top-down model nor a bottom-up model, but rather an interactive model that was more effective. Stahl, Duffy-Hester, and Stahl (1998) developed a set of principles for effective phonics instruction based on their review of the literature.

The NRP (NICHD, 2000) examined the scientific research of 38 studies to determine whether evidence exists to support phonics instruction as a means of assisting children to learn to read more effectively than other approaches. They discovered many different approaches were used in the classroom to systematically teach phonics. These included synthetic phonics, analytic phonics, analogy-based phonics, and embedded phonics, each differing in many respects.

They reported that systematic phonics instruction produced higher reading scores than nonphonics instruction. Systematic phonics helped children learn to read more effectively than programs with little or no phonics instruction. In fact, phonics instruction facilitated reading acquisition in both younger and older readers. However, the effect of phonics instruction to facilitate reading progress was significantly greater when phonics was used in the first years of education rather than in later years after children had been exposed to alternative methods.

Research has demonstrated that children who become proficient readers are sensitive to linguistic structure, recognize redundant patterns, and accurately and unconsciously are able to connect letter patterns with sounds and syllables. Effective teaching of reading entails these concepts, represented in an order in which children can learn them (Moats, 1994). Ehri (2004) stresses the importance of professional development to enhance the efficacy of teacher effectiveness. She also charges educators and policymakers to become cognizant of the place of phonics in beginning reading programs. However, phonics, in and of itself, will not lead to the development of proficient readers because phonics instruction is only one element of a comprehensive reading program.

Vocabulary and Background Knowledge

Vocabulary refers to stored information about the meanings and pronunciations of words necessary for communication and consists of both decoding tasks as well as immediate recognition of high function words. Davis (1942) describes reading as being a task consisting of two components: word recognition (vocabulary) and reasoning (comprehension). Since then, psychological models of the reading process have reported the unchallenged importance of the vocabulary component of reading acquisition and reading comprehension (Anderson & Freebody, 1981; Beck, McKeown, & Omanson, 1987; Kintsch, 1977; Nagy & Herman, 1987; Rumelhart, 1985; Samuels, 1985).

Correlational studies have shown the presence of a concomitant relationship between vocabulary and comprehension. In fact, Whipple (1925) states, "Growth in reading power means, therefore, continuous enriching and enlarging of the reading vocabulary and increasing clarity of discrimination in appreciation of word values" (p. 76). Furthermore, McGuinness (2004) states that there are two propositions regarding vocabulary and reading. The first contends that "vocabulary causes reading" (p. 215). The premise of this theory is that reading is easier when there are more words stored in memory. The second proposition contends that "reading causes vocabulary" (p. 215). The basis of this theory is that many new words are learned through expansive reading. However, research studies that attempt to establish a causal link between vocabulary development and reading comprehension are inconclusive (Baumann & Kame'enui, 1991; Baumann, Kame'enui, & Ash, 2003; Beck, McKeown, & Omanson, 1987; Stahl & Fairbanks, 1986). This is substantiated by the 2000 NRP report that contends that there is a correlation between reading vocabulary knowledge and reading comprehension (Anderson & Freebody, 1981; Baumann et al., 2003) even though the causality is undetermined (Stanovich, 2000). The report also found that both direct, explicit vocabulary instruction as well as learning words from context are very effective for vocabulary development and acquisition. Although research has demonstrated the importance of vocabulary instruction, this component of reading has been minimized over the past years (Biemiller, 2003).

Teacher candidates should become aware of the research that has demonstrated that a variety of methods used for vocabulary instruction assists students to increase the number of words learned as well as increase the depth of their word knowledge (Baumann et al., 2003; Beck & McKeown, 1991; Nagy & Scott, 2000). The 2000 NRP report concluded that vocabulary growth can be a result of incidental learning, but teachers must also choose words for explicit vocabulary instruction. Most teachers rely on the vocabulary identified by the publishers of the basal reader. However, Hiebert (2005) questions the sagaciousness of allocating instructional time to these targeted words that are usually so rare that they infrequently reoccur in future reading. Thus, candidate preparation should focus on evidence-based practices for teaching vocabulary as well as strategies for selection of words to be taught.

Reading Fluency

Fluency is reading with speed, accuracy, and proper expression without conscious attention. Despite over four decades of research in oral reading fluency, there is some variability among definitions (see Strecker, Roser, & Martinez, 1998, for a discussion). One widely accepted definition is that of the NRP in which fluency is defined as "reading text with speed, accuracy, and proper expression" (NICHD, 2000, p. 3-1). Even though a unified definition of oral reading fluency does not exist, most researchers agree that fluency is a complex, multifaceted skill that is an aggregate of three discrete components which generate a distinct process. These three components are (1) accuracy of word recognition, (2) speed of word recognition, and (3) prosody. Also, most all of the current definitions of fluency tend to regard the components of fluency as outcomes of learned skills (Wolf & Katzir-Cohen, 2001). Once the reader masters skills in lexical, phonological, and syntactical processes, the result is effortless reading with good comprehension.

Numerous studies on reading fluency literature report a link between fluency and reading proficiency (Anderson et al., 1985; Chard, Vaughn, & Tyler, 2002; Dowhower, 1994; Kuhn & Stahl, 2003; NICHD, 2000; Rasinski & Hoffman, 2003; Strecker et al., 1998). Recent research has shown oral reading fluency to be a predictor of reading comprehension (Fuchs, Fuchs, Hosp, & Jenkins, 2001; NICHD, 2000; D.E. Wood, 2006). The National Assessment of Educational Progress (NAEP) study (Daane, Campbell, Grigg, Goodman, & Oranje, 2005; Pinnell et al., 1995) reported that there was a strong relationship between the various components of oral reading fluency (fluency, accuracy, and rate). Furthermore, it was found that fluency scores highly correlated with reading comprehension, as measured by the NAEP 2002 reading assessment. On average, the students that attained the highest level of reading performance were the students that had the highest rating on the NAEP oral reading fluency scale score. Fluency represents a level of reading expertise that supersedes the skills of accurate and fast word recognition such that comprehension may be aided (NICHD, 2000).

Empirical data suggest strong, positive correlations between reading fluency and comprehension, thereby removing any doubt concerning the existence of the interrelatedness of oral reading fluency and reading comprehension (Allinder, Dunse, Brunken, & Obermiller-Krolikowski, 2001; Fuchs et al., 2001; Nathan & Stanovich, 1991). Furthermore, researchers claim that an increase in performance in one area leads to an increase in the other area. The NRP's (NICHD, 2000) examination of the literature reported that fluency is directly associated with the process of comprehension because it allows for "preliminary interpretive steps" (p. 3-6). They acknowledge that when reading rate is increased, comprehension increases. However, there is no definitive response regarding the direction of the relationship. The question arises whether multiple readings of a passage increase both reading rate and comprehension because of the several opportunities to interact with the text, or do multiple readings prompt understanding of the written text, in turn facilitating speed of word identification. If this is the case, comprehension could directly facilitate rapid word recognition (Massey, 2007).

The NRP (2000) reviewed the studies on reading fluency with the goal of examining how concepts of fluency were changing and to determine the effectiveness of guided oral reading and repeated reading as instructional practices to promote fluency development. They confirmed the importance of reading fluency, which can be positively affected through instruction for children in grade 2 through high school, for both good and poor readers alike. Their findings demonstrate that repeated and guided oral reading significantly affected word recognition, fluency, and comprehension. There was little evidence, however, to support the effectiveness of independent reading activities such as Sustained Silent Reading, a finding that has been disputed in response to the NRP findings (Krashen, 2001).

Comprehension Strategies

The 2000 NRP report states that reading "comprehension is critically important to the development of children's reading skills and therefore to the ability to obtain an education" (p. 1-3). Reading comprehension is the construction of the meaning of a written text through a reciprocal interchange of ideas between the reader and the message in a particular text (IRA, 2002a). It is referred to as a process that incorporates decoding skills, vocabulary knowledge, prior knowledge, and activation and execution of pertinent strategies to gain meaning of the printed text (Block & Pressley, 2002; Kintsch & Kintsch, 2005). According to Armbruster, Lehr, and Osborn (2001), comprehension is purposeful and active and is enhanced by instruction.

A key element in the comprehension process is the reader. A reader's experience, knowledge of language, and knowledge of syntactic structure affect the comprehension process. Lack of this knowledge prohibits comprehension, regardless of vocabulary knowledge and application of strategic skills. For example, a child may be able to sound out an unknown word but may not be able to determine the meaning. Block and Pressley (2002) determine that more than 30 cognitive processes are integrated as a reader activates the process of comprehending. These include clarifying meaning, summarizing, drawing inferences, and predicting, just to name a few.

Research has demonstrated the efficacy of teaching reading comprehension strategies and interventions for both general education students and students who have been identified as learning disabled (Block & Pressley, 2002; Mastropieri, Scruggs, Bakken, & Whedon, 1996; Pressley, Johnson, Symons, McGoldrick, & Kurita, 1989; Swanson, Hoskyn, & Lee, 1999; Talbott, Lloyd, & Tankiersley, 1994) to improve comprehension of new text and topics via teacher-guided strategy instruction. Good readers engage in comprehension strategies before, during, and after reading (Pressley & Wharton-McDonald, 1997). Struggling readers typically do not, but can, improve comprehension when they are explicitly taught specific strategies. The teacher should model these strategies and then scaffold or support the children through the process (NICHD, 2000). Pressley and Block (2002) also recommend that teachers first practice the strategies in their own reading to determine how they function so they will be better equipped to transfer these skills to their students. However, researchers have determined that many students are not benefiting from comprehension instruction because teachers dedicate only a fraction of instructional time to teaching and demonstrating the skills and strategies that are seldom acquired without conscious effort or that can be self-taught, but could assist students to comprehend (Durkin, 1978/1979; Pressley, 1998), despite the evidence from empirical studies.

Reading comprehension strategies are plans that readers consciously and flexibly apply, adopting to varied texts and tasks as needed (Pearson, Roehler, Dole, & Duffy, 1992). Additional criteria for comprehension strategies—that they be "specific, learned procedures that foster active, competent, self-regulated, and intentional reading"—are offered by Trabasso and Bouchard (2002, p. 177). The mature reader possesses a wide variety of reading strategies for the specific reading situation (Pressley & Afflerbach, 1995). Cognitive strategy instruction has been shown to increase memory and comprehension in children (Pressley, 2000). The NRP concluded that when

> readers are given cognitive-strategies instruction, they make significant gains on measures of reading comprehension over students trained with conventional instruction. Teaching a variety of reading comprehension strategies in natural settings and content areas leads to increased learning...to transfer of learning, to increased memory and understanding of new passages.... (NICHD, 2000, p. 4–6)

The NRP found evidence of seven comprehension strategies to be highly effective pedagogical techniques out of the 203 studies on comprehension-strategy instruction. These included cooperative learning, comprehension monitoring, graphic organizers, story structure, question answering, question generation, and summarization. Teachers are expected to teach these seven strategies, but they are not limited to only these techniques. It must be noted that isolated strategies result in improvements in comprehension, but there are many cognitive processes occurring simultaneously during the reading process. Efficient readers often implement more than one strategy; therefore, instruction in multiple strategies is most effective, as this guides students how to be flexible in strategy selection and to use them according to the specific task (Block & Pressley, 2002).

In addition to the NRP report, findings from the RAND Reading Study Group (RRSG) (Snow, 2002) are also pertinent in thinking about candidate preparation in the teaching of reading comprehension. In 1999, the RRSG was charged with the responsibility of reviewing extant literature on reading comprehension instruction and to set an agenda for future research. Their research was framed by a dynamic model of reading comprehension that envisioned thinking of reading comprehension as an interaction among the reader, text, and activity within a sociocultural context. Snow concludes that we have much to learn from research about how best to prepare candidates to be most effective in the teaching of the complex and dynamic act of reading comprehension.

Motivation

One factor that tends to affect reading comprehension is a reader's ability to maintain engagement with the text, or motivation (Snow et al., 1998). As Guthrie and Wigfield (2000) assert, "a person reads a word or comprehends a text not only because she can do it, but because she is motivated to do it" (p. 404). In their review of the research literature on motivation, Guthrie and Wigfield point out that motivation involves active engagement and is psychologically and sociologically multifaceted. They also observe that motivation changes over time. Indeed, independent reading decreases as students progress to higher grades (Guthrie & Wigfield, 2000), unless students possess intrinsic motivation. Furthermore, practitioners need to become proficient in the use of new technologies to teach these components in integrated and motivational ways (Education Development Center, 2004). These technologies include programs that focus on the reading components as identified by the NRP (NICHD, 2000).

Conclusion

Snow (2004) contends that anyone inclined to study or teach reading regardless of the perspective does so with the intent to facilitate children's learning with the outcome of creating productive citizens. However, even though one would not negate the fact that there are many excellent educators who teach well without the knowledge of empirical data to guide reading instruction, the literature demonstrates that teachers whose instruction and educational decisions are governed by scientific research produce students that reap greater benefits (Spear-Swerling & Sternberg, 2001).

It is the responsibility of IHEs to create a curriculum that instructs candidates on the science and history of reading and to explore their own beliefs based on both experience and professional knowledge (Vacca et al., 2005). Candidates with such an opportunity for professional growth are armed with the knowledge and expertise to adequately guide their reading instruction and minimize the "chasm that exists between classroom instructional practices and the research knowledge-base on literacy development" (Moats, 1999, p. 7). Snow (2004) further states that teacher preparation curricula should ensure that teacher candidates and inservice teachers are not only grounded in the research, but are also accoutered with the skills "to identify, read, respect and apply the findings of scientific research to their practice" (p. 23). This affords them the foundational knowledge not only to make informed decisions and solve problems but also to proffer rebuttals against mandated decisions from administrators and policymakers. It also gives teachers the knowledge to disprove the prevalent and potentially harmful educational fads that are marketed to guarantee dramatic improvements in one or all the components required for reading proficiency.

FURTHER READING

Alexander, P.A., & Fox, E. (2004). A historical perspective on reading research and practice. In R.B. Ruddell & N.J. Unrau (Eds.), *Theoretical models and processes of reading* (pp. 33–68). Newark, DE: International Reading Association.

This chapter highlights the past 50 years of reading research and practice.

Education Development Center. (2004). *Technology and teaching children to read.* Retrieved December 15, 2007, from www.neirtec.org/reading_report

This report aligns key components of the 2000 National Reading Panel report with research in technology.

Fresch, M.J. (Ed.). (2008). *An essential history of current reading practices.* Newark, DE: International Reading Association.
In this volume, experts in the various components of reading instruction outline the history and research for each topic.

International Reading Association. (2004). *Preparing reading professionals: A collection from the International Reading Association.* Newark, DE: Author.
This publication presents articles that extend and elaborate on topics such as the development of reading research and reading instruction due to the influences of linguistics, psycholinguistics, cognitive psychology, and sociolinguistics. Furthermore, the book presents foundational knowledge on the issues of multiculturalism, language acquisition, and literacy research.

Rayner, K., Foorman, B.R., Perfetti, C.A., Pesetsky, D., & Seidenberg, M.S. (2001). How psychological science informs the teaching of reading. *Psychological Science in the Public Interest*, 2(2), 31–74.
This is a comprehensive monograph presenting research, theory, and practice relevant to how children learn to read English.

Robinson, R.D. (2005). *Readings in reading instruction: Its history, theory, and development.* Boston: Allyn & Bacon.
Robinson provides a collection of primary source readings related to foundations of reading instruction.

Sweet, R.W. (2004). The big picture: Where we are nationally on the reading front and how we got here. In P. McCardle & V. Chhabra (Eds.), *The voice of evidence in reading research* (pp. 13–44). Baltimore: Paul H. Brookes.
Sweet presents a succinct account of the history of reading research and instruction and the cultural and societal influences that shaped this development. Three decades of reading research and instruction are detailed.

The CaseNEX case study selected for Standard 1 specifically addresses theories of learning (Element 1.1). For Element 1.1., there is a possibility of scoring a high of 11 and a low of 0 for writing off topic (see Standard 1 Rubric, Appendix, p. 142).

Case Study for Standard 1: Foundational Knowledge

Reprinted from CaseNEX LLC, founded at University of Virginia's Curry School of Education. Reprinted with permission.

Conducting Learning

Some say teaching is like juggling plates, like pulling teeth, like walking a tightrope. And some say that because Martha Kueffner teaches gifted first graders in a self-contained classroom, her job is a piece of cake. To her, on good days, it's more like conducting an orchestra. Simultaneously, she's building independence in her students, beefing-up their technology skills, teaching the writing process, adhering to the prescribed curriculum, providing arts enrichment, and matching activities to various intelligences and learning styles.

Leaning over the tiny tables, chairs, and students, Martha works to check homework while keeping an eye on all that is happening in her busy classroom.

As the morning progresses, she encourages her students to recall all the steps they've used to draft and revise a recent writing project. She's been focusing on increasing students' responsibility for evaluating and improving their work and helping students support one another as they move through the writing process.

One student, Meghan, is clearly comfortable speaking in front of her classmates. Martha regularly reminds herself not to lean too hard on Meghan when she needs to keep a class discussion moving. After years of teaching, she knows how important it is to give everyone a chance to speak, especially those students who are new to the United States and working to master English. These students, and their peers, need just as much practice speaking and listening as reading and writing.

Whenever she can, Martha integrates the arts into the curriculum. Her focus on visual art, drama, and music makes good use of nearby Manhattan's resources. Organizing trip logistics and guest artists is challenging, but in the end Martha always returns to this teaching hook.

Attend the Queens Symphony
Discuss how music can express feelings

Listen to a piece of music with the class
What feelings does it bring out in them

Write a story that fits the music or might depict the feelings in the music that the composer is trying to make us feel

Make books out of their stories

Examine the instruments in the orchestra download pictures and descriptions of the instruments they can color and put together in a book *Free rehearsals. Contact while Orchestra Sec - Mets Lincoln Cent*

Music Enrichment 2
Attend the Nutcracker Ballet at Lincoln Center New York State Theatre evening performance

View the video of the Nutcracker Ballet in

Martha can't stop grinning as she helps her students pack up for the day. She's continually amazed by their ability to function as a cohesive group and pull together creative projects. She realizes that her students' gifts make her job look easy. But, Martha knows better.

Question for response: Think about the many activities Martha uses in her classroom. Briefly describe three activities and explain how these activities are examples of specific theories of learning discussed in this and previous classes. Be sure to include a rationale (or your reasoning) that links the activity with the theory.

Context of Administration

Candidates were provided with this case study as a take-home assignment at the end of a course focusing on diagnosis of reading difficulties. This reading course emphasized theoretical foundations and the responses included here are from candidates who were in their first year (second semester) of a degree-seeking graduate reading program. The instructor (Peggy) shared the rubric with the candidates so that they would be familiar with the evaluation criteria. Candidates watched the accompanying video and read the case in class and were provided time to ask questions. An honor statement was signed before leaving class indicating that responses would be individual, yet discussion of the case would be allowed. Time for collaboration was not provided in class, so any discussion of the case would be done on the candidates' own time. One week later the response was turned in to the instructor. Before scoring, two faculty members brainstormed foundational theories related to the case, appropriate possibilities, and theories that could be linked to practice for the rationale section. These brainstormed lists provided the minimum criteria from which to begin scoring responses.

Responses

The first response received a content score of 0 and a rationale score of Novice because the content focuses on the teaching techniques with no mention of theories behind those techniques. The rationale is weak and is really a mere summary of the case.

After watching the video on Conducting Learning involving Marta's first grade self contained Gifted/ELL class, I saw the following examples/evidence of specific theories of learning. Marta's instructional and ESOL strategies she used in her classroom which were individualized work, pairing, cooperative group work, peer tutoring/correction/monitoring and modeling. Marta's structured daily morning routines which select students were assigned the duties and responsibilities of taking the attendance and writing the morning announcements on the board. Then some of the students as a group read aloud the morning announcements with Marta monitoring them. The purpose of these activities was to help the students strengthen and increase their writing, spelling, oral reading, listening, punctuation, grammar, questioning, correcting, sharing, work recognition/meaning, and monitoring skills. Marta's activities were based on what her students already knew, their prior knowledge, which she activated by tapping in on their interest and experiences. Marta gave her students outside exposure (fieldtrips), time to explore (computer research) and hands on (experience learn by doing) activities. Marta also integrated visual arts into her activities by having the students to draw and create their own book using their words, thoughts, ideas and visual images. Last but not least Marta focused all her activities on helping ELL learn by speaking, reading, writing, experiencing, exploring and exposure.

As teachers we must remember that creating is nothing more than using our prior knowledge to help make predictions, asking questions, sketch ideas, then write or draw those ideas on paper (organizing). And finally blend them together (connect). Like the sweet sounds of an orchestra.

The second response provides more of a theoretical basis for practices than the previous response. The response received a content score of 7 because essential aspects of Vygotsky's theory are provided, along with applications. The response received a rationale score of Sufficient because an emergent conceptual understanding is evident.

Martha utilizes various activities in her class that incorporates strategies that are based on the theories of Vygotsky and Bruner's constructivist perspectives of learning. She provides her students with a rich and stimulating environment dependent on social interaction and learning that leads to their cognitive development. Her classroom provides space for collaboration, peer and small group instruction. Martha's teaching methods actively involve students in engaging activities based on their various intelligences and learning styles that assist them in becoming independent learners. The instructional designs of materials to be learned are structured to promote and encourage students' interaction and collaboration of assignments. Her class consists of untraditional means of communication between teacher and student. Instead of dictating her meaning to her students, Martha collaborates with them to create meaning in ways that students can make their own and learning becomes a reciprocal experience for her and the students. The process of learning, retaining, and applying information from peer to peer and peer to teacher interaction takes place. Under Martha's guidance the students perform tasks and become independent problem solvers through peer collaboration which leads to their zone of proximal development. This zone, according to Vygotsky, bridges the gap between what is known and what can be known as learning. Through Martha's effective scaffolding and reciprocal teaching strategies, the zone of proximal development is accessed and students are given the opportunity to extend their current skills and knowledge of technology, the writing process, the curriculum, and art enrichment activities engaging to the their interest that motivates them to pursue her instructional goals and thus creating a classroom that becomes a community of learners.

The third response received a content score of 11 with a Distinguished rationale because it shows a strong conceptual understanding of how theories are enacted within literacy practices.

Martha Kueffner's classroom provides a learning environment where all students have the opportunity to develop their academic skills. The classroom provides all the necessary elements to provide differentiating instruction, the use of multiple intelligences, and the incorporation of technology available for the student's use. She provides reading, writing, researching, and cooperative learning in a classroom with students having the chance to learn at their own pace and develop knowledge that will help scaffold their learning experience with the teacher as facilitator of the learning journey.

The goals of education, according to Bruner, are to free society and assist students in developing their full potential. Jerome Bruner would like Martha Kueffner's classroom because Bruner believes that education is a process of discovery and Martha's classroom provides an environment where students can make educational discoveries. Martha provides materials, activities, and tools to facilitate the developing cognitive capabilities of her students. Martha's classroom uses the principles of Bruner by providing experiences that motivate the students to learn in a structured environment where the material is easily accessed. All experiences and instruction are designed to facilitate the student's exploration of knowledge and provide material that goes beyond what is expected. Bruner also believes to keep pace with the ever increasing changes of technology education should focus on the basic skills that will be needed to manage this technology. These skills should continuously be updated as technology grows more complex. Skills in handing, seeing and imaging and symbolic operations (especially as they relate to technology) are also worthwhile learning. Martha provides various opportunities for her students to develop the necessary skills to make technology part of their educational process which will prepare the students with real world experiences.

Learning is an active, social process, in which students construct new ideas or concepts based on their current knowledge (Bruner). Students realize that, as they learn, they are able to access information that they were previously unable to utilize. This reward and excitement perpetuates the student to learn even more. Educators should assist with this. Martha excels in the motivation and development of the student's interest in learning. Louise Rosenblatt would approve of how Martha creates an atmosphere where the students and teachers feel comfortable and permit a personal response to the educational process. Martha helps students create a live circuit between what they are learning and their lives. She takes them on field trips so they have the opportunity to develop schemas which, in turn will improve their ability to comprehend new ideas in the classroom because it develops personal relevance in their lives

(Rosenblatt). According to "Improving Reading Comprehension" it is important the teacher help connect to the student's prior knowledge with new information. The Schema Theory explains how knowledge is stored in the mind and the importance of activating this knowledge. The schemas contain related concepts and it is obvious in Martha's Music Enrichment plan that she finds this theory important in the development of the students' acquisition of new material. She includes field trip, discussion, listening to music, writing, creating books, and playing instruments in her lesson. While developing the schemas, she is also using Gardner's theory of Multiple Intelligences by using a variety of activities to challenge different skills of her students. They students use the various intelligences throughout the music plan; linguistic through discussion and writing assignments, logical-mathematical by writing stories that fit the music and also the understanding of how the instruments are made, musical through the listening and appreciation of the music, kinesthetic by playing instruments, Interpersonal through the understanding of the purpose of the composer, and intrapersonal through the understanding of their feelings to the music.

The students in Martha Kueffner's class have the freedom to develop independently through the use of differentiated instruction and on- on-one contact with the teacher, but they also develop through cooperative learning that created peer tutoring and reciprocal learning that provide interaction of the students where they help scaffold one another through the transference of their knowledge in a relaxed educational environment. Martha is the facilitator of the entire proves, interjecting when necessary to provide necessary instructional ideas.

Martha Kueffner's classroom is one that most teachers can only dream of creating. She has designed her environment and instruction to align with the ideas and educational theories that motivate, interest, encourage, and develop students who are destined for academic success.

The fourth response also received a content score of 11 with a Distinguished rationale because it demonstrates a strong understanding of how theories are present in the teaching recorded on the case video.

The activities Martha uses in her classroom are clear examples of the Constructivist theories of learning studied in class, specifically those of Piaget, Bruner, and Vygotsky. In our classes we learned that constructivist theories view knowledge as something constructed by the learner as he or she engages in the learning process. In Martha's classroom, knowledge is not transmitted in its entirety by the teacher, but rather, through her careful choice of activities, Martha allows her students to construct meaning, either on their own (cognitive oriented constructivist theories, like those of Piaget and Bruner) or through interactions with the teacher and/or their peers (socially oriented constructivist theories like Vygotsky). Piaget's influence can be seen in the kinds of materials and activities Martha chooses for her students. Martha knows that her gifted first graders are leaving the preoperational stage, where intelligence is naturally instinctive, and entering the concrete operational stage, where the cognitive structure is logical in nature but depends on the concrete as a reference. She therefore plans activities that build cognitive and linguistic skills, like having her students classify musical instruments, discuss the relationship between the Nutcracker play and the Nutcracker story, or discuss how some music expresses feelings.

Martha's activities and strategies also reflect the Constructivist Theory of Bruner. According to Bruner's theory, students learn by constructing meaning, based mostly on current or past knowledge and schema, or cognitive structure, and the teacher's job is to guide their students to discover this knowledge on their own. In Martha's classroom, students write the morning message, conduct research on the computer, and write, edit, and publish their own books. One aspect of Bruner's theory evident in Martha's interaction with her students is what Bruner refers to as "socratic learning" where the teacher and students engage in dialogue and discussions about what is being learned to clarify and/ or expand on ideas. One example of "socratic learning" in the video clip is when Martha asks a boy about his editing and he responds that he noticed he was missing some letters a period and he fixed it. Another example is when Martha has her students recall the steps they used in writing and revising their stories. In her dialogues with students, Martha uses the process of metacognition, or thinking about thinking, to monitor her students' progress and cognitive development.

Bruner's four key elements of his theory are also evident in Martha's classroom activities. One of these elements is the "spiral curriculum" where the skills learned build upon each other and are repeated until the student gains mastery. An example of this is the writing process: Martha engages her students in many and varied writing activities which reinforce the skills of drafting, revising, editing, and publishing and help her students become better, more proficient writers.

Martha's classroom activities for music enhancement also show evidence of Bruner's three modes of reasoning. Attending the Nutcracker ballet and watching the Nutcracker video to discuss the differences is an example of the iconic mode (visual recognition and compare/contrasting). Making their own Nutcracker storybooks and making and playing their own musical instruments are both examples of the enactive (manipulating objects) mode. Finally, discussing how music can express feelings, or listening to music and talking about the feelings it brings out in them are examples of the symbolic (abstract) mode of reasoning.

Many of the activities in Martha's classroom promote social interactions as reflected by Vygotsky's social development theory where social interactions play an important role in the student's full cognitive development. Martha's students collaborate with her and each other in various reading and writing activities throughout the day. The clip shows several examples of students collaborating with each other. Take for instance the morning message: a student writes the message on the board, and then calls her classmates to come listen to her read. After reading it aloud, she then calls on a student to make corrections where needed. In another corner of the room, one student is showing another one how to print what she just researched on the computer. Later in the day, Meghan, one of the girls in the class, shares her Nutcracker story and art with classmates at the Reader's Chair.

Martha also collaborates with those students that need her help, using her knowledge of their zone of proximal development (ZPD) to guide them as they solve problems that arise. One example is when she works with a boy that is writing a sentence; she has him say the sentence aloud and then write it, thus scaffolding his learning. Martha's classroom, both in its activities and its physical design, truly exemplifies Vygotsky's theory of a community of learners as well as the constructivists' framework of cognitive development.

CHAPTER 2

Learning About and Assessing Standard 2—Instructional Strategies and Curriculum Materials

There are many ways to approach reading curriculum and instruction in P–12 classrooms. Differentiated instruction has garnered attention as an effective means to meeting students' diverse literacy learning needs (Tomlinson, 2003). Heacox (2002) reports that reading lessons can be differentiated by changing the content, the process, or the product of instruction. The content can be customized to learners' needs by changing the curriculum taught to focus on what should be mastered or providing students with choices of subtopics to investigate, relating to the main topic of study. For example, when reading historical fiction, novels at different reading levels are provided, or students choose to research the setting or characters' occupations to learn more about the time period in which the story takes place. Teachers who differentiate the process enable their students with various strategies or activities to learn about the content (i.e., modeling and teaching divergent comprehension, metacognitive or word attack strategies). Finally differentiating the product (or evaluation of the content learned) allows students to demonstrate their knowledge in varied ways.

To differentiate literacy instruction in these three areas, teachers must be adept and knowledgeable of practice, curriculum, and methods. Standard 2 recommends that "candidates use a wide range of instructional practices, approaches, methods, and curriculum materials to support reading and writing instruction" (IRA, 2004, p. 8). Thus, the elements that make up Standard 2 include the following:

- Grouping practices during reading instruction
- Instructional approaches and methods
- Curriculum materials and effective reading instruction for all learners

Whereas reading programs can contribute to effective instruction, teachers are the most important variable in the teaching and learning instructional milieu (Bond & Dykstra, 1967/1997; Darling-Hammond, 1999; Fitzgerald, 1999; Pressley, 2002). In fact, according to Nye, Konstantopoulos, and Hedges (2004), effective teachers outweigh the impact of student ethnicity, family income, school attended, or class size; therefore, high-quality literacy teachers are instrumental in closing the achievement gap (Sanders & Rivers, 1996).

Element 2.1

Use instructional grouping options (individual, small-group, whole-class, and computer-based) as appropriate for accomplishing given purposes.

Inclusive classrooms and increasing student diversity solidify the need for different grouping configurations, or differentiated instruction, during reading (Burnett, 1999), particularly for children requiring supplementary instruction (Allington, 2002a; Snow et al., 1998; Vaughn, Hughes, Moody, & Elbaum, 2001). Generally, students are grouped based on homogenous or heterogeneous ability levels in groups containing 5–9 students and are either taught by a teacher, reading specialist, or paraprofessional. Research such as Pinnell, Lyons, Deford, Bryk, & Seltzer (1994) and Vellutino et al., (1996) indicates that small groups are more effective with fewer students (i.e., 2–3 students) and when instructed by teachers or reading specialists (Achilles, 1999; IRA, 1994). Other characteristics of effective small-group instruction include high levels of interaction among the students, texts at appropriate levels of difficulty (i.e., instructional reading level), and explicit instruction of strategies (Swanson & Hoskyn, 1998).

Whereas ability grouping (grouping students by low, middle, or high ability levels) has been widely used during reading instruction, problems using this approach have been identified (Barr, 1995). Students in low-ability groups may experience low self-esteem (Barr, 1995), fall even further behind their peers in middle or high groups (Juel, 1988), and receive different types of instruction than those in higher groups (Allington, 1983; McGill-Franzen & Allington, 1991). In addition, classroom management is an issue for many teachers while working with ability groups (Morris, 1999). However, in a study investigating teachers and schools with differing achievement levels, Taylor, Pearson, Clark, and Walpole (1999) find, among other characteristics, that the most effective schools' teachers spent the majority of their reading instructional time in small, homogenous reading groups. The difference between these ability groups and others was the flexibility noted by the researchers. Systematic assessment guided the teachers in placing students in groups for early intervention instruction. As students progressed, they were moved across groups in a flexible grouping environment. Taylor and colleagues demonstrated that fluid, flexible homogenous grouping of students is key and can lead to higher reading achievement.

Dynamic grouping practices (Fountas & Pinnell, 2001) have also proven to be successful with struggling, grade level, and above grade level readers (Morris, 1999; Temple, Ogle, Crawford, & Freppon, 2005). Dynamic groups provide targeted guided reading opportunities and involve the creation of several kinds of reading/writing groups throughout the school day (Temple et al., 2005). It is important to understand that dynamic grouping alone does not guarantee success for every reader. Rather, it is what the teacher does during specific blocks of time with dynamic grouping that raises achievement. Early interventions using one-to-one instruction or small groups such as Reading Recovery (Clay, 1993), Success for All (Slavin, Madden, Karweit, Dolan, & Wasik, 1994), or guided reading (Avalos, Plasencia, Chavez, & Rascón, 2007; Cunningham, Hall, & Sigmon, 2000; Fountas & Pinnell, 1996) have proven to be effective in raising reading achievement levels. Again, flexible grouping is essential when using these approaches to teach reading.

According to Marzano, Pickering, and Pollock (2001), grouping for cooperative learning should include small, heterogeneous groups so that students achieving at higher levels are able to assist those who need help. Student engagement and participation is encouraged when using smaller groups, as comfort levels are generally higher. This is especially important for ELLs (Hill & Flynn, 2006).

Students may also have a choice in forming groups. For example, when using literature study groups, teachers may allow students to choose a book from five to six selections and form groups based on the students' choices. It is recommended that students indicate a first and second preference so that there is flexibility in forming groups (Harp & Brewer, 2005). Five to eight students per group would be ideal as less than five does not generally offer much stimulation for discussion, and more than eight inhibits all students from participating.

Whole-class instruction is also appropriate for teaching certain skills at grade level; however, the teacher must be aware of students' instructional needs so that, if necessary, the concept(s) can be reviewed or taught in different ways when differentiated instruction is provided.

Recently the Response to Intervention (RTI) movement has promoted a tiered approach to grouping for instruction (Fletcher, Francis, Shaywitz, Lyon, Foorman, Steubing et al., 1998; Siegel, 1989; Stanovich, 1991; Vellutino, Scanlon, & Lyon, 2000). The use of the IQ-discrepancy formula, or wait-to-fail model, as a means of identifying children with reading disabilities came under attack in part because students who demonstrated reading difficulties did not receive preventive interventions prior to being diagnosed with a reading disability (Stage, Abbott, Jenkins, & Berninger, 2003). As a result, the reauthorization of Individuals With Disabilities Education Improvement Act (IDEA) of 2004 introduced a new operational definition of learning disabilities to include domain-specific definitions that assist in more reliable identifications of at-risk students and to supplement the discrepancy concept that has been the primary standard for learning disabled (LD) identification. There is no longer the need to compare a student's measured ability and their score of achievement as determined by a standardized test of intelligence (i.e., IQ) to determine eligibility for special education. Now, there is the option of implementing an RTI approach as a means to identify reading disabilities. The general principle of the RTI model involves using classroom-based teacher intervention evaluation and response and data-driven assessments to determine the presence or absence of a reading disability. There are variations of how different states have operationalized RTI; however, the basic premise is the same: A student is only identified with a reading disability when his response to an effective educational intervention is dramatically inferior to that of his peers (Compton, Fuchs, Fuchs, & Bryant, 2006).

In most states, the RTI model involves three levels of instruction: Tier 1, Tier 2, and Tier 3. Every child is enrolled in Tier 1 reading instruction, which takes place in the general education classroom. This reading program provides both small-group and whole-class instruction. Progress is monitored by continuous assessment throughout the academic year. Students who do not demonstrate progress within the general education curriculum are referred to Tier 2 intervention. At this level, differentiated instruction consists of more concentrated interventions to meet students' learning needs in key areas of reading (phonological awareness, phonics, fluency, vocabulary, and comprehension). The specific interventions take place in addition to the regular reading block during the school day. Students stay in Tier 2 until they master the skill and then return to Tier 1 instruction. If the student does not respond to instruction at the Tier 2 level, as monitored by assessment scores, they are referred to a more intense level of intervention (Tier 3).

Although RTI helps to prevent reading problems by providing early intervention, teachers are even more accountable than before because they are responsible for designing and implementing differentiated instruction to address the needs of all children. Now more than ever teacher education programs need to be aware of the value of preparing teachers to implement differentiated instruction on a regular basis (Schumm & Arguelles, 2006).

In sum, the commonalities among effective grouping practices include knowing students' instructional needs, being flexible in grouping practices, and ensuring that all students have the opportunity and comfort levels needed to actively participate in the learning.

Element 2.2

Use a wide range of instructional practices, approaches, and methods, including technology-based practices, for learners at differing stages of development and from differing cultural and linguistic backgrounds.

There are a multitude of research-based instructional practices that could be used as Standard 2 indicates. In fact, a book could be written for this element alone, and there are many available that are helpful in addressing varied, effective instructional approaches (see Beers, 2003; Fang, 2005; Hill & Flynn, 2006; IRA, 2002a; Marzano et al., 2001). For the purpose of this chapter, the focus of this review covers three aspects of reading instruction: (1) a comprehensive approach to literacy instruction, (2) the need to integrate the language arts, and (3) how technology can effectively be used for reading instruction. However, it is important also to note the impact of time spent reading on achievement. One distinguishing factor between more and less effective teachers at the elementary level has been the actual time students spend reading (Pressley, Allington, Wharton-McDonald, Block, & Morrow, 2001; Taylor et al., 1999a). Teachers who had their students read at least 45 minutes each hour allocated for reading instruction were most effective (i.e., 90 of the 120 minutes allocated for reading instruction). Allington (2001) recommends a minimum of 90 minutes of actual reading time for children at the elementary level; hence, although using varied instructional approaches are important, it is also critical that students spend a good amount of instructional reading time actually reading at their instructional level.

Comprehensive Literacy Instruction

There have been disagreements in the past concerning "the" most effective way to teach reading; however, more recently scholars have agreed there is not a "one-size-fits-all" approach (Beers, 2003; Cox, 2005; Fitzgerald, 1999; Harp, & Brewer, 2005), and diverse methods and materials are necessary to create independent readers (Stoicheva, 1999). A comprehensive approach to reading instruction balances instruction in *all* areas, from phonics and comprehension, to systematic skill and systematic strategy, to using multiple text types (decodable to literature-based), depending on the needs of the learners (Fitzgerald, 1999; Harp & Brewer, 2005). Baumann and Ivey (1997) studied strategy instruction in a literature-rich environment and looked at student outcomes after one academic year. They found that the students in participating classrooms (diverse second graders) made instructional reading level gains; were highly engaged with texts; developed skills in word identification, fluency, and comprehension; and grew in writing/composition skills. After analyzing observational data, Baumann and Ivey credit the gains students made to the balance between a literature-rich environment and contextualized strategy instruction as well as a balance between teacher-initiated instruction and instruction in response to students.

A comprehensive approach to instruction requires reading teachers to make many decisions based on student needs, thus emphasizing the importance of the teacher in the instructional process (Bond & Dykstra, 1967/1997; Darling-Hammond, 1999; Fitzgerald, 1999; Pressley, 2002). Spiegel (1999) developed criteria to assist teachers in finding the balance between teacher-directed explicit instruction and student-directed discovery that is right for each student (see Table 4). She posits that teachers must first look at the student and then at the task to find an appropriate approach (skills-based versus holistic) and use for assessment (standardized versus authentic). If the student has the tendency to fall behind others in the class when not receiving teacher-directed instruction and has a lower confidence level, the teacher should move toward a more teacher-directed means of instruction. On the other hand, if the student is typically able to induce learning strategies, completes tasks independently, and easily becomes bored, a more learner-directed approach to reading instruction is warranted. If the majority of students need to know a strategy or concept, or if that strategy is needed now, a more teacher-directed approach is appropriate. If the concept or strategy can be learned through exploration and is not a foundation for other concepts or needed immediately, a more learner-directed approach should be used. In addition, a learner-directed approach would be beneficial if the students are not engaged in the curriculum or are not taking responsibility for their own learning.

Spiegel (1999) also suggests that teachers use more of an isolated skill or strategy focus if the student demonstrates a limited number of strategies when reading and a more holistic focus on texts when the student demonstrates the strategy using only artificial texts, appearing to need assistance in transferring the strategy to authentic texts. The holistic approach is also needed when a student does not spontaneously integrate the strategy with other strategies.

Finally, to find a balance between standardized and authentic assessments, the teacher may use a more formal measure to compare student progress with other students as a group, or if parents and other stakeholders need a measure of achievement that is meaningful to

TABLE 4. Criteria for Balanced Literacy Instruction

	Teacher-directed	Learner-directed
Student	• Falls behind peers without teacher assistance • Low self-confidence	• Typically able to induce strategies on his or her own • Completes work independently • Easily becomes bored
Task	• When the majority of students need the strategy or concept • When the strategy is needed now	• When the strategy or concept can be learned through students' exploration of texts • Not a foundational concept or strategy, nor needed immediately
	Isolated skill emphasis	**Whole texts**
Approach	• When student demonstrates few strategies while reading • Student needs to focus on the strategy to internalize it	• When student only demonstrates the strategy using artificial texts • When students need assistance in transferring the strategy to authentic texts • When a student does not spontaneously integrate the strategy with other strategies
	Standardized assessment	**Authentic assessment**
Assessments	• To compare student progress with other students as a group • When parents and other stakeholders need a measure of achievement that is meaningful to them	• When data demonstrates individual student progress or processes • To validate or invalidate formal test scores

them. To determine individual student progress or processes or to validate or invalidate formal test scores, teachers could use more authentic assessment measures. Whenever important decisions are made about individual children, a single, formal test score should not be the only data used in making those decisions. Comprehensive literacy instruction requires teachers who know the learning needs of their students, ways to meet those needs, appropriate instructional approaches for differentiating instruction, and how to best measure student outcomes.

Integrating the Language Arts

The integration of reading, writing, listening, and speaking is another important variable in effective literacy instruction (Anderson et al., 1985). The language arts are not isolated from one another but rather build upon each other and develop simultaneously. Studies investigating classroom time spent reading, writing, listening, and speaking, however, demonstrate that not all of the language arts receive equal treatment in the classroom (Cox, 2005). Students typically listen 45% of the school day (mostly to teacher talk focusing on explaining and evaluating), speak 30%, read 16%, and write 9% (Rankin, 1928). Although these findings were first published over 80 years ago, little attention has been paid to teaching listening skills even though actively teaching listening has been demonstrated to improve listening ability (Brent & Anderson, 1993; Devine, 1978; Funk & Funk, 1989; Winn, 1988).

Although students spend a good part of the school day speaking, oral language development is another area that has been ignored. Cox (2005) points out that this is generally the case because reading and writing have traditionally been used to measure achievement; however, listening and speaking are important correlates to writing and reading achievement, particularly for diverse learners or students from differing cultural or linguistic backgrounds (Dyson, 1994; Meier, 2003). Morrow (2005) suggests both structured question and answer sessions and conversations as two organizational formats that lend themselves to promoting oral language and developing vocabulary in the classroom. Providing open-ended questions during question and answer sessions affords more opportunity for students to talk. Conversations occur best in small-group settings of 3–6 students. Morrow points out that within these conversations incorporating different types of talk is important for developing language in varied social settings. She explains "aesthetic talk" generally responds to literature (e.g., interpreting what was read or listened to), "efferent talk" is used to inform or persuade (e.g., discussing themes studied), and "dramatic activities" provide ways for students to share experiences, explore understandings, or interact with peers (e.g., formal role playing or dramatic play, puppetry). An environment rich in opportunities including all three types of talk motivates students to speak, thus developing oral language.

There are numerous instructional methods facilitating a comprehensive literacy approach while emphasizing the importance of reading, writing, listening, *and* speaking. Among these are the Four Blocks Program (Cunningham et al., 2000), Modified Guided Reading (Avalos et al., 2007), Collaborative Strategic Reading (Klingner & Vaughn, 1999), and others (cf. Beers, 2003; McCaster, 1998; Smith, 2000).

Technology in Reading Education

Technology has long been accepted as a tool for literacy learning (McNabb, 2005; Reinking, 1997); however, empirical studies investigating the impact of technology as a means to teach literacy are few and far between (Kamil, Intrator, & Kim, 2000). Kamil and colleagues reviewed the literature on reading and writing from 1986 to 1996 and found less than 5% of articles addressed technology-related issues. Schrum (2005) indicates that it is not easy to explore the impact that technology has on learning due to the "messiness of classrooms, the complexity of students' access to technology throughout their 'away from school' lives, and the ethical issues of disadvantaging some learners" (p. 113).

According to Smolin and Lawless (2003), there are differing levels of technology use in the classroom. A text-based view of literacy is one level in which technology is used in a fashion similar to a traditional approach to literacy learning, namely building skills and developing students' reading and writing abilities. In this type of classroom, skills-based computer software, online worksheets, and electronic dictionaries would be used; therefore, technology is used to facilitate reading and writing development in much the same way that individual seatwork-type activities are used. Using technology in this way has had mixed results, with some studies demonstrating positive links to improving achievement (Mann, Shakeshaft, Backer, & Kottkamp, 1999; Salerno, 1995) and at least one study finding no significant differences between classrooms using a computer program and text-based approaches (Paterson, Henry, O'Quin, Ceprano, & Blue, 2003).

Of the articles included in Kamil and colleagues' (2000) review, only two areas of literacy learning had sufficient research to indicate strong conclusions could be drawn from the literature: writing and hypermedia. Research concerning the use of technology to facilitate writing instruction has shown that students using word processing generally develop better writing skills than students not using word processing for composition (Kulik, 2003). Montgomery and Marks (2006) found that software for word processing and organization of writing enabled students with disabilities to become more independent in their writing. Beneficial features included graphic organizers or templates for brainstorming, word prediction, voice output, spell checker, and a thesaurus (see Table 5). A note of caution, however, research indicates that spell checkers can be problematic, as they sometimes fail to identify misspelled words, identify correctly spelled words as misspelled words, and do not offer the writer a foolproof way of identifying the correctly spelled word from the list of possible spellings (as cited in Montgomery & Marks).

Watson and Lacina (2004) make five suggestions based on lessons they learned from integrating technology within a writing workshop approach. First, model the writing process using a digital projector or other visible monitor. Students will benefit when they see a proficient writer actually writing, editing, revising, and publishing on-screen. Second, encourage risk taking by having students maintain an online "writer's notebook" (the teacher should also keep one that is accessible to all students as a model). The notebook should contain students' writing that is based on techniques used by authors after discussing their work in class. For example, some authors utilize bolded text in their stories to draw attention to certain words or concepts. Students could write a paragraph in their Writer's Notebooks, bolding text that serves to focus the reader's attention on the desired words or concepts. Watson and Lacina point out that blogs (web-based tools used to create webpages arranged chronologically) are good places to house the online writer's notebooks.

Third, synchronous writing conferences can be web-based using chat rooms or course management systems (i.e., Blackboard or WebCT) with up to five students participating in each conference. Peer editing can also take place by exchanging drafts and inserting comments directly into the text. Fourth, since writers need resources that are often available on the Internet, create a curriculum homepage with links to resources and tools that will be accessed frequently when students are writing. The resources on the curriculum page should be changed often to reflect the genres, content-rich sites, and annotations that pertain to the focus of what is being studied as well as the skills being emphasized during

Table 5. Software That Facilitates Writing Composition

Software feature (phase of writing process)	How writing is facilitated	Programs available
Organization (prewriting)	• Templates allow students to brainstorm using multiple sources • Facilitates synthesizing material	Inspiration or Kidspiration (available free online as trial programs at www.inspiration.com)
Word-Prediction (drafting or writing)	• Provide correctly spelled word choices, minimizing the spelling demand placed on students during the composing phase and allowing them to write at a level corresponding with oral proficiency	Co:Writer or Aurora (trial versions available online at www.qurora-systems.com)
Voice output (drafting or revising)	• Increases length of text • Improves grammatical cohesion and lexical density • Improves word identification skills and ability to identify errors independently	
Spell checker (editing and revising)	• Higher confidence and independence levels • Fewer errors	Microsoft Software
Thesaurus (revising)	• Provides vocabulary that enables writers to vary word choice • Enriches vocabulary learning	Microsoft Word and other word processing programs

Adapted from Montgomery, D.J., & Marks, L.J. (2006). Using technology to build independence in writing for students with disabilities. *Preventing School Failure, 50*(3), 33–39.

writing workshop. Finally, publication possibilities are endless when using computer software that assists in creating graphics or illustrations. For example, Story Book of Kids, by Kids, and for Kids (www.kids-space.org/story/story.html) is organized by different "shelves" (e.g., original stories, class works, folk tales, monthly themes) within the current and previous years, offering space for children to upload their writing. Kidscribe (www.brightinvisiblegreen.com/kidscribe) is a bilingual site (English/Spanish) that provides children with thoughtful questions or prompts (e.g., "What does peace mean to you?") to answer either in English or Spanish. Children can write their responses and post them for sharing in either language. Another website that offers publishing opportunities is ZuZu (www.zuzu.org/cati.html). Many different writing genres are encouraged to be shared.

Using computers during a writing workshop is another example of a text-based approach that integrates technology with literacy instruction. Whereas another level of technology integration focuses on the development of multiple literacies (discussed in more detail later), many learners are motivated by and do well when given the opportunity to work on computers (Martin, 2003). Martin provides some valuable Internet guidelines for reading instruction. Begin by choosing Internet sites that keep reading a priority while complementing the curriculum. Integrating technology with reading and other content area (math, science, social studies) instruction and using a before-, during-, and after-reading format assist the teacher in deciding how and when technology should be used. Martin suggests using technology in one of the before-, during-, or after phases as an induction phase for students and teachers until all have become more comfortable with technology. When exploring Internet sites to decide which to bookmark, ask yourself questions about the site (e.g., Will this information enrich the lesson? Is the reading level appropriate? Is the information accurate?). Reflect on the lesson after using the site(s) and make notes for the future about the appropriateness of the website. It is also important to revisit websites shortly before using them as the Internet is always changing and sites are not always available. Last, have students work in small groups and construct tasks that make readers accountable to ensure a shared responsibility among all students. For example, tasks that include creating questions, sending letters via e-mail, role-playing, and completing graphic organizers foster accountability among all students.

With regard to hypermedia, McNabb (2005) explains that printed text structure is unilinear in that authors typically choose a narrative or rhetorical text structure and make assumptions about the audience to inform their use of vocabulary, extent of knowledge presented, and motivational language used. Reinking (1997) points out that hypermedia texts contain large portions of text that are linked together in nonsequential ways. Hypertexts provide choices for the reader to determine the sequence of content, making the reading multilinear. Heller (1990) reviewed initial studies about reading hypertext. Results of her review found "evidence of reader disorientation, cognitive overload, lack of commitment, and unmotivated rambling among readers of hypertext," especially among students with limited self-monitoring strategies (p. 438). Successfully reading a hypertext document requires readers to develop their own "internal narrator and rhetorical structure" (p. 438), creating demands on the reader that are not present when reading a traditional text. Conversely, the interactive features of hypertext have been shown to improve comprehension of texts (Anderson-Inmann & Horney, 1998; McKenna, 1998). Additional positive effects when using digital texts to teach reading include links to vocabulary definitions, graphic concept maps, summaries, translations, and repeated low frequency vocabulary in meaningful context.

A final view of technology applications in classrooms incorporates a broader perspective of literacy instruction with the goal of developing multiple literacies (Leu, 2002). In this type of classroom, for example, groups of students begin by examining local business partners' brochures to investigate what it means to be bilingual (Smolin & Lawless, 2003). They create interview protocols, record the interviews of community business owners using digital and video cameras, and analyze/synthesize the data using computers with the objective of sharing their interview findings with the school or local community. In addition to engaging students in text-based literacy instruction, teachers with this broader vision of technology integration also aim to develop technological, visual, information, and intertextuality literacies.

Technological literacy exceeds knowing how to use technology by incorporating how to use it in conjunction with increasing academic achievement. Smolin and Lawless (2003) point out that students completing the interview scenario above are not only learning how to use different technologies (cameras and computers), they are also learning how to work effectively in groups, express their ideas, and communicate with a diverse audience. Many language arts standards list these as important and desirable outcomes.

One definition of visual literacy is "a group of vision-competencies a human being can develop by seeing and at the same time having and integrating other sensory experiences" (Debes, 1969, p. 27). This aptitude is especially significant today as children must be able to make meaning from multiple sources, including visual information. Images and text bombard readers now more than ever; new understandings can be developed from the use of visual actions, objects, and symbols. Smolin and Lawless (2003) mention that a visually literate child is able to successfully convey their understandings in multiple and creative ways.

Information literacy entails finding, evaluating, analyzing, and synthesizing information to construct knowledge. As the students use the computers to create their interview protocol, they search websites preselected by the teacher and discuss what makes certain websites better sources of information than others. From this information, the teacher, with student input, develops a rubric to assist in determining useful resources on the Internet. A plan to further students' understandings of using the Internet as a resource, along with an authentic use of the preselected websites, enables students to analyze and synthesize information to construct new knowledge.

Furthermore, intertextuality involves synthesizing and integrating information from a variety of sources to gain a deeper understanding of the topic (Kristeva, 1984). Exposure to a variety of text-based sources is essential for students to understand that sources build on one another to create deeper insights about the topic. The interview assignment scenario provides students with multiple sources of information (Internet, books, and community business materials) and allows students to build their knowledge base of the topic by combining those resources for multiple outcomes.

A comprehensive research agenda needs to be developed and acted upon to inform our use of technology for reading instruction (McNabb, 2005). Adding to the need of acting upon a formal research agenda, there is a lack of technology professional development among English language arts teachers in the United States (McNabb, Hassel, & Steiner, 2002). Most language arts teachers rely on "computer teachers" in a lab setting to integrate technology into the language arts. It has been noted that technology creates a new layer for professional development that goes beyond assisting teachers in using the equipment and software. Multifaceted understandings of how technology relates to curriculum goals are necessary for technology to be successfully integrated and sustained during instruction (Staples, Pugach, & Himes, 2005). In other words, the curriculum should be the framework for deciding when and how technology is integrated with instruction. Teachers need to be well informed about reading processes and pedagogy to effectively support and enhance reading instruction with technology.

Element 2.3

Use a wide range of curriculum materials in effective reading instruction for learners at different stages of reading and writing development and from different cultural and linguistic backgrounds.

According to the National Council of Teachers of English (NCTE, 2004), instructional materials comprise not only published reading programs, but also novels, magazines, computer software, videotapes, and more. Teacher- or student-generated materials (e.g., letters to the editor, personal stories) should also be considered as curriculum materials that facilitate effective reading instruction. NCTE points out schools ought to develop their own criteria for materials selection, keeping in mind that (a) there must be connections to established learning goals and objectives and (b) the selected materials need to attend to the needs of the learners, more specifically at the appropriate level of difficulty. When using literature, the teacher's judgment about the readability of the text is more accurate when considering the complexity of plot, text organization, abstractness of the language, familiarity of vocabulary, and clarity of syntax. Most classrooms have children reading at several instructional levels; therefore, materials seen as inappropriate for whole-class instruction might be more suitable for small groups or individuals.

Materials that students can relate to and that prompt use of preexisting knowledge to aid their comprehension are also desirable. Unfamiliar texts should be included in the curriculum as well; however, teachers will need to support their students more by building background knowledge when using materials with unknown topics or contexts.

Teachers who are well versed in learning objectives, best practices, and how the selected text fits within the medium, genre, epoch, or such that it represents should be involved with the decision making concerning materials. Furthermore, in determining which materials should be selected, teachers must not only keep in mind the learning objectives and needs of the learners, but they should also be able to defend the choices made.

It is clear that the same instructional materials are not appropriate for all learners (NCTE, 2004; Snow et al., 1998). Snow and colleagues call attention to the fact that publishers are not required to evaluate their reading-related materials in terms of effectiveness. They suggest that districts (a) set explicit performance standards to evaluate student outcomes when making decisions about program or text adoptions and (b) in light of the amount of money spent on purchasing reading instructional materials, highlight the urgency of requiring publishers to substantiate the efficacy of their products. IRA (2002b) offers the following recommendations and advice for teachers, parents, and policymakers when selecting reading instructional materials:

- It is unethical for reading professionals and publishers or manufacturers of materials or devices to claim or guarantee success for all learners. Individuals who seek to purchase reading programs and materials should examine evidence of instructional success in guiding their purchase decision or product selection.

- The adoption, purchase, or recommendation for instructional services, methods, and materials should be based on publicly available studies of effectiveness. Purchasers of reading improvement programs should ask for results of unbiased and independent evaluations.

- The research and evaluation information provided by the publisher or distributor should describe the students for whom the materials have been successful and the conditions under which they were implemented; some materials might be successful with some learners, but not for others. (n.p.)

Though the selection of reading materials for classroom use may be limited by policy decisions, legislation, or publishers' offerings, teachers are usually able to select literature for classroom libraries, reading aloud, and at times for instructional purposes. Tunnell and Jacobs (2007) state that all literature used for instruction in the classroom should be of high quality. There are several guidelines used to determine if a book is of high quality, including the author's use of language and writing techniques (skill in manipulating the language), characters, plot, illustrations, pacing, setting, tension, visual design and layout, mood, accuracy, tone, point of view, and theme.

Children's books often have themes of family, friendship, honesty, acceptance, justice, or growing up. The theme of a book should be evident, but not overpowering, so that many interpretations are possible depending on the prior experiences of the readers. Readers who need support would do well with books that have predictable plots, but developing or skilled readers generally like more challenging texts. Additionally, high-quality plots reflect the reality of the character's world and age. As the reading level of the text increases, multiple story lines or flashbacks are sometimes used by the author to add complexity to the plot.

A setting can be central to the story (i.e., historical fiction takes place during a specific time period) or vague so that the story can take place in any city or rural area. Books that have realistic characters that readers can relate to are considered to be high quality. Often we remember an unforgettable character's actions, words, thoughts, or deeds after the other elements of the story are forgotten. Last, style is the author's choice of words, how those words are arranged in sentences, the pace, and structure of the story. Rather than distract the reader, style should enhance the story (i.e., language that paints a picture or dialogue that reveals a character's personality).

Multicultural literature selection guidelines include the following criteria as noted by Pang, Colvin, Tran, and Barbra (1992):

- Cultural pluralism—Literature should value diversity and sensitively address cultural assimilation.

- Positive portrayals—Empowered, rather than stereotyped, characters from diverse backgrounds should be positively portrayed.

- United States settings—Characters from diverse backgrounds should be portrayed in American settings.

- Plot and characterization—A well-constructed plot, good writing, and accurately portrayed characters should be found in all children's literature.

- Accurate illustrations—Characters' dress, mannerisms, speech, and physical features should not be stereotypical.

Literature that is culturally aware depicts many types of diversity (ethnic, linguistic, religious, socioeconomic, and so forth) and should be made available to all students. It is important for teachers to be aware of their students' home language or dialect and experiences. Children need to see themselves reflected in books, poems, plays, and other texts to validate their ways of knowing and doing (Cisneros, 1993). Ethnosensitivity is an important principle of effective literacy instruction when teaching students from diverse cultural and linguistic backgrounds (Avalos, 2006; Cox, 2005).

Conclusion

Grouping students, employing instructional methods, and selecting materials all require teachers to make complex decisions on a daily basis. Different grouping structures should be used, depending on the goals of literacy instruction, student needs, and desired level of student interaction. According to research, changing groupings based on students' instructional needs is the key to successfully using ability grouping to improve students' reading outcomes. Comprehensive literacy instruction provides a balanced approach to literacy learning. Instructional methods should integrate reading, writing, listening, and speaking holistically, providing sufficient time for students to develop expressive and receptive oral language skills. Technology should be seen as a tool to further literacy learning as well as critical thinking skills, team work, and leadership abilities. Finally, selected materials should be authentic and reflect diverse populations, multiple genres, narrative and expository texts, and high quality literature at students' instructional levels.

FURTHER READING

Calderón, M. (2007). *Teaching reading to English language learners, grades 6–12: A framework for improving achievement in the content areas.* Thousand Oaks, CA: Corwin Press.

This is a concise guide to language learning and literacy teaching for success in all areas, debunking myths for secondary ELLs.

Farstrup, A.E., & Samuels, S.J. (Eds.). (2002). *What research has to say about reading instruction* (3rd ed.). Newark, DE: International Reading Association.

This text covers the gamut of possibilities with regard to research findings in literacy learning, from phonemic awareness to new literacies and preparation for high-stakes testing.

Garcia, G.G. (Ed.). (2003). *English learners: Reaching the highest level of English literacy.* Newark, DE: International Reading Association.

In the book's three sections, the authors address the following: Teaching English Learners to Read: Current Policy and Best Instructional Practices; Teaching English Language Development: Rethinking and Redesigning Curriculum; and Optimizing Culture as a Bridge to Literacy Learning.

International Reading Association. (2004). *Preparing reading professionals: A collection from the International Reading Association.* Newark, DE: Author.

This publication compiled articles from IRA journals that extend and elaborate on effective instructional approaches.

Mason, P.A., & Schumm, J.S. (Eds.). *Promising practices for urban reading instruction.* Upper Saddle River, NJ: Pearson, Merrill Prentice Hall.

Organized around 10 rights to excellent instruction and assessment practice, the chapters address how fundamental and urgent these rights are for children in urban classrooms.

Reutzel, D.R., & Cooter, R.B. (2005). *The essentials of teaching children to read: What every teacher needs to know.* Upper Saddle River, NJ: Pearson, Merrill Prentice Hall.

This book is a good guide to basic literacy instruction in a succinct, yet comprehensive format.

The CaseNEX case study selected for Standard 2 specifically addresses reading instruction for an English-language learner (Element 2.2). For Element 2.2, there is a possibility of scoring a high of 9 and a low of 0 for writing off topic (see Standard 2 Rubric, Appendix, p. 146).

Case Study for Standard 2: Instructional Strategies and Curriculum Materials

Reprinted from CaseNEX LLC, founded at University of Virginia's Curry School of Education. Reprinted with permission.

Matchmakers, Scene 2 (pertaining to Marta only)

"These things are nasty," Jennifer said, taking another bite of her doughnut and brushing powdered sugar off her cropped khakis. "I gotta run. Got some new students to meet this morning and a high school student visiting."

Greyfield County was encouraging high school seniors to explore education careers by spending time shadowing teachers in their schools. Jennifer generally liked the idea, so she had volunteered to help. She headed across the parking lot to the secondary school, carrying her bulging tote bag on her shoulder, deep in thought. She was in a contradictory mood, feeling thankful that the district had finally funded an ESOL specialist and yet disappointed that they'd only come up with enough money for a part-time position. She felt frustrated by families that relocated six weeks into the school year while also feeling a tenderness toward whatever circumstances might have made their moves necessary.

Just as she entered the school she caught a glimpse of herself in the glass door and noticed that in her morning rush she had put on one white and one yellow sock. Nothing seemed to match that day! She chuckled to herself as she walked the hall leading to the sixth-grade wing to meet Suzanne, the high school student with whom she would spend the day. So far, Suzanne had been a helpful weekly companion, providing both another set of eyes and the ability to pose pointed questions in a non-threatening way.

"Hey, Ms. Harris. Nice socks!"

"Yeah, thanks. It's been one of those mornings. Want a doughnut?" Jennifer pulled the now wrinkled paper bag from her tote along with her testing schedule for the day.

Jennifer and Marta work through Marta's reading assessment.

"No thanks. Who are we testing today?"

Although this was their second day testing together, Jennifer wasn't quite sure how to include Suzanne in these reading assessments. She just figured Suzanne could watch now and ask questions later. They found Marta Perez's name and class schedule in Jennifer's notes and headed toward their first meeting with this new student. Marta's transfer folder had arrived the day before, and it contained generally positive notes about work habits, neat handwriting, and reasonable English progress given the length of time Marta had been in the United States. When they arrived at her math class, Marta was seated in her desk near the window working on her warm-up exercises.

"Hi, Marta. I'm Mrs. Harris. I'd like to read with you for a few minutes to make sure we've got you in the right classes, OK?"

"OK. Should I bring my books?" Marta seemed happy for the distraction, gathered her things, and accompanied Jennifer and Suzanne down the hallway to the media center for her assessment.

Marta's Vocabulary Assessment (video transcript)

Jennifer:	We're going to start with a word list and we're just going to read them one time through.
Marta:	OK.
Jennifer:	And then we'll go back and I'll have you use them in a sentence for me or just tell me another word that means the same thing. OK?
Marta:	I have to read this?
Jennifer:	Uh-hum.
Marta:	Decided, Served, Amazed, Silent, Wrecked, Improved, Certainly, Entered, Realized, Interrupped.
Jennifer:	Now *decided* in a sentence?
Marta:	I *decided* to go to the store with my Mom. Today I *served* lunch. My mom. I am. He was *amazed* when he saw when he went to Disney World. Um... We...Um...We have to be *silent* when someone's speaking. Um. Two guys *wrecked* the party. I *improved* on my math test.
Jennifer:	Certainly.
Marta:	I *certainly* want to go to Disney World. I *entered* the door. I *realized* I was being wrong and I *interrupted* uh, *interrupted* a class.
Jennifer:	Let's go back to *entered* one more time.
Marta:	I *entered* the house.
Jennifer:	Right. Entered.
Marta:	Considered. I *considered* a gift for my mom.
Jennifer:	Say that one more time.
Marta:	I *considered* a good gift is something. UnhH!
Jennifer:	That's OK. You can take your time. What were you considering?
Marta:	A gift or something.

Jennifer:	OK. A gift. I *considered* a gift...
Marta:	I *considered* a gift of something special.
Jennifer:	OK. Let's go back to *discuss*.
Marta:	I *discussed* my homework to my dad.
Jennifer:	If you *discussed* it what did you do?
Marta:	Um explaining, telling him.
Jennifer:	Talking to each other?
Marta:	Yeah.
Jennifer:	Now, let's go back to *considered* for a minute. If you consider something, what are you doing?
Marta:	Keeping it into myself. Like I know...
Jennifer:	I *considered* going to the party. What are you doing?
Marta:	Like I'm going, like I'm considering like I'm going to that party.
Jennifer:	If you consider going to a party, do you go or are you thinking about it?
Marta:	Yeah. I'm thinking about to go.

Marta Reads a Nonfiction Passage *(video transcript)*

Jennifer:	Based on that, I would consider giving, let's see. She did 100% decoding and 100% meaning on fourth. She went to 100% decoding, about 60% meaning on fifth so I'm going to administer a fifth-grade running record and see how she does for comprehension.
Marta:	The elephant is the largest animal in the world that lives on land. A full-grown elephant may have a weight of about four tons and may be nine feet tall. Because elephants are so large, they have no natural enemies other than man. Since elephants have so few enemies, they are usually easy to get along with, ah, along with, and always act friendly. Elephants usually live in herds with around thirty members of all ages. The female or lady elephant is called a cow. The herd usually has a cow as a leader who is in charge of all the other elephants. During the hottest part of the day the herd will huddle together and attempt to find shade. Near sundown the entire herd usually goes to the nearby river or lake for a drink. Elephants normally continue to stay together in the herd for most of their lives.

Marta Answers Comprehension Questions *(video transcript)*

Jennifer:	What is the largest animal in the world?
Marta:	It's...what is the largest animal?

Jennifer: The largest animal in the world that lives on land?

Marta: Elephant.

Jennifer: OK. How heavy might a full grown elephant be?

Marta: Tons.

Jennifer: How many tons?

Marta: Ten tons. A thousand.

Jennifer: Ten?

Marta: Ten.

Jennifer: Ten tons?

Marta: More than...yeah.

Jennifer: OK. Why do elephants have no natural enemies other than man?

Marta: Why are they what?

Jennifer: Why do elephants have no natural enemies other than man?

Marta: They...charge of female cows.

Jennifer: OK. Why are elephants almost always easy to get along with or why do they act friendly?

Marta: With the female elephants called cows? With the female.

Jennifer: OK. What is a herd?

Marta: Herd?

Jennifer: Um-humm. "Elephants usually live in herds with around thirty members of all ages."

Marta: Like a place.

Jennifer: OK. How many elephants usually live in a herd?

Marta: A lot.

Jennifer: Can you tell me how many? Do you remember how many it said usually live in a herd? Not sure?

Marta: Uh-huh.

Jennifer: OK. Who is usually a leader of an elephant herd?

Marta: The woman. The elephant cow.

Jennifer: The female is the cow.

Marta: Yeah.

Jennifer: What do elephants do during the hottest part of the day?

Marta: They go in the shade.

Jennifer: What do elephants usually do near sundown?

Marta: During sundown?

Jennifer:	Yeah. Near sundown. When the sun is going down.
Marta:	They come out to the herd.
Jennifer:	OK. What do they go and do?
Marta:	Down the trees to get the shade. I don't know what it's called.
Jennifer:	OK. What did it say that would make you think that elephants usually like each other?
Marta:	What did?
Jennifer:	What did it say at the end that made you think that elephants usually like each other?
Marta:	I don't know. 'Cuz it's a girl. I don't know.
Jennifer:	OK.
Suzanne:	[While Jennifer finishes making notes, Suzanne makes an attempt to use something from her third period Spanish class] ¿Como te va en la escuela, Marta? [*How are you doing in school, Marta?*]
Marta:	[Giggling] It's fine.
Suzanne:	No, no. ¡En español, por favor! [*In Spanish, please!*]
Marta:	OK. [Giggles again and offers a rapid-fire reply that leaves Suzanne wide-eyed]
Suzanne:	¡Mas despacio, por favor! [*More slowly, please!*]

Jennifer was glad that Suzanne could offer a little levity to what could otherwise be a stressful testing situation.

After a short break, Jennifer handed Marta a piece of lined paper. "Marta," she said. "I'd like you to write a paragraph. It could be about anything you like, but lots of students like to write about a problem they had with a friend or a time they got in trouble. You can take as long as you like."

Marta sat stolidly, chewing on her pencil, without writing, for several minutes. Jennifer glanced at her watch just as Marta sat up straight and asked, "Can I write about why I should get a present?" Jennifer nodded, glad that inspiration had hit.

Marta wrote quickly, stopping only to erase and rewrite a few words. She smiled proudly as she handed the paper to Jennifer and giggled as Suzanne attempted one more time to converse in Spanish. They walked Marta back to math class and summarized her assessment.

READING ASSESSMENT SUMMARY

Name: Marta Perez

Grade: 8th

Marta scored 100% on the fourth-grade word list and 60% on the fifth-grade list. Here, she had difficulty showing an understanding of several words, including: scanty, acquainted, escaped, and grim. She read the fourth-grade passage fluently with minor errors, and scored 85 percent on the comprehension questions. Marta read the fifth-grade non-fiction passage fluently with few minor errors. However, she scored only 30 percent on the comprehension questions.

1. *Question for response: List one objective for Marta (in objective format, i.e., "The student will...") that you feel should be a priority for her instructional plan. Describe the instructional plan for your objective. Be sure to include technology as a part of your instructional plan.*

2. *Rationale for response—state why you responded as you did. What was or were the rationale(s) for your response?*

Context of Administration

Candidates were provided with a case study as an in-class assignment during a reading foundations course. The responses included here are from candidates who were in their first year of a degree-seeking graduate reading program. The instructor (Mary) shared the rubric with the candidates so that they would be familiar with the evaluation criteria. Candidates were given 20 minutes to view and discuss the case and ask the instructor clarifying questions. Then they were given 30 minutes to write responses using a computer for word processing purposes. Before scoring the responses, the instructor and a graduate assistant brainstormed what they felt were the prominent issues of the case, appropriate instructional plan possibilities, and theories that could be linked to practice for the rationale section. These brainstormed lists provided the minimum criteria from which to begin scoring responses.

Responses

The first response received a content score of 1 and a rationale score of Novice. Although the bullets adequately reflect the issues of the case, the response and rationale sections do not demonstrate a strong understanding of an appropriate objective, technological applications, or research-based instruction.

1. *Summarize the issues of the case; bullet the issues that need to be addressed.*

· Marta is an ESOL student who's been in the country a short time
· Although she has positive work habits and neat handwriting, she is still acquiring the English language
· Marta seems anxious and unsure of herself
· She needs explicit vocabulary instruction

- Marta has some fluency issues and requires extra reading practice
- Comprehension is also lacking

2. *Respond: List one objective for Marta (in objective format, i.e., "The student will...") that you feel should be a priority for her instructional plan. Describe the instructional plan for your objective. Be sure to include technology as a part of your instructional plan.*

"The student will be able to read fluently with expression and intonation." Marta will be given opportunities to work cooperatively to practice reading skills through Readers' Theatre. After thorough practice and repetition, the student will read her part of the script aloud. She will also participate in buddy reading activities to further enhance her reading skills. Every effort will be made for Marta to listen to stories on tape or computer (eBooks), paying particular attention to the reader's fluency. She will then type 2-3 questions on the computer in relation to the feelings and emotions of the characters in the story. These questions will be shared with her buddy to help build her confidence.

3. *Rationale for response—state why you responded as you did. What was or were the rationale(s) for your response?*

Due to the fact that Marta is still acquiring the English language, repeated readings and practice will enable her to become more comfortable in her abilities as a reader. Providing her with opportunities to feel successful will strengthen her abilities. As she listens more intently to stories, she will gain the confidence and understanding that will assist in her fluency, vocabulary, and comprehension of the material. Using technology offers extra support. Learning to type questions about her readings and sharing them with others also enhances Marta's rate for success.

The second response is more substantive than the first response, however there still is an emerging conceptual understanding of the issues as they are basically glossed over and generic wording such as "research says" is used. In addition, the website listed is geared for teachers (general lesson plan ideas, distance learning opportunities, and so forth) rather than an instructional tool for students. A content score of 5 was awarded with a Novice rationale.

1. *Summarize the issues of the case; bullet the issues that need to be addressed.*

- Jennifer needs to administer a reading and writing assessment to two English language learners (ELLs).
- Marta is one of the eighth grade students Jennifer evaluated.
- Marta is an ELL.

· According to Marta's reading assessment, she reads fluently at the 4th and 5th grade level, but she seems to have an issue with comprehension at the 5th grade level.

2. *Respond:* List one objective for Marta (in objective format, i.e., "The student will...") that you feel should be a priority for her instructional plan. Describe the instructional plan for your objective. Be sure to include technology as a part of your instructional plan.

Objective: The student will be able to read and comprehend the information read.

Instructional Plan:

The stated objective will be met with teacher support and the use of graphic organizers and an internet-based reading program. Marta will receive guided reading time. Guided reading will be set up into two parts: teacher-student instruction and an internet-based reading comprehension program. At first, the teacher will work with the student to scaffold the student's learning. The instruction will begin at the fifth grade level.

To begin with, the teacher will do a lot of modeling in order for the student to understand how to use graphic organizers. Depending on the benchmark covered in class, the teacher can choose a graphic organizer and story, accordingly. For example, if the benchmark is main idea, the teacher can choose a graphic organizer that enhances comprehension for that benchmark. The graphic organizers will be used as a before, during, and after reading activity.

After the first couple sessions, Marta will begin to work on the website internet4classroom.com. This website allows the student to work at his/her independent or instructional level. The teacher will have the website ready for the student to work interactively. First, the student should read the story. Then, the student should complete the graphic organizer with teacher support. After that, the student should answer the comprehension questions provided on the website.

3. *Rationale for response*—state why you responded as you did. What was or were the rationale(s) for your response?

Based on Marta's reading assessment, she should receive instruction on comprehension. Although Marta is in eighth grade, she should receive instruction at the fifth grade level. The goal of Reading First is for all students to read at grade level. Therefore, in order for Marta to reach this goal, she must receive instruction at the fifth grade level. The purpose of the instructional plan is for Marta to enhance her comprehension; thus, increasing her reading level.

In addition, research has found that if graphic organizers are used effectively as a before, during, or after reading activity, comprehension is enhanced. Technology is another effective tool that can be used to increase the student's comprehension. The website internet4classrooms.com is a credible source. Trainings for teacher are available. This website provides support with comprehension which is one of the components of the Big Five. Moreover, the use of graphic organizers and technology will be productive for Marta's growth.

The third response has many activities listed that are appropriate for Marta. The rationale demonstrates a good understanding of the benefits for ELLs behind the activities mentioned. The two computer applications listed are also suitable for ELLs. The response would be stronger, however, if the candidate had mentioned the need to use texts at Marta's independent and/or instructional reading levels for these activities, as well as grounding the ideas or activities in research or theory. The content score awarded was 9, with a Proficient rationale.

1. Summarize the issues of the case; bullet the issues that need to be addressed.

- There is not enough funding for a ESOL specialist, therefore the school has only been allocated a part-time position
- Suzanne, the high school senior who was exploring the education field, was watching Mrs. Harris test.
- Marta is in the eighth grade
- Marta Perez had been paced in a remedial math class
- Marta was a new transfer student to Greyfield schools
- Marta's transfer folder had arrived the day before, and it contained generally positive notes about work habits, neat handwriting, and reasonable English progress given the length of time Marta had been in the United States.
- Marta was very eager and enthusiastic about going with Mrs. Harris.
- When Marta was given the vocabulary assessment, she was able to read the fourth grade list
- She had some difficulty reading the fifth grade list, scoring 60%.
- Marta had difficulty using the words in sentences.
- Marta read the fourth grade non-fiction passage, fluently with small errors.
- Then she read the fifth grade passage with small errors.
- Marta did not do well on the comprehension questions, as she scored on 30%.
- When Marta was handed a paper to write a paragraph she sat thinking for several minutes.
- Marta's writing showed a lack of grammar knowledge, usage and coherence.

2. *Respond: List one objective for Marta (in objective format, i.e., "The student will...") that you feel should be a priority for her instructional plan. Describe the instructional plan for your objective. Be sure to include technology as a part of your instructional plan.*

Objective: The student, after working in small guided reading groups, will be able to read a fifth grade passage with 70% comprehension.

In guided reading groups the teacher will focus on comprehension. Some activities that will be used in small groups are literature circles, reader's theater, graphic organizers, reciprocal teaching and think-pair share. The student will also use River Deep and Accelerated Reader to chart their progress.

3. *Rationale for response—state why you responded as you did. What was or were the rationale(s) for your response?*

I believe that Marta will benefit more from small group work. She needs extra help and support on her comprehension skills. While working in small group I suggest a couple of different activities for them to work on. One activity is literature circles, where the students in the group read the same book, and later discuss it as a team. I believe this is a great strategy because they are formulating their own discussion as well as their own questions. The students are able to feel more relaxed in this environment as well as they are able to use different comprehension strategies to discuss the book. Another strategy that can be used in small group is reader's theater. This always proves to be a fun strategy for student to use in the class. The students take a story and act it out. I think the students are able to grasp and understand the story better. They are using a more hands on approach, as well are personalizing the material, and making it their own through their experience.

While using the aforementioned strategies, the students should incorporate graphic organizers to facilitate their recollection of the material. Different graphic organizers that can be used are two column notes, where the students are reading and writing a statement from their reading, and reflecting upon that statement. They can also use KWL chart, this way they can chart their knowledge before they read and then see what they have learned after their reading. Another strategy the teacher can incorporate into small group is reciprocal teaching. This way the teacher can model what she expects the students to be doing throughout their thinking process, and then one of the students takes on the role of the teacher. The students will first summarize what they read, then they will ask questions using higher order skills, then they will clarify any information or vocabulary which was not understood. Finally they will predict what they think will happen. The last strategy is think pair-share, the use of this strategy will help the students answer each others' questions, and discuss what they think about the story. All of the above strategies help increase comprehension, as well as help build their oral communication skills.

The students should also work on programs such as River Deep and Accelerated Reader. These two programs can help them practice their comprehension skills through the use of different passages and stories. They can also help monitor and assess the students' progress over time. Every time the student reads a passage their responses will be charted in the program. This way the child can see how they are performing as well as the teacher can monitor their progress over time. Accelerated Reader also helps see what level the student is working at and can suggest the level the student should be reading.

All of the above strategies can help Marta with her decoding, vocabulary, fluency and comprehension. Through the use of the aforementioned activities Marta will gain various skills. She will be able to develop questions, build oral communication, extend her vocabulary, use skills as before, during and after reading, provide feedback etc. I believe these are some great strategies to help Marta increase her reading comprehension.

The fourth response not only demonstrates a strong understanding of possible instructional foci but also links research or a credible source to the suggested activities throughout the rationale. The response received a score of 9 for content and Distinguished for rationale. (The response has been edited to include references.)

1. Summarize the issues of the case; bullet the issues that need to be addressed.

· The first student tested in this case was Marta. Her transfer papers had positive notes about her work habits, neat handwriting, and reasonable English progress given the amount of time Marta has been in the U.S.A.

· Marta was given a Vocabulary test in which she scored 100% on the 4th grade worded list and 60% on the 5th grade worded list.

· She scored 85% on the comprehension questions after reading a 4th grade passage and a 30% after reading a 5th grade reading passage.

2. Respond: List one objective for Marta (in objective format, i.e., "The student will…") that you feel should be a priority for her instructional plan. Describe the instructional plan for your objective. Be sure to include technology as a part of your instructional plan.

Objective: The student will improve reading comprehension to successfully understand and retell details to questions from 5th grade texts using a variety of instructional learning strategies such as questioning, graphic organizers, and technology.

First the teacher should note what interests Marta. The teacher should find reading materials that capture her interests and that are at her independent reading level. Marta should be placed in a guided reading group that targets her level of comprehension. Marta should be engaged in various activities before reading the text to activate schemata, brainstorm and utilize before, during and after reading strategies. Activities such as Anticipation Guides (graphic organizers), Story Impressions, and the use of Twin Texts using fiction and non-fiction books related to the topic will help familiarize her to the text. During Reading, the teacher can get Marta involved in active instruction that will help her monitor her comprehension as she reads the text. These activities can include DR-TA, Reciprocal Teaching, and Questioning/Questioning the Author. After Reading activities can include graphic organizers such as Main Idea Frames, SWBS, QAR, and Story Frames to help her review what she read. After completing a graphic organizer, Marta should be asked various lower and higher level questions in which she is guided to refer to the organizer to answer the questions.

Technology also plays an integral part as a tool for reading and literacy instruction. Marta can receive computer time by working on Brainchild, FCAT Explorer, or reading Tumble Books, in which she is able to continue practicing the skills she learned in her guided reading group. The teacher can also have Marta read electronic books on the computer to support reading at her instructional level.

3. *Rationale for response—state why you responded as you did. What was or were the rationale(s) for your response?*

If a child is reading fluently but does not demonstrate comprehension, then the child is not reading; he/she is merely reciting words (Anderson, Hiebert, Scott, & Wilkinson, 1985). It is important that a child who is struggling with retelling of details from a text is actively engaged in before, during, and after reading activities using various styles of reading and reading strategies to help build comprehension. According to the National Reading Panel (NICHD, 2000), one of the essential components of the Big 5 is comprehension in which the goal is that students have an understanding of what they are reading. It is very important to tap into students' schemata to activate prior knowledge that they become familiar with what they will read (Rumelhart, 1980). Students must make connections with what they are reading and what they already know to help them remember what they read. By doing this, it helps facilitate the comprehension process and enable students to construct knowledge by interacting with what they read.

Teachers need to model explicit instruction that guide students through Think Alouds so they are able to build comprehension. According to Vygotsky's (1978) zone of proximal development, this supports the idea that knowledge is socially constructed and students should receive the help they need until they are able to perform independently as a result of the teacher's guidance. Also, the use of technology has shown to improve reading achievement. Ms. Zapata-Romero, a technology specialist who visited our class, also stated that reading skills improve when students are exposed to technology. She recommends programs that monitor student progress and show learning gains, so the teacher is able to monitor the students' progress and use this information to help guide her instruction. Students can read text online that are specific to their reading level. The use of eBooks help to differentiate instruction and keep students engaged in the lesson.

References

Anderson, R.C., Hiebert, E.H., Scott, J.A., & Wilkinson, I.A.G. (1985). Becoming a nation of readers: The report of the Commission on Reading. Washington, DC: National Academy of Education, Commission on Education and Public Policy.

National Institute of Child Health and Human Development. (2000). Report of the National Reading Panel. Teach children to read: An evidence-based assessment of the scientific research literature on reading and its implications for reading instruction (NIH Publication Non. 00-4769). Washington, DC: U.S. Government Printing Office.

Rumelhart, D.E. (1980). Schemata: The building blocks of cognition. In R.J. Spiro, B.C. Bruce, & W.C. Brewer (Eds.), Theoretical issues in reading comprehension (pp. 33-58). Hillsdale, NJ: Erlbaum.

Vygotsky, L.S. (1978). Mind in society: The development of higher psychological processes. Cambridge, MA: Harvard University Press.

CHAPTER 3

Learning About and Assessing Standard 3—Assessment, Diagnosis, and Evaluation

I n an age of increased emphasis on accountability and high-stakes testing, it is particularly important for educational professionals to be fluent in the administration of tests, interpretation of test scores, and data-based instructional decision making. Sometimes referred to as "assessment literacy" (Lukin, Bandalos, Eckhout, & Mickelson, 2004), the development of professional competency in the administration and interpretation of mandated accountability assessments (Abu-Alhija, 2007) as well as in the development, administration, and interpretation of classroom-based assessments (McMillan, 2001, 2003; Shepard, 2001) has steadily become more common in teacher education.

For years, teacher preparation in assessment has been marginal at best. Campbell and Collins (2007) provide evidence that for more than 50 years researchers have recognized this lack of preparation. This has not gone without notice in the professional community of teacher educators in literacy. In 1994, IRA, in collaboration with NCTE, approved guidelines for assessing reading and writing. In 2000, IRA in its position statement *Excellent Reading Teachers* (IRA, 2000a) emphasized the importance of teacher preparation in assessment. More recently, IRA's Teacher Education Task Force (IRA, 2007) examined excellent teacher preparation programs in reading. Their findings included recommendations for teacher preparation in assessment. Likewise, The National Academy of Education Committee has commissioned two volumes of recommendations for teacher preparation based on an analysis of effective teacher preparation. Both documents, *Preparing Teachers for a Changing World: What Teachers Should Learn and Be Able to Do* (Darling-Hammond, Bransford, LePage, Hammerness, & Duffy, 2005) and *Knowledge to Support the Teaching of Reading* (Snow et al., 2005), offer recommendations for professional development in assessment.

While becoming more prevalent in preservice teacher education, assessment literacy among practicing teachers who have on-the-job, incidental, or no training in this area is in need of improvement. Thus, the need for both preservice and inservice professional development in assessment is vitally important. Standard 3 recommends that "candidates use a variety of assessment tools and practices to plan and evaluate effective reading instruction" (IRA, 2004, p. 14). The elements that make up Standard 3 comprise the following:

- Use of a wide range of assessment tools
- Identification of students' strengths and challenges in reading

- Use of assessment data to plan reading instruction for students representing a wide range of instructional needs

- Communication of assessment results to key stakeholders

Element 3.1

Use a wide range of assessment tools and practices that range from individual and group standardized tests to individual and group informal classroom assessment strategies, including technology-based assessment tools.

Few topics in education have generated as much discussion in the past decade as assessment (e.g., Amrein & Berliner, 2002; Linn, 2001; Murphy, Shannon, Johnston, & Hansen, 1998). The passage of NCLB was the result of years of growing concern among policymakers and the general public about the status of basic skills instruction in the United States (see Reutzel & Mitchell, 2005, for a brief chronology). The student performance data now required for states and school district accountability has spawned a focus on assessment unprecedented in the history of the United States. These assessment requirements have fueled heated discussion among policy makers, educational professionals, parents, students, and the community at large. For example, in response to human error in scoring the third-grade Florida accountability exam, *The Miami Herald* (Shah & deLuzuriaga, 2007, p. 1B) reported, "Parents hate it. Students dread it. Teachers live and die by it. Like it or not, high-stakes testing will remain a way of life in Florida and across the nation." It is difficult not to concur that the consequences of high-stakes tests are high and getting higher. For the present, states and local districts must comply with the law or lose federal funding, state funding, or both. This public policy is laced with stakes and consequences.

What are the stakes of high-stakes tests? Test results can have an impact on students, teachers, and institutions (Thomas, 2005). For students, stakes are related to promotion, retention, graduation from high school, placement in special needs or remedial classes, and access to student loans in postsecondary programs. For teachers and administrators, test scores can determine eligibility for awards or sanctions. In some states, the idea of linking scores of students being taught by alumni of teacher education programs is being considered as a factor in determining eligibility for accreditation. For schools, school districts, and states, test scores are related to accreditation, funding, and school grades. The stakes for the lives of individuals and institutions are high and getting higher.

What are the consequences of high-stakes tests? Birenbaum (2007) writes that the consequences are both intended and unintended. Intended consequences are stated benefits of testing that are purported to improve student achievement, to serve as a means of accountability, and to provide guidelines for instruction at individual student, school, district, and state levels. Unintended consequences include heightened student, parent, teacher, and administrative anxiety; reduced instructional time; teaching to the test; reducing the reading curriculum to basic skills only; increased drop-out rates; and unethical behavior such as student or teacher cheating (Birenbaum, 2007; Cimbricz, 2002; Kohn, 2000). Loss of instructional time and redundancy in tests are also cited as unintended consequences (Invernizzi, Landrum, Howell, & Warley, 2005).

Critics of large-scale assessments pose questions related to appropriate measurement for ELLs, minorities (Abedi, 2001, 2006; Paul, 2004; Valencia & Villarreal, 2003), and students with disabilities (Cizek, 2001). Another concern for all students is the stress and anxiety and demoralization that high-stakes testing can impose (Thomas, 2005). Some concerns are related to the measures themselves, including the validity of standardized measures in terms of their ability to go beyond measuring reading subskills to gauging real-life literacy demands (Damico, 2005; Goodman, 2006; Johnston, 2005). In some cases, alignment of standards with the assessment instrument is questionable (Conley, 2005), and standards may be so narrowly defined that the ability of a single measure to include all standards in the item pool is not feasible (Popham, 2006). Another concern is related to the misinterpretation of standardized test score results. As several researchers point out (e.g., Valencia & Riddle Buly, 2004; Wilson, Martens, & Arya, 2005), students with similar test scores can have very different instructional needs when additional formal and informal assessments are resolved.

Abu-Alhija (2007) has identified both the benefits and pitfalls of high-stakes (or as he phrases it, "critical") tests for a range of key stakeholders (i.e., students, teachers, administrators, policymakers, and parents). The bottom line is that not enough longitudinal research has been concluded to fully understand the ramifications of current policy on the lives and futures of students (Abu-Alhija, 2007; Cimbricz, 2002; Conley & Hinchman, 2004). As Abu-Alhija points out, "Ultimately, there is a tremendous need for research to provide evidence and develop professional knowledge regarding testing roles and uses of large-scale testing results as well as factors that make testing more precise and more useful" (2007, p. 65).

With the current highly charged assessment climate in the United States, the need for teachers and administrators to develop assessment literacy is obvious. The educational futures of students depend heavily on the knowledge and expertise of professionals charged with their care. Element 3.1 defines proficiency in the use of multiple assessment tools (both formal and informal)—including technological applications—as important components of assessment literacy. It is imperative for teacher education programs to include opportunities for teacher candidates to explore their personal beliefs about current public policy regarding assessment, to understand a range of mandatory assessments including their appropriate and ethical use and interpretations, and to see how high-stakes testing fits into a comprehensive assessment plan.

Use of Multiple Assessments

What is assessment? *The Literacy Dictionary* defines assessment as "the act or process of gathering data in order to better understand the strengths and weaknesses of student learning, as by observation, testing, interviews, etc." (Harris & Hodges, 1999, p. 12). By definition, assessment emphasizes the importance of using a variety of data collection tools.

Serafini's (2000/2001) definition of assessment underscores the function of assessment as inquiry and role of educators as decision makers when planning for curriculum and instruction. Cooper and Kiger (2008) emphasize the need for varied tools and techniques allowing literacy assessment to be continuous and discrete, producing results to inform instruction and the organization of the learning environment.

In an analysis of existing reading assessments, Kame'enui (2002) and later Reading First (Barone, Hardman, & Taylor, 2006) identified four general purposes for the assessments reviewed: (1) screening, (2) diagnosis, (3) progress-monitoring, and (4) outcomes. Recognizing that student outcomes can be used for multiple purposes, Schumm and Arguelles (2006) define the purposes of assessment as follows:

- To screen students for initial grouping, instruction, and needs for further assessment.
- To identify individual student strengths and areas in need of improvement in reading and writing.
- To monitor ongoing progress in reading and writing development.
- To determine student outcomes in reading.
- To evaluate the strengths and weaknesses of instructional programs at the classroom, school, district, state, and national levels.
- To account to parents, administration, community, and policy makers. (p. 36)

Clearly, no one test can or should meet all purposes in a reliable and valid way. Guskey (2007) sums it up this way: "one point on which both advocates and critics agree is that they [i.e., large-scale assessments] represent but one, potentially limited, indicator of student learning that might be considered in making high-stakes decisions about schools and students" (p. 19). Nonetheless, Guskey further points out that whereas many educators acknowledge the importance of using multiple measures, particularly for high-stakes decisions such as rating the performance of schools and student promotion or placement, the development of defensible models for how to use multiple measures is still in progress. Similarly, Riddle Buly and Valencia (2003), recognizing that "multiple indicators of achievement has long been advocated but rarely implemented," call for using multiple measures that both "require teacher knowledge and decision-making and, most importantly, are perceived by teachers as helpful in everyday instruction" (p. 22). As you will read in the next section, many professional organizations encourage the use of multiple measures particularly in the case of critical decisions such as promotion, retention, and placement in remedial courses or services for exceptional children.

Professional Guidelines

Understanding the ethical, responsible, and legal use of assessment tests and their results is an important aspect of professional development for teachers and administrators. One way for teacher candidates to become familiar with appropriate use is to review the guidelines, position statements, and standards for assessment that various educational professional organizations set. Although individual organizations differ in procedures, typically a committee of organization members with expertise in assessment (and in some cases other groups, including the general public) draft such guidelines and standards. Drafts are often sent to a number of additional members for review. Finally, the board of directors of the organization votes on adoption of the final draft. These documents are likely to change from time to time. Therefore, a periodic review of relevant professional documents is warranted.

The American Educational Research Association (AERA), American Psychological Association (APA), and National Council on Measurement in Education (NCME) publish *Standards for Educational and Psychological Testing* (AERA, 2000). This monograph contains guidelines for test construction, evaluation, and documentation; fairness in testing; and testing applications. Whereas standards do recognize the importance of professional judgment, they also do provide a framework for appropriate use of tests. The AERA, APA, and NCME along with the American Speech-Language-Hearing Association, the National Association of School Psychologists, and the National Association of Test Directors have a *Code of Fair Testing Practices in Education* (Joint Committee on Testing Practices, 2004). Consistent with the standards monograph, the *Code* was recently revised and includes recommendations for test developers and test users in the following areas of testing: development/selecting, administrating/scoring, reporting/interpreting, and informing test takers (IRA, 2008).

In 1994, IRA, in collaboration with the NCTE, developed guidelines for assessing reading and writing. In addition to this monograph, in 2003 the Delegates Assembly of IRA passed a resolution regarding formal and informal literacy assessment. All the documents mentioned here address the importance of using multiple measures.

A number of professional organizations have position statements on assessment practices and high-stakes testing (e.g., AERA, 2000; IRA, 1999). Like most of such position statements, IRA's position statement *High-Stakes Assessments in Reading* (IRA, 1999) and the National Reading Conference policy brief *High Stakes Testing and Reading Assessment* (Afflerbach, 2005) express the potential dangers of using a single measure for critical decisions. *High-Stakes Assessments in Reading* (IRA, 1999) states,

> The Board of Directors of the International Reading Association is opposed to high-stakes testing. High-stakes testing means that one test is used to make important decisions about students, teachers, and schools. In a high-stakes testing situation, if students score high on a single test they could be placed in honors classes or a gifted program. On the other hand, if students score low on a high-stakes test, it could mean that they will be rejected by a particular college, and it could affect their teacher's salary and the rating of the school district as compared with others where the same test was given. (n.p.)

Key to the understanding of use of multiple measures is their ethical use. The IRA's *Code of Ethics* (IRA, 2008) states,

> Professionals in reading must possess suitable qualifications for engaging in consulting, diagnostic, or remedial work. Unqualified persons should not engage in such activities except under the direct supervision of one who is properly qualified. Professional intent and the welfare

of the person seeking services should be given in all consulting or clinical activities such as counseling, administering diagnostic tests, or providing remediation. (n.p.)

In the next section, we discuss different types of assessments that might be included in teacher preparation programs. In considering the use of a variety of assessment tools, teacher educators should review technical manuals and instructions for using any formal or informal measures to help candidates understand their ethical and responsible use.

Types of Assessment

Assessment instruments fall into three general categories: norm-referenced, criterion-referenced, and informal or classroom-based (Schumm & Arguelles, 2006). The National Research Council (2001) has recommended a balanced model of assessment that incorporates a variety of carefully selected measures as part of a comprehensive assessment plan.

Norm-referenced tests are administered according to a set of standard procedures. Student scores are compared with a norming group on which the test was standardized (McMillan, 2001). Norm-referenced tests are typically used for large-scale, high-stakes assessments and due to high development costs are often commercially published instruments. The scores generated include raw scores, scaled scores, stanines, percentiles, and grade-equivalent scores. Norm-referenced tests typically are less useful for making specific instructional decisions than are criterion-referenced or informal assessments (Invernizzi et al., 2005; McMillan, 2001).

Curriculum-based measurement (CBM) is a type of norm-referenced assessment in that it is a standardized measure of classroom performance. Rather than using commercially prepared tests, teachers using CBM evaluate the academic content children learn in the classroom for screening and progress-monitoring purposes (Good, Kaminski, Smith, Laimon, & Dill, 2001; Haager, Klingner, & Vaughn, 2007). Based on a model of fluency, CBM tools include brief snapshots of student achievement that are to be administered periodically during the school year (Invernizzi et al., 2005) that can be used to inform instruction.

Criterion-referenced tests gauge student mastery of target skills (Cooper & Kiger, 2008). Usually a predetermined goal or level of performance is set to determine mastery (McMillan, 2001). They can be either commercial or teacher made and can be administered with standard or informal procedures depending on the measure.

Informal assessments or classroom-based assessments can be either commercial or teacher made. This category represents a wide range of data collection tools including tests and quizzes, teacher observation, student self- or peer-evaluation, benchmark tests, portfolios, rubrics, and checklists (Harp, 2006).

The classic assessment tool, the informal reading inventory (Betts, 1946; Paris & Carpenter, 2003; Schumm, 2006), falls in this category. Unlike many informal assessments, the informal reading inventory necessitates professional training and practice to develop a high level of proficiency in its administration and interpretation.

Other types of informal assessments include portfolio assessment, performance assessment, and authentic assessment (Afflerbach, 2007). Portfolio assessment involves collection of student work samples to provide both formative and summative evaluation of students' reading and writing. Portfolios offer the benefit of gauging not only student products, but the learning process as well (Hewett, 1995; Tierney, Carter, & Desai, 1991). Performance assessments go beyond traditional criterion-referenced tests that are typically in a multiple-choice performance. Students actually need to produce a product or demonstrate/perform a task and then performance is gauged using a checklist or rubric. A related, but somewhat different type of assessment, is authentic assessment. Afflerbach (2007) describes authentic assessment as (a) "embedded in classroom routines of instruction and learning and conducted during regular activities of the classroom," or (b) "focus[ing] on their relationship to real-world reading" (p. 92). Thus, performance assessment tools can be authentic or not, depending on the nature and setting of the performance task.

Assessments of all types can be timed or untimed, individual or group, or administered orally or with paper and pencil or computer. Similarly, assessments can be designed for the purposes of screening, diagnosis, monitoring, or determining student outcomes.

With such an array of assessment tools, it is important that educators thoroughly understand assessments mandated by a state or school district. Moreover, when educators (either as individuals or as a committee) have the flexibility to select assessment tools, it is vital that they have the knowledge and skills to critique and select possible measures. Afflerbach (2007) offers the CURRV acronym to identify domains to consider in test selection: consequences, usefulness, roles, reliability, and validity of the instrument. To this, we would add a review of test fairness, freedom of bias, and appropriateness of the assessment tool for the developmental level of students as well as students with different cultural, linguistic, and academic differences (Invernizzi et al., 2005).

Technology-Based Assessment

Given the accelerated use of technology in schools in the past decade, incorporation of technological applications in teacher education programs is imperative. Technology-based applications in assessment are also morphing at a rapid rate. Thus, both teacher educators and candidates need to make a concerted effort to keep abreast of developments at the local and national levels.

Any specific listing of competencies is beyond the scope of this review and likely to be dated by the time of publication. The following five competencies are important for planning professional development in technology and assessment for teacher candidates: (1) data collection (including assessment construction), (2) record keeping, (3) data scoring and analyzing, (4) reporting, and (5) use of data for instructional planning (Roeber, 1995). We will discuss each one briefly with supporting examples.

Data Collection. Technology can be used to improve the efficiency and effectiveness of data collection. Computer software and Internet resources can be used for aiding with test construction (including test item banks from textbook publishers) and in construction of assessment checklists and rubrics.

Reading assessments have been criticized in the past because when students are administered a test that is at an inappropriate level, teachers cannot accurately assess student reading proficiency (Fry, 1971; Hewitt & Homan, 2004). Computer technology has the potential to resolve this dilemma through adaptive testing (e.g., STAR Early Literacy, www.renlearn.com/sel/). Adaptive tests use a branching procedure to determine items from a pool that are most appropriate for the individual test taker (Cohen & Cowen, 2008).

Personal Digital Assistants (PDAs) are increasingly being used as a data collection tool (Cohen & Cowen, 2008). For example, in many districts, handheld devices are being used to enter, store, and submit data from the Dynamic Indicators of Basic Early Literacy Skills (DIBELS; Good et al., 2001) as the test is being administered.

Record Keeping. Record keeping is an important aspect of teacher accountability to students, parents, and administration. Electronic grade books are quickly becoming the rule rather than the exception. In many cases, parents and students can access the data input at home to facilitate ongoing communication and progress monitoring. Teacher preparation can provide candidates with suggestions for the ethical use of electronic grade books, ways to keep parents and students informed about policies and procedures for its use, and tips for how to make data entry more efficient and less tedious.

Technology can facilitate record keeping through the use of electronic or e-portfolios (Cohen & Cowan, 2008) where students can store their digital work and reflections. In addition, paper and pencil work samples can be scanned into the e-portfolio document. Creating portfolios of their progress through a teacher education program can help candidates develop the skills needed to teach their own students how to create a portfolio that documents their progress as a reader and writer.

Data Scoring and Analyzing. The use of technology for data scoring and analysis can streamline the amount of time teachers need for grading and developing progress reports. Use of computer software, data scanners, and web-based test administration can provide teachers and students with immediate feedback about performance. For example, with the Accelerated Reading program (www.renlearn.com/ar), after reading a tradebook, students can take a quiz and get immediate feedback about their performance.

Reporting. Computer technology has an enormous capacity for generating reports. The reports can be for individual students or for a group (e.g., class, school, district, state). Data reports can also be produced for a variety of audiences (e.g., students, parents). Teacher preparation in this area can concentrate on interpretation of data from mandated reports as well as guidelines and procedures for preparing reports from other data sources including teacher-made tests. Reports are particularly important for students and parents to help them track progress in learning to read and write.

Use of Data for Instructional Planning. Programs that use technology for data-based instructional planning are becoming more available. Partridge, Invernizzi, Meier, and Sullivan (2003) point out, "Without a bridge to instructional strategies, assessment results serve a limited purpose" (p. 11). In their research on Phonological Awareness Literacy Screening (PALS), Partridge and colleagues developed a web-based assessment tool that enables teachers to link student assessment data with appropriate instructional activities. In addition to generating a variety of reports, PALS has the capacity to assist teachers with data-based decision making.

Blanton and Menendez (2006) observe that using technology in the classroom involves knowledge of the resources available as well as classroom organization that will promote regular, systematic use of technology. They contend,

> the key to understanding and sustaining effective computer-mediated reading instruction is the provision of sufficient professional development and support to the classroom teacher—and this varies tremendously across applications. Some publishers provide teachers with little more than a scanty manual or a one-shot introduction to the application. (p. 437)

This statement applies to technology for assessment as well. Professional development in this area can provide candidates with a foundation for ongoing proficiency in technology applications as they emerge.

Element 3.2

Place students along a developmental continuum and identify students' proficiencies and difficulties.

The process of assessment as inquiry necessitates use of both formal and informal measures to place students on a developmental continuum and to plan appropriate instruction. Reading experts have offered a number of continua including overall stages of reading (e.g., Chall, 1983), emergent literacy (e.g., McGee & Richgels, 2007), word recognition (e.g., Ehri, 1995, 1998), spelling (Gentry & Gillet, 1993), as well as word recognition and spelling (e.g., Bear, Invernizzi, Templeton, & Johnson, 2008). Thus, researchers and states/school districts may differ in their definitions and guidelines for determining a "developmental continuum." Cooper and Kiger (2008) offer the following developmental continuum based on an examination of professional literature: early emergent literacy, emergent literacy, beginning reading and writing, almost fluent reading and writing, and fluent reading and writing. Within these levels, students may actually exhibit behaviors on different levels depending on the area of literacy being assessed (e.g., word recognition, comprehension). Thus, using a variety of measures for screening, diagnosis, and monitoring of students in the various areas of the reading curriculum is an important aspect of teacher education in reading. Emphasis in assessment instruction should be on both identification of areas of student strengths and on areas that need more intensive instruction (Reutzel & Cooter, 2005).

Teachers can use the data to form flexible groups and to differentiate instruction (Schumm & Arguelles, 2006; Walpole & McKenna, 2007). Walpole and McKenna (2007) caution,

> Using assessments to form needs-based groups is not an exact science and we are glad of that!... assessment results are always imperfect—they merely estimate the proficiencies we wish to target....Your experiences interacting with children once a needs-based group is formed may cause you to reconsider your initial conclusions. (p. 30)

This level of teacher decision making is quite sophisticated and demands knowledge of developmental levels of reading and writing as well as a variety of assessment tools. Reading researchers focusing on teacher professional development recommend using student-based data as an instructional tool (Hayes & Robnolt, 2007; Walpole & McKenna, 2004). Teacher educators can also use case studies, demonstrations, simulations, and classroom or clinical practica (Avalos & Pazos-Rego, 2006) to scaffold instruction for teacher candidates.

A critical aspect of Element 3.2 is professional knowledge of assessment as it relates to referring students for special services (e.g., resource rooms in reading, special education, programs for ELLs). Classroom teachers play a critical role in identifying students with special needs and in the process for referring students for additional assessment. Teachers also participate in prereferral or RTI initiatives to see if intensive support and instruction can circumvent the need for time-consuming and costly assessment and potential placement in special classes or programs (Vaughn, Bos, & Schumm, 2007). Given issues such as the disproportional representation of minority students in special education, it is vital for teachers to have knowledge of appropriate assessment for all students (Harry & Klingner, 2005). Teacher knowledge of federal, state, and local policies as well as assessment tools and procedures is imperative to refer students to appropriate testing beyond the classroom and appropriate instruction to meet their individual needs.

Element 3.3

Use assessment information to plan, evaluate, and revise effective instruction that meets the needs of all students, including those at different developmental stages and those from different cultural and linguistic backgrounds.

In synthesizing the literature on teacher education in reading, IRA's Teacher Education Task Force (IRA, 2007) emphasized the importance of addressing the assessment–instruction link in teacher education: "Not only do beginning teachers need to learn how different assessment strategies, models, and approaches test student learning, they also need to be taught how to interpret assessment data critically and adjust classroom instruction accordingly" (p. 5). The element is both inclusive and recursive in nature. It is inclusive in that it recognizes meeting the needs of all students, including those with academic, linguistic, and cultural differences. To plan, evaluate, and revise effective instruction that meets the needs of all learners, candidates need to think clearly about the assessment tools used and how those tools tap what students know and need to learn. It is recursive in that assessment and instruction can and should be ongoing.

First, for the assessment–instruction link to occur, candidates must understand curricular standards and how they relate to the specific assessment tool being used—whether the assessment tool is mandatory or teacher-selected. This should occur up front before the instrument is administered.

Second, the measure needs to be evaluated to determine whether or not it is appropriate for all students—particularly for students who are ELLs (Avalos, 2006) and students with other specialized needs (Schumm & Arguelles, 2006). Can the assessment be used with accommodations such as increased time, use of a scribe, or special formatting (Thurlow, Elliott, & Ysseldyke, 2003)?

Third, when adaptations to tests are not sufficient to accommodate the needs of an individual with disabilities, alternative assessment measures may be appropriate (Byrnes, 2004). "Alternate assessments are data collection procedures used in place of the typical assessment when students cannot take standard forms of assessment" (Ysseldyke & Olsen, 1997, p. 1). Byrnes (2004) writes that performance-based assessments and portfolios of student work are typical examples of alternate assessments.

Fourth, after the assessment is given, teachers need to decide issues related to grading, reteaching, and further assessment. Making assessment–instructional connections is complicated particularly when multiple measures are used (Opitz & Ford, 2006).

Teacher candidates can work through this maze by becoming familiar with resources that help make those connections (e.g., Caldwell & Leslie, 2005; Shea, Murray, & Harlin, 2005; Taberski, 2000). Instructional decisions can be short term for the particular group of students or long term for future instructional planning. Student performance can be the basis for teachers to reflect about how assessment or instruction might be changed in the future.

For high-stakes assessments, states have some flexibility in determining what constitutes appropriate test adaptations and alternative assessments to document student mastery of state curriculum standards. Knowing how to find this information from school districts and websites is important so that teacher candidates can provide students as well as parents and caregivers with appropriate information. Most state department of education websites provide an overview of accommodations and adaptations allowed for their state-administered high-stakes tests.

Element 3.4

Communicate results of assessments to specific individuals (e.g., students, parents, caregivers, colleagues, administrators, policymakers, policy officials, community).

Imagine that you are a third-grade teacher. You are the only third-grade teacher in the school. Thus, when test results for third-grade students are released on your school district website, it is obvious to administrators and the community at large whose class is represented in the data. You have two students who have not met the state cut-off score requirement for promotion to fourth grade. How would you report these findings to the parent, student, and the administration at your school? Do you have evidence from a variety of measures that indicated screening, diagnosis, monitoring, and outcome efforts? Have you provided key stakeholders sufficient information during the academic year? Can you explain options to parents for remediation or alternate routes to promotion approved by your state? Can you report data to a variety of audiences with dignity and clarity?

The days when student outcomes on standardized tests are buried in cumulative records are gone. Therefore, candidates must be able to understand test scores; validate instructional practice based on screening, diagnosis, progress monitoring, and outcome measures; and report student data in an ethical manner that is appropriate for the intended audience. In discussing the responsibility of reporting test results, Birenbaum (2007) recommends the following:

> The proposition regarding *reporting* is that the score reports are *accurate*, include *sufficient* information, and are *clear* to the stakeholders. This holds both for reports generated by test developers/publishers to help test users interpret test-results correctly, and for teacher-made tests where feedback to the learner is at issue. (p. 40)

Thus, it is not sufficient for candidates in teacher education programs simply to memorize assessment terms for an in-class test. Reading professionals must be fluent in their knowledge of assessment terms and be able to explain assessment results to a variety of audiences in appropriate ways.

Different Audiences

Students. The individuals who feel the impact of assessments and their consequences most directly are students. Students need to know more than if they passed or failed a test. If assessment and instruction are to be linked, it is critical that students are provided with assessment opportunities in which they learn not only what they understand well, but also what they need to improve concerning the content evaluated. Thus, students have the right to learn, in a developmentally appropriate manner, the nature of the tests they will be taking (content and format), how the tests are scored, how to best prepare for the test, what the consequences of the test might be, and how they performed on the test. The APA (1988) has developed a "Bill of Rights" for test takers that is useful in orienting students of their rights as a test taker, but also for their responsibilities in terms of test-taking ethics. The document can sensitize candidates to the valid and fair treatment of students in the assessment process including the practice of reporting results to students. Providing teacher candidates with opportunities to plan and implement the full spectrum of assessment activities including student assessment conferences (with appropriate supervision) can help them experience the process.

In addition, getting students at a young age and beyond engaged in self-assessment is a way to help students learn to monitor their own strengths and challenges as a learner as well as to monitor their own progress (Wormeli, 2006). IRA's position statement *Making a Difference Means Making It Different: Honoring Children's Rights to Excellent Reading Instruction* (IRA, 2000b) states, "Children have a right to reading assessment that identifies their strengths as well as their needs and involves them in making decisions about their own learning" (n.p.).

Parents and Caregivers. More than ever, parents and caregivers need clear information about general policies and procedures for assessment and (more significantly) their own child's status in learning to read and write. Although family members have greater access to student data than ever before, the high-stakes testing climate has the potential to escalate fear and anxiety among parents and caregivers. School websites, newsletters, parent workshops, and family conferences can be used to keep parents informed. Carefully planned family conferences are an important aspect of communication and an area sometimes neglected in teacher education programs. Cooper and Kiger (2008) stress the importance of family conferences and offer guidelines for their planning and implementation. Crucial to successful conferences are teacher understanding of the community, use of jargon-free language that is respectful to parents and caregivers, and involvement of students when appropriate.

Parents and appropriate caregivers can and should be involved not only in receiving reports of student outcomes but also in the assessment process. Edwards (2004) calls for a curriculum for teacher candidates that goes beyond superficial parental involvement to true partnerships. Edwards (2005) also encourages educators to have parent conferences serve more as parent conversations during which teachers can learn more about home literacy activities. Parents can also provide artifacts, such as favorite books and writing samples, to show teachers about a student's literacy journey.

School-Based Colleagues and Administrators. There are numerous ways that teachers use student data in conversations with school-based colleagues and administrators. When students are referred for special services, classroom teachers, special education teachers, and other school-based personnel discuss student assessment data in light of the referral or prereferral process. To engage in such conversations, teachers must recognize regulations for the ethical use of student test scores, be prepared to discuss and interpret data presented, and have a working knowledge of the types of assessment data school psychologists provide. This holds true in individualized education program (IEP) meetings and high-stakes meetings dealing with student placement, promotion, and retention. As Snow and colleagues (2005) relate, "we would be appalled if our medical care was delivered by different specialists who failed to check with one another about their diagnosis or about what drugs they were prescribing" (p. 195).

Snow and colleagues (2005) also suggest that assessment can be a topic for teacher learning groups. Sharing student data (with identifying information removed) with discussions about scoring, interpretation, and next steps for assessment can be a part of formal and informal teacher professional development.

The discussion of assessment outcomes includes discussions that occur with school-based administrators. The role of administrators as *instructional leaders* has continued to evolve to meet the accountability requirements of NCLB and standards-based instruction at the state and local levels (Womble, 2006). Administrators may delegate assessment oversight to an assistant principal or reading coach (Bean, 2004; Walpole & McKenna, 2004). Regardless, at school-based administrative levels those responsible must account to parents, school-district officials at local and state levels, and to the community at large. Teachers who are assessment literate, keep accurate records, and are knowledgeable about their students' strengths and challenges can be supportive of administrators in their school-accountability responsibilities as well as in their interactions with individual parents and students. Teacher education can prepare candidates for these important functions by providing direct instruction and experience in assembling student data for various audiences, record keeping, and in developing ways to articulate student data and problem solve critical cases in professional ways.

Conclusion

Campbell and Collins (2007) state that the underlying assumption behind NCLB and IDEA is that all teachers not only be skilled in assessment but also be capable of using assessment results to inform practice and decision making; therefore, teachers must be assessment literate, and teacher preparation in assessment must be strong.

Standards 2003 provides a general template for professional development of assessment literacy. However, what competencies and skills constitute assessment literacy are likely to vary from state to state and among institutions of higher education. In the absence of a unified core curriculum in assessment (McMillan, 2003), research on teacher preparation in assessment indicates variability in what is taught (Campbell & Collins, 2007) and how it is taught (Cuevas, Schumm, Mits Cash, & Pilonieta, 2006).

In using the rubric related to Standard 3, teacher candidates should include some mandatory artifacts (e.g., responses to case studies) to demonstrate each of the elements, but also some discretionary artifacts based on individual student self-assessed strengths and weaknesses, professional goals, and faculty member recommendations for areas in need of improvement.

> Just as teachers think of their students as individuals, those who train teachers in assessment should remember that preservice and inservice teachers, too, are individuals, each with a different style, strengths, and weaknesses, working in a unique environment. We should not standardize our advice about assessment practices because teachers and their needs, goals, and contexts are not standardized. What may work well for one individual may not work well with another (McMillan, 2003, p. 42).

FURTHER READING

Afflerbach, P. (2007). *Understanding and using reading assessment, K–12.* Newark, DE: International Reading Association.

This is an excellent tool to help teacher candidates choose and evaluate reading assessments. The book provides a framework for evaluating potential instruments considering consequences, usefulness, roles and responsibilities, reliability, and validity.

Barrentyne, S.J., & Stokes, S.M. (Eds.). (2005). *Reading assessment: Principles and practices for elementary teachers*. Newark, DE: International Reading Association.

This is a collection of articles from *The Reading Teacher* that addresses various topics related to assessment.

Harp, B. (2005). *The handbook of literacy assessment and evaluation* (3rd ed.). Norwood, MA: Christopher-Gordon.

This book provides descriptions of a wide variety of formal and informal assessment instruments.

Thomas, R.M. (2005). *High-stakes testing: Coping with collateral damage*. Mahwah, NJ: Erlbaum.

This is a thought-provoking book that examines the impact of high-stakes tests on students as well as other key stakeholders.

The CaseNEX case study selected for Standard 3 addresses Element 3.1, requiring candidates to use a wide variety of assessment tools. Element 3.1 has a highest possible content score of 7 and lowest possible score of 0 (see Standard 3 Rubric, Appendix, p. 149).

Case Study for Standard 3:
Assessment, Diagnosis, and Evaluation

Reprinted from CaseNEX LLC, founded at University of Virginia's Curry School of Education. Reprinted with permission.

Matchmakers, Scene 2 (pertaining to Allen only)

Jennifer did a double-take as Allen walked towards them. He was so small and fragile-looking. It was hard to believe he and Marta were in the same grade.

As they walked beside him down the hall, Jennifer made a couple of attempts at small talk and saw quickly that either Allen was a shy one or his English skills were minimal. Suzanne thought she might have better luck, so she slipped in between Allen and Jennifer, offering, "Hola, Allen. How are your new classes? ¿Que es escuela?"

Allen struggled to provide answers to Jennifer's questions.

Suzanne didn't get more than a feeble, "OK," in response. She dropped back a step, caught Jennifer Harris's eye, and shrugged. They settled for a quiet walk with Jennifer wishing she could remember some of her high school Spanish.

Once back in the media center, Jennifer pulled out her assessment materials, glad that she'd brought a wide range with her. She had a feeling that Allen's teachers were right to be so concerned about him.

Allen's Reading Assessment (video transcript)

Jennifer: I want to double-check to see how you're doing on all your letters and sounds. OK? Let's do that. Want to?

Allen: Uh-huh.

Jennifer: I'll point to it and just tell me, just tell me up to here [Uses a pencil to indicate a line on the sheet of paper] what the letter is. What are these called? Are these the lowercase or the capital letters?

Allen: Capital letters?

Jennifer: Uh-huh, capitals. OK, what's that one?

Allen: B. E. G. No. J.

Jennifer: OK.

Allen: N. K.

Jennifer: [There is a pause as Jennifer writes on the paper]. OK. This one.

Allen: U. X. Is that a *B*?

Jennifer: A what?

Allen: A *B*?

Jennifer: A *B*?

Allen: Yeah.

Jennifer: [Writes on the paper] OK. This one.

Allen: Y.

Jennifer: OK. This row.

Allen: Z.

Jennifer: Say that again?

Allen: Z.

Jennifer: Z? [Jennifer makes a notation on the paper] OK.

Allen: F. Y. [Jennifer makes notations] L. O. K. [Allen makes a slight pause and Jennifer makes notations] T. S. Z. D. A. H. K. N. R. D. P. W.

Jennifer: OK. These down here, I want you to tell me the letter and the sound that it makes and if you know a word that starts with the sound. OK? What's that letter?

Allen: D.

Jennifer: What does D make?

Allen: T?

Jennifer: What letter, what sound does D make, like when you're trying to…you know what D makes?

Jennifer: OK. [Jennifer makes a notation] How about that letter?

Allen: G?

Jennifer: Let's hear your G sound.

Allen: I don't really know. [Under his breath he says, "geee, geee"]

Jennifer: No? OK.

Allen: L. A.

Jennifer: OK. This one.

Allen: P. G? [Jennifer makes more notations]

Jennifer: This one?

Allen: T?

Jennifer: Umhumm. What's the sound of T?

Allen:	T-t-t-t-t-t-t.
Jennifer:	Are you doing the sound right now?
Allen:	It's T…S? T…No.
Jennifer:	How about this one?
Allen:	O.
Jennifer:	You know all your letters, don't you? Almost all of them.

Allen's Reading Minilesson, Part 1 (video transcript)

Jennifer:	OK. One more thing. We're going to try this. Um. Can you read that letter? That word?
Allen:	Dig? No?
Jennifer:	Does that say dig? How about this?
Allen:	Get.
Jennifer:	OK, now you said this is dig. If I cover this up, how would you start that word?
Allen:	D.
Jennifer:	What's your starting sound?
Allen:	Leyday?
Jennifer:	Duh.
Allen:	Duh?
Jennifer:	Duh. What's the middle sound?
Allen:	I?
Jennifer:	Yeah, but what is the sound?
Allen:	Uh?
Jennifer:	'Cuz you said that was dig, right? Ih, that's your second sound.
Allen:	I?
Jennifer:	Ih.
Allen:	Dike?
Jennifer:	Duh-ih-ggg.
Allen:	Dike?
Jennifer:	Allen, dig. Do you know that word *dig*? Do you know what that word means? *Dig*?

Allen's Reading Minilesson, Part 2 (video transcript)

| Allen: | Cat? |

Jennifer:	What's your first sound?
Allen:	C.
Jennifer:	You said this was cat, right? What's that word start with?
Allen:	Kuh?
Jennifer:	What's the first sound you hear? Kuh, Kuh.
Allen:	K?
Jennifer:	C can say the K sound, too. What's the middle sound?
Allen:	Ay? Anh?
Jennifer:	Anhhh. So these are the sounds that they're making, huh? So the letter is C but the sound can either be "ssss" or "kuh." So what's our second sound for A?
Allen:	Ah?
Jennifer:	Open your mouth really wide.
Allen:	Anhh.
Jennifer:	There it is. Say it again.
Allen:	Anhh.
Jennifer:	Yeah. What's our third sound?
Allen:	T-t-t-t-t
Jennifer:	Yes. So when Mrs. Harris is asking you what sound it makes, what is the sound for T?
Allen:	T-t-t-t-t
Jennifer:	OK. So let's do it one more time.
Allen:	Cat.
Jennifer:	Let's just do our sound. Kuh. Anhhh. T-t-t-t-t. Cat. But when we do it we do it really fast, don't we? We go cat.

Jennifer wondered if there was any point in attempting to collect a writing sample with Allen, but she didn't think it could hurt to try. "Allen," she smiled. "I'd like you to write something about your birthday party."

Allen's face remained impassive as Jennifer handed him paper and pencil. "Your birthday party," she repeated, inadvertently raising her voice a bit. "Okay? What happened at your birthday party?"

Suzanne chimed in, hesitantly, "Your compleaños?"

Allen looked even more uncomfortable, but he picked up the pencil, and began writing. After twenty minutes, he quietly placed his pencil neatly parallel to his paper. He was done.

Allen's Writing Sample

On their way back to the library after dropping Allen off at his next class, Jennifer shook her head, saying, "That was a disaster."

"How can you even tell if he understood what to do?"

"Good question...I don't really know." Jennifer was afraid she wasn't being much help to Suzanne. "Let's look at the summaries to make sure we covered everything." Jennifer wondered if Allen might have some special education issues and just how this might be determined.

READING ASSESSMENT SUMMARY

Name: Allen Ramirez

Grade: 8th

Allen was able to identify most letters of the alphabet and could distinguish between lowercase and capital letters. He had significant difficulty naming letter sounds and offered responses that seemed almost random. He was able to sound out a couple of simple words (such as cat), but could not name the sounds made by each letter without significant coaching.

Question for response: Name three other assessments you would administer to Allen in order to determine Allen's learning needs. Why did you choose those three?

Context of Administration

The context of administration was a literacy assessment course. Candidates were allowed to preview the case in class and write a response at home over the week before the next class met. Collaboration in discussing the case was allowed, however, the actual written responses were to be completed independently.

Responses

Note that we were unable to gain permission to use actual candidates' responses for this case; therefore, we created sample responses to provide you with an idea of probable anchor responses. For the first response, the Burns and Roe IRI and CTOPP assessments suggested are appropriate for Allen; however, the WRMT-R is inappropriate for a student who is having difficulty with phonological awareness. There is no mention of any issues concerning second language literacy or technology as a tool for assessment. The rationale is weak and little evidence of conceptual understanding is demonstrated concerning Allen's language and literacy assessment needs. A content score of 2 was awarded with a Novice rationale.

Allen needs to improve his reading. He does not know all the letters of the alphabet and cannot blend sounds together. I would give Allen an informal reading inventory, such as the Burns and Roe IRI to determine the grade level he is presently reading. It is necessary to determine his independent, instructional and frustration reading levels. Once these have been established, Jennifer can give him work at his independent and instructional reading levels.

I would also want to give Allen the Comprehensive Test of Phonological Processing (CTOPP in English) to evaluate his auditory processing and phonological awareness skills. This test has various substests including: Elision, Blending Words, Sound Matching, Memory for Digits, Nonword Repetition, etc. This test will see how well he manipulates and blend sounds. Another assessment I would give Allen is the Woodcock Reading Master Test-Revised (WRMT-R). This will test his passage comprehension in silent reading.

The second response provides two appropriate formal assessments for Allen's case, but the CASAS is a group administered adult assessment. The content score of 2 was awarded because there are two appropriate formal assessments and one inappropriate formal assessment suggested, with no informal assessment suggested. In addition, there is no mention of a technology-based assessment tool. The rationale is minimal but demonstrates an emerging conceptual understanding of Allen's assessment needs; therefore, a Sufficient rationale score was given.

Allen is having difficulty with identifying letters and also with the grapheme-phoneme connections. I would want to know how proficient Allen actually is in English. The CASAS —Comprehensive Adult Student Assessment Systems —used for assessing listening, writing, and speaking skills would help me to make this determination. Once I have completed this I would like to assess Allen's phonological awareness by using the CTOPP. Since there is such a discrepancy between Allen's age and his actual achievement I would want to have the results of the complete psychoeducational battery (WISC IV) to gather information of his psychological processes and inform me if there are any underlying issues I should be aware of when designing his instruction.

The third response demonstrates a good understanding of literacy and language transition from Spanish to English, as well as the need to determine if the difficulties Allen is experiencing are due to acquiring a new language or are also present while reading in the primary language. The CTOPP is an appropriate formal assessment to determine phonological processing in both languages. The *Ekwall/ Shanker Reading Inventory* (Shanker & Ekwall, 1999) has appropriate subtests for emergent readers (which Allen is, at least in English) and is an excellent informal measure to guide instruction. The STAR and Accelerated Reader (AR) programs are computer based and will assist the teacher in monitoring Allen's reading practices outside of language arts instruction. A content score of 6 and a Proficient rationale were awarded for this response.

Allen is in eighth grade and cannot recognize all of his letters proficiently. When asked letter sounds he was very uncomfortable and seemed to be guessing the sounds. In blending sounds it became apparent that Allen struggled. The teachers in the case study seemed to believe that he was not proficient in English. In fact, on a few occasions they tried to speak to him in Spanish. For this reason it seems that whatever tests are done need to be administered in both Spanish and English to rule out the possibility that Allen is having reading difficulties due to lack of English proficiency. Allen was able to sound out some words like "cat" but could not name the sounds made by each letter. In order for someone to read unknown words, they need to be able to recognize letters and connect those letters to the sounds they represent. This is called the grapheme-phoneme relationship and connection. Before this can occur individuals must be able to discern the individual sounds in words. It seems that although Allen is in eighth grade he has difficulty with phonological awareness. For this reason I would administer the CTOPP in both Spanish and English which assesses phonological processing.

I know that Allen cannot decode words but I would be interested in getting information on his other foundational reading skills. For this reason I would administer the Ekwall Shanker Informal Reading Inventory reading passages with comprehension questions and subtests to determine Allen's instructional reading level, as well as other possible reading skills that need explicit instruction. Finally I would also use the STAR assessment and Accelerated Reading program to assist Allen in choosing books at his appropriate reading level. The AR program also helps to monitor students' reading habits and comprehension, with the computer tracking books read and percentage of correct comprehension questions.

The fourth response, a Distinguished response with a content score of 7, indicates a solid understanding of biliteracy development (second language literacy development builds on first language literacy skills and knowledge), as well as knowledge of different assessments and their purposes. DIBELS is a web-based tool that will assist in monitoring progress in phonological awareness, an obvious instructional need for Allen. (References for the response are included.)

According to the reading assessment summary, Allen, an 8th grade student, was able to identify the majority of the letters in the alphabet and could distinguish between lower and uppercase letters. He could only sound out a few simple words and required much coaching to identify individual letter sounds. The case study did not indicate as to when Allen entered the United States and since he is in the 8th grade and unable to identify all of the letters of the alphabet, I will assume that this is a recent migration. Therefore, I would conduct an initial assessment as governed by federal statutes and outlined in the No Child Left Behind (NCLB) Act (2001) to identify ELLs in order to provide the necessary provisions to guarantee a successful school career. Selection of assessment tools would be limited to those that have high reliability and validity as research has established the importance of these factors for ELLs.

Since the purpose of assessment would be to assess Allen's academic skills in order to implement instructional strategies to match his particular skills and needs, building on his prior knowledge, I feel that the assessments need to be administered in Allen's native language whenever possible. Allen may possess skills in reading in his first language that can be transferred to English and facilitate learning English language literacy skills (August, Calderon, & Carlo, 2001). Also, assessing Allen in his first language is indicative that there is value in Allen's past literacy acquisition (Goodman, 1998). Furthermore, standardized tests in English are unable to distinguish a poor score due to Allen's inability to perform the targeted skills or due to Allen's inability to interpret the vocabulary.

The first assessment that I would administer to Allen would be the Comprehensive Test of Phonological Processing (CTOPP) in Spanish to evaluate his phonemic awareness and auditory processing skills. Phonemic awareness is the ability to hear, identify, and manipulate the individual sounds in spoken words. Cisero and Royer (1995) found evidence of cross-linguistic transfer of phonological awareness skills among kindergarten and first-grade English- and Spanish-speaking students. Since there is a vast discrepancy between Allen's grade level and ability level, the CTOPP will identify if Allen's deficit in English is mirrored in his first language. If the discrepancy exists, then I would recommend that Allen undergo a battery of psychological testing to determine if there is a specific learning disability.

It would be also be essential to assess Allen's language proficiency as well. According to Baca and Cervantes (1984) it is recommended that a child be tested in both languages to develop prescriptive measures for interventions. I would recommend the Language Assessment Scales, Reading and Writing Test in the Spanish form and English form. The results would determine Allen's reading and writing ability on one of three levels: non-reader/writer; limited reader/writer; and competent reader/writer. The Woodcock Language Proficiency Battery, English and Spanish forms could be administered to test receptive and expressive semantics. The information from this assessment could offer information as to which skills Allen already possesses that can be transferred to the acquisition of literacy in English as well as indicate which skills need to be developed because they are below grade level.

I would also recommend informal assessments to determine Allen's attitude toward reading, his perceptions on the reading process and to identify how he feels about his own reading. One example could be the Reading Interest Survey in the Ekwell/Shanker Informal Reading Inventory. Assessments give insight to the constructivist view of reading as they can identify Allen's strengths and weaknesses in literacy acquisition through the types of reading strategies he uses, and how factors such as background experiences, vocabulary knowledge, and interest influence his reading comprehension (Garcia, 1992).

After determining instructional needs, I would also administer the Dynamic Indicators of Basic Early Literacy Skills (DIBELS) as I begin instructing Allen to monitor progress in English phonological awareness, alphabetic principle, fluency with connected text, vocabulary development, and reading comprehension. The DIBELS is designed for K–6 students and although Allen is in eighth grade, he demonstrates the needs of an emergent reader, one of the targeted populations for which DIBELS was developed. DIBELS is an online assessment tool that assists teachers in storing, analyzing, and reporting data for progress monitoring.

References

August, D., Calderon, M., & Carlo, M. (2001, February). The transfer of skills from Spanish to English: A study of young learners. Washington, DC: Center for Applied Linguistics (CAL). Summary article available: www.cal.org/pubs/articles/skillstransfer-nabe.html

Baca, L., & Cervantes, H. (1984). The bilingual special education interface. St. Louis: Time Mirror/Mosby.

Cisero, C. A., & Royer, J. M. (1995). The development and cross-language transfer of phonological awareness. Contemporary Educational Psychology, 20, 275–303.

Garcia, E.E. (1992). Effective instruction for language minority students: The teacher. Journal of Education, 173(2), 130–141.

Goodman, E. (1998, April 20). The bilingual question. Currents, 2(34). Santa Cruz, CA: University of California Santa Cruz (UCSC) Public Information Office. Available: www.ucsc.edu/oncampus/currents/97-98/04-20/crede.htm

CHAPTER 4

Learning About and Assessing Standard 4—Creating a Literate Environment

The interconnection between the environment and human behavior has been important within reading and literacy research. Barker (1978) found that human behavior is adapted to meet the needs of the setting. These conclusions can be generalized to classroom environments (Morrow, 2007). In fact, Bandura's (1969) sociocultural theory of learning explains how a learner's social and personal competencies are modified as a result of the social environment in which learning occurs. Bandura analyzed the role of children's environments on their academic development and success. His analysis revealed that several factors can affect observational learning, such as the developmental age of the observer, and the model's own feelings of self-efficacy. Further, Bandura found that observers are influenced by their feelings about the model. They will be more likely to adopt a behavior observed if they admire and trust the model. In addition, Bandura concluded that in observational learning the observer learns from the consequences that the behavior has for the model (see also Bower & Hilgard, 1981). The interconnection between the environment and human behavior has been especially important within the field of reading and literacy.

There is evidence to support the significant role played by literacy-rich classrooms in reading instruction of elementary age students (Noyes, 2000). In fact, experts who study the field of reading and classroom environments have clearly established that classrooms rich in print can positively affect students' reading achievement (Wharton-McDonald, Pressley, Rankin, Mistretta, & Ettenberger, 1997; Morrow, 2007; Morrow, Tracy, Woo, & Pressley, 1999; Pressley, Rankin, & Yokoi, 1996; Taylor et al., 1999b). NCTE (1997) contends that providing students with a rich literate environment is the foundation of literacy development. McGee and Richgels (2004) state,

> Literacy-rich environments provide child-centered, developmentally appropriate support for children's literacy learning. All children, whether they have many or few home literacy experiences, whether they speak English or another language at home, and whether they have special learning needs, thrive in such classrooms. (p. 145)

In investigating the effects of a literacy-rich environment on vocabulary in low-income classrooms, Snow, Barnes, Chandler, Goodman, and Hemphill (1991) conclude that classrooms that provided ample opportunities to interact with literacy materials, were motivating and diverse, granted opportunities to visit libraries, and improved students' knowledge of vocabulary. In other words, Snow and colleagues found that students who were engaged in literacy-rich environments had greater knowledge of vocabulary than their peers who did not have these experiences.

Hoffman, Sailors, Duffy, and Beretvas (2004) point out that not only have we confirmed through this research the role that literacy-rich environments play, but a trend is evident in that the research has expanded from being descriptive and investigative of the components in the literacy-rich environment to investigating and understanding the association between literacy development and literacy-rich environments. Hoffman and colleagues also point out that these areas of research began with investigations focusing mainly on trade books and preschools but now include all elementary grades as well as a variety of print materials in various settings. As research in this area has expanded, it has become clearer that classroom environments rich in print and literacy exposure positively affect students' literacy development.

A literacy-rich environment is designed with an emphasis on the language arts (reading, writing, listening and speaking, viewing and presenting) and allows students to engage in activities that cultivate these language forms. The classroom appearance, peer and teacher interactions, and available materials are important contributors of the literacy-rich environment (American Institutes for Research, 2007).

The value of literacy-rich settings has also been highlighted by IRA which designated "Creating a Literate Environment" as Standard 4 of their recommended practices for reading professionals. IRA's emphasis on literacy-rich environments can be interpreted as a requirement of professional competence in all teachers. Therefore, teacher education programs need to focus on preparing candidates who understand and are effective in crafting classroom settings that promote and foster literacy, and in turn create lifelong readers. It is important to note that Standard 4 builds upon Standards 1 through 3, discussed in previous chapters, because the reading teacher needs to be able to incorporate foundational knowledge (Standard 1), skills for diverse instructional practices and curriculum materials (Standard 2), and broad knowledge of assessment materials and practices (Standard 3) in order to develop a classroom that is rich in literacy opportunities for students. Standard 4 specifically recommends that "candidates create a literate environment that fosters reading and writing by integrating foundational knowledge, use of instructional practices, approaches and methods, curriculum materials, and the appropriate use of assessments" (IRA, 2004, p. 16).

The elements that make up Standard 4 comprise the following:

- Use of students' interests, abilities, and backgrounds as foundations for instruction
- Materials and technology
- Modeling reading and writing
- Motivating learners

Element 4.1

Use students' interests, reading abilities, and backgrounds as foundations for the reading and writing program.

Differentiating instruction is important when building a student-centered literacy program. Tomlinson (2003) states that for educators to successfully differentiate instruction they need to provide accommodation for every student in their classroom, possess a great deal of common sense, and base their practices on a strong foundational background in research and theory. Hall (2002) contends that

> to differentiate instruction is to recognize students' varying background knowledge, readiness, language, preferences in learning, interests, and to react responsively. Differentiated instruction is a process to approach teaching and learning for students of differing abilities in the same class. The intent of differentiating instruction is to maximize each student's growth and individual success by meeting each student where he or she is, and assisting in the learning process. (p. 2)

The principle of differentiated instruction is based on the idea that every student's background, experiences, and culture are important factors to consider when designing lessons. Teachers who do not consider adjusting their lessons will most likely find that their teaching addresses the needs of a slim minority. Differentiated instruction has its roots in the idea that we teach best when we consider who the learner is (Tomlinson, 2003).

Schumm and Arguelles (2006) discuss the five different dimensions that affect differentiated instruction and that should be considered when planning literacy instruction (see Table 6). These five dimensions vary in intensity from low to high and involve (1) group size, (2) strategies and materials, (3) instructor, (4) time, and (5) practice, support, and feedback. The effective teacher should think about these five dimensions when making educational decisions to better address the needs of individual students and decide which level of intensity is appropriate to apply.

Whereas differentiated instruction will assist teachers in creating a foundation for student-centered reading programs, student diversity should also be considered. Orlich, Harder, Callahan, Trevisan, and Brown (2004) point out that diversity encompasses ethnicity, race, language, and physical, religious, and ability differences. In addition, social issues greatly affect the classroom environment and need to be considered by educators when designing a literacy-rich environment and reading programs. Students need to see themselves reflected in the materials, and their backgrounds should be an integral part of the curriculum and instruction (Allen, 1994; Hefflin & Barksdale-Ladd, 2003). As Orlich and colleagues (2004) state,

> A society's schools mirror its values and inject them into curricula, and instructional practices. But schools are also deeply affected by social factors, and in many cases these factors impact one of schooling's most important premises: that students show up at the schoolhouse door ready to learn. (p. 12)

TABLE 6. Dimensions That Have an Impact on Planning for Differentiated Instruction

Dimensions	Grouping	Strategies and materials	Instructor	Time	Practice support feedback
Low intensity	• Whole class • Mixed ability	• No evidence	• Untrained volunteer	• Low length of time and frequency	• None
Medium intensity	• Small groups or pairs • Mixed or same ability	• Moderate scientific evidence or previously used in classroom with success	• Classroom teacher	• Moderate length of time and frequency	• Peer supported • Not specific or delayed
High intensity	• Individuals • Same ability	• Strong scientific evidence with similar populations	• Reading specialist	• High length of time and high frequency	• Immediate • Specific

Adapted from Schumm, J.S., & Arguelles, M.E. (2006). No two learners are alike: The importance of assessment and differentiated instruction. In J.S. Schumm (Ed.), *Reading assessment and instruction for all learners* (pp. 27–59). New York: Guilford.

Teachers should also be aware of current social issues that have an impact on the lives of their students. Orlich and colleagues (2004) mention some of these factors, highlighting that in the United States, 31% of children are a part of a single parent family and 17% of children live in poverty. Further, of all the children living in poverty, the majority are either African American or Latino, compared with 35% of Caucasian children.

Types of Diversity

Racial Diversity. Consisting of physical or biological traits shared by a group, particularly skin color, body structure, and facial features (Orlich et al., 2004), racial diversity is the most evident type of diversity. Candidates should be aware that within a racial group there are different cultures and the racial group does not define a cultural group. The experiences shared by individuals with similar racial characteristics are comparable and these experiences affect the school and learning environment. Similarly, regional diversity includes the differences found among people from different regions of a country or of the world in terms of beliefs, values, and practices.

Language Diversity. Often when teachers are asked how they differentiate instruction they recount experiences with students who are culturally or linguistically diverse. Indeed, cultural and linguistic diversity are important factors to consider when tailoring instruction and have become one of the reasons why differentiated instruction has received such interest in the United States. As noted in Chapter 1, a large increase of ELLs in U.S. public schools requires instruction that is responsive to diversity. It is clearly established that when compared to the majority, ELLs have experienced greater retention as well as dropout rates (U.S. Department of Education, 2000), and an overrepresentation in special education categories (Donovan & Cross, 2002; Ortiz & Yates, 2001).

Physical Diversity. For years societies have glorified beauty and have imposed the ideal image for a female or male. In U.S. culture where certain stereotypical features are valued and beauty is celebrated, differences in physical traits can possibly expose some children to negative experiences. Physical features include age, gender, physical condition or traits, and physical disabilities (Orlich et al., 2004). A child with a physical disability thus has two challenges to face: overcoming the obstacles imposed by the disability and dealing with the rejection they face from society. These obstacles are real in the lives of many children, and teachers need to be prepared to face the challenge of embracing these students as well as considering them when developing literacy lessons.

Religious Diversity. Orlich and colleagues (2004) posit that students who attend public schools bring with them their religious beliefs and faiths that should not be ignored. Their beliefs are a big part of who they are. The role of the teacher is not to promote one belief over the other but to accept all students regardless of their religious beliefs, even when they are very different from the teacher's personal beliefs. The First Amendment to the U.S. Constitution governs the relationship between religion and government entities, including public schools (U.S. Department of Education, 2003). First Amendment rights not only prevent the government from establishing a religion, it also protects individuals' rights of religious expression and activities from government discrimination and interference. Guidelines for dealing with religious expression in schools are available online at www.ed .gov/policy/gen/guid/religionandschools/prayer_guidance.html#1.

Ability. Whereas an influx of ELLs and minority numbers in public schools have helped to focus the attention of educators on providing differentiated instruction to all students, issues related to special education placement have also forced educators to address differentiated instruction. Another critical issue in special education's modern history that strongly affects general education is the inclusion movement. In response to legislation and philosophical trends, the field of special education has steadily moved toward the goal of providing instruction to all students in the least restrictive environment. For many students this setting is the general education classroom (Vaughn et al., 2007). In fact, the number of students with special needs serviced in the general education setting has increased by 20% in the last few years (U.S. Department of Education, 2000). As outlined in Chapter 2, Response to Intervention (RTI) is the use of differentiated instruction to meet instructional needs before placing the student in a special setting. It is therefore essential that all teachers are well prepared to adapt instruction to service *all* students.

Despite the fact that considering reading performance level is good practice in planning literacy instruction, studies demonstrate that teachers generally do not make adaptations for their students of differing abilities. Elbaum, Vaughn, and Schumm (1997) found that students favored teachers who made adaptations for students who needed them. Teachers who provide accommodations relevant to ability allow each student to receive what is needed instructionally. J.W. Wood (2006) suggests that teachers adapt the learning environment, lesson plans, teaching techniques, format of content, assessment, evaluation, and grading to meet the needs of all children.

Teacher education programs need to emphasize preparing candidates to implement differentiated instruction on a regular basis (Schumm & Arguelles, 2006). In fact, Manson (1999) argues that teacher education programs may become accountable for preparing candidates to be aware and sensitive to children's differences. Manson researched ways in which teacher education programs could prepare teachers to become effective in implementing differentiated instructional practices. This qualitative study measured teacher perceptions of cross-ethnic and cross-racial instruction. The analysis of responses to the Manson Teacher Inventory revealed that participating teachers felt there was still room for improving teacher education programs in the area of strategies for teaching diverse student populations. More specifically, participants felt that these strategies should be directly modeled early in the academic programs, emphasizing the opportunity for candidates to work directly with students from different ethnic and cultural backgrounds. When candidates are able to design reading and writing lessons based on student's interests, abilities, and backgrounds, they are likely to achieve success in engaging and motivating their students (Noyes, 2000).

Element 4.2

Use a large supply of books, technology-based information, and nonprint materials representing multiple levels, broad interests, and cultural and linguistic backgrounds.

In a resolution statement, the NCTE stated that a rich literate environment is indispensable to literacy development in children (NCTE, 1997). In fact, it urged professionals to develop language arts instruction that included a variety of materials to enhance the print environment. Students need to be immersed in print-rich environments early on that allow them to manipulate language in all of its forms. In fact, there is a strong relation between the amount of texts available to students in a classroom and their reading achievement (Morrow, 2007). Research has demonstrated that print-rich environments are not easily found in classrooms today (Clark & Kragler, 2005). Often teachers may not understand the importance of integrating a variety of materials, and they may be impeded by time constraints or the pressure to deliver a script-like curriculum.

To encourage and develop lifelong readers and writers, a wide array of materials need to be available in classrooms. For example, Morrow and Weinstein (1982) found that when library areas in kindergarten classrooms were attractive to children and filled with books, students gravitated more often to these centers and interacted with the print-rich environment. Some examples of these materials include, but are not limited to, phone books, dictionaries, menus, recipes, labels, signs, books, and research materials. A variety of fiction and nonfiction materials need to be available as well so that students can experience literacy in different forms. Providing access to texts, literacy materials, and technology along with a variety of opportunities to interact with diverse materials positively affects a child's literacy development. Relevant to this investigation were the findings by Snow and colleagues (1991) who found that literacy-rich environments could help close reading skill gaps found in low income populations.

According to McGee and Richgels (2004), "the main objective of the literacy-rich environment is to encourage students to become reflective as well as motivate individuals who use reading and writing to learn more about themselves and their environments" (p.186). For this goal to be attained, certain characteristics need to be a part of the classroom environment in which these children learn, including an abundance of materials and opportunities to engage daily in various forms of literacy. The curriculum in the ideal literacy-rich classroom must be culturally sensitive and guided by assessment and should integrate language arts with various disciplines. Another important component of this classroom includes careful planning of its layout or design. Classrooms should offer students an inviting and motivating environment in which they are enthusiastic about reading and writing. The teacher should strive to diversify instruction by creating different grouping opportunities for students to work together or individually and also include different teaching strategies to keep students motivated.

Valid instruments to measure and assess the quality of print rich literacy environments have been developed (Hoffman et al., 2004; Wolfersberger, Reutzel, Sudweeks, & Fawson, 2004). Hoffman and colleagues created and validated an instrument (TEX-IN3) designed to assess the quality of the classroom literacy environment to measure (a) the physical text environment, (b) how texts are used in the classroom, and (c) the understanding and valuing of texts in the classroom environment. Using rubrics that evolved over the two-year development period, the TEX-IN3 requires a text inventory to categorize text types into 17 categories (e.g., leveled books, reference materials, student/teacher published work, tradebooks), two separate ratings of the holistic text environment using different scales (one for published materials and the other for teacher/student print), and interviews with children about their understandings and use of the print in the classroom. Findings from Hoffman and colleague's research indicate solid empirical support for the three major components of the TEX-IN3 with regard to student reading comprehension growth.

The Classroom Literacy Environmental Profile (CLEP) was also developed, field tested, and validated to serve researchers and practitioners (Wolfsberger et al., 2004). Characteristics of print-rich classroom environments were identified, defined, and categorized using the literature, classroom observations, teacher focus groups, and an audit trail to substantiate the data collection and analysis process for validation. The CLEP uses 33 separate scales to evaluate literacy tools (the quantity, utility, grouping, accessibility, interactions with, and appropriateness of); text materials (quantity of, genres, levels, format and content of); print used for classroom organization; classroom literacy product displays; reference materials; written communications; writing utensil, surfaces, and publishing materials; furnishings; storage and display containers; accessories to support literacy events (e.g., puppet stage, masks, costumes); classroom areas (locations, boundaries, and types); classroom library; participation in literacy events (if encouraged and inviting); authentic literacy settings and events; record keeping of literacy interactions; and literacy products (variety and sharing of). After calculating the scores from the different scales, results are provided for two main areas: (1) provisioning the classroom with literacy tools and (2) arranging classroom space and literacy tools, gaining students' interest in literacy events, and sustaining students' interactions with literacy tools. Both the TEX-IN3 and the CLEP can be used by candidates, teachers, administrators, or researchers to improve, enhance, investigate, and revamp classroom literacy environments for preschool and elementary classrooms.

Taylor, Blum, and Logsdon (1986) explored creating literate rich classrooms with 13 teachers. The study revealed that participating teachers who received instruction in creating literacy-rich settings had students who outperformed their peers in all measures of reading. Similarly, McGill-Franzen, Allington, Yokoi, and Brooks (1999) researched the value of supplying classrooms with books and training teachers to develop instructional activities that incorporated these materials. They divided their sample into three groups or classrooms. The first group was given the materials and the instruction on how to employ them. The second group was given only books, and the third was considered the control group, receiving neither materials nor instruction. The investigation found that not only did materials help to augment the benefits of the classroom for children's literacy development, but teaching teachers to employ these materials effectively was critical. Students in group one scored the highest compared with their peers in reading achievement scores. Effective teachers create literate rich environments and consequently produce better readers.

Element 4.3

Model reading and writing enthusiastically as valued lifelong activities.

Teachers play an important role in helping students to develop a lifelong love for reading and writing. Teachers can nurture student literacy by modeling reading and writing enthusiastically. Schunk (2003) points out that "vicarious" learning is that which occurs through observing others and that this type of learning is as powerful as "enactive" learning when people learn through their own experiences. In vicarious learning the observer not only learns from the behavior, but also from the consequences that the action has for the model they observe. Depending on those consequences, the observer may opt to imitate the behavior or refrain from it.

Modeling provides opportunities and examples for learning (Cambourne, 1988). Functions of print and pleasures gained by reading are first demonstrated by family members and later by teachers and society (Bus, 2001; Johns & VanLeirsburg, 1994; Sonnenschein,

Brody, & Munsterman, 1996). Preschoolers who have been exposed to print will hold books, turn pages, and "read" the story as others have modeled for them. Children will strive to imitate attitudes and daily activities of significant role models who are admired and respected; to model literacy activities is to influence in a powerful way (Spiegel, 1994). The most effective model in schools is a teacher who genuinely loves books and reading as students will notice, catch, and benefit from the teacher's enthusiasm (Johns & VanLeirsburg, 1994; Wilson & Hall, 1972).

Reading aloud is one way to model enthusiastic reading as it has been compared to giving a commercial for the pleasure of reading (Trelease, 1995). Teacher implementation of the read-aloud session determines its influence on students' reading (Fisher, Flood, Lapp, & Frey, 2004). Expressive and enthusiastic read-aloud sessions model fluency, allow students to hear literature above their independent reading levels, boost comprehension, and positively affect student writing (Martin, 2003; Morrow, 2003; Pinnell & Jaggar, 2003; Sipe, 2000). Studies investigating the benefits of reading aloud to children also provide evidence of increased vocabulary (Beck, McKeown, & Kucan, 2002; De Temple & Snow, 2003; Greene Brabham & Lynch-Brown, 2002; Sharif, Ohuah, Dinkevich, & Mulvihill, 2003), listening comprehension (Morrow & Gambrell, 2002; Stanovich, Cunningham, & West, 1998; Teale, 1986), syntactic development (Chomsky, 1972), and word recognition (Stahl, 2003).

Teale (2003) suggests teachers consider the amount of time, choice of text, the method (use of gestures, expression, and voices), and the fit of the text with the curriculum to select daily read-alouds. Rewarding experiences with read-alouds can lead to positive attitudes toward reading, encouraging engagement with other literacy activities. McKenna and Kear (1990) also demonstrate that a positive attitude about reading is linked to higher reading achievement.

One of the main goals of teaching literacy is to foster a love of reading and help students become enthusiastic readers and writers for life. Everts Danielson and Everts Roberts (2000) posit that enthusiasm cannot be taught but must be passed on in order for children to feel the power and impact that lifelong reading can have. Thomas (2000) reflects on her love of literacy and middle school reading practice, recommending literature circles as an important tool to get students into books for life. Literature circles enable students to discuss novels based upon their own diverse viewpoints and experiences without the worry of having a "wrong" answer. She also creates themes for her literature circles based on the novels being read; thus the students have a focal point for their discussions. Other practices Thomas suggests include drama activities or role playing, poetry reading and writing. A framework of engagement, exploration, collaboration, and celebration guides her instruction and leads her students to passionate reading. Thomas recognizes as crucial to creating lifelong readers the need to give her students choices, varied opportunities to become engaged in literature, time to read, and chances to share their perspectives.

Routman (2003) often asks teachers to reflect and make a list of the "top five things" they do to ensure that students become excellent readers. Among the responses, "Read good literature to them," "Share our love of literature," and "Model" are typically included (p. 42). It is important for teachers to make their own reading lives public and model how to behave, think, and talk as readers for their students (Gambrell, 1996; Routman, 2003). By doing so, they will immerse students in literacy, promote an implicit love for reading and writing, and help assist in developing students' skills to understand the nature of reading and writing.

Element 4.4

Motivate learners to be lifelong readers.

Although the affective domain of reading has received increased interest, specifically dealing with reading attitudes and motivation (Cramer & Castle, 1994), there is still much to learn about this important part of the reading equation. Cramer and Castle acknowledge that illiteracy is a big problem but speculate that alliteracy, or lack of a reading habit among capable readers (Harris & Hodges, 1981), is an even bigger problem. Cramer and Castle hypothesize the causes of alliteracy to include the following: the cultural belief that affective characteristics are personal and not a matter for public examination, the tendency of teachers to believe that affective aspects are built into reading programs and children will develop positive attitudes spontaneously over time, assumptions that affective reading elements are difficult to evaluate and grade, and little or no training in the affective aspects of teaching reading for prospective teachers.

Researchers have recognized that some children need to be motivated to read and interact with literacy (Baker & Wigfield, 1999; Ivey, 1999). Guthrie and Wigfield (1999) state that motivation to read is made up of the student's personal goals and beliefs with relation to reading, and these ideas influence how the individual interacts and learns with the text. Element 4.4 of the IRA standards establishes that effective teachers need to have the ability to motivate students to become lifelong readers.

Mastropieri and Scruggs (2007) define motivation as "the extent to which students desire to succeed in school" (p. 196). It can be classified as intrinsic or extrinsic. Extrinsic motivation occurs when the desire to succeed is caused by an external incentive. For example, a child may be motivated to finish reading a book in order to get a gift from the classroom treasure box. The gift is an extrinsic motivator for the academic task to be completed. Intrinsic motivation, on the other hand, is internal and evident only in situations when the student applies effort solely for curiosity, or a desire to learn, succeed, or to contribute (Mastropieri & Scruggs, 2007). Some teachers may avoid extrinsic motivators because they fear that this will hinder the development of intrinsic motivation in children. Research suggests, however, that some forms of extrinsic motivation may actually be helpful in motivating struggling readers to engage in literacy practices (Baker & Wigfield, 1999; Gambrell, 1996; Hidi & Harackiewicz, 2000). It is important to note that students who are intrinsically motivated will apply every effort to fulfill their own curiosity, quest for learning, or desire.

Most strategies for motivating students are based on the "expectancy x value theory," which states that the effort a student is willing to apply to a task is the result of their expectation for success on the task as well as how much they value the reward that results from the task (Brophy, 2004). Consequently, teachers need to understand that they must teach children not only to become effective readers but also to have confidence and the desire to read. They must also ensure that students value reading and view it as a lifelong pursuit (Irwin, 2006). In this way, according to the "expectancy x value theory," students will read for pleasure and will feel rewarded by the literacy experience. The challenge for educators is to find ways to motivate students.

Gambrell (1996) found that book-rich classroom environments, student opportunities for choice to interact socially with others and become familiar with many books, and appropriate reading incentives lead to environments that foster reading motivation. Tunnell and Jacobs (2007) suggest that teachers set an example, provide books, make time for reading books, create a reading atmosphere, work with parents, and choose meaningful activities and assignments in order to motivate children to read. Struggling readers are motivated when teachers determine their attitudes toward reading, immerse learners in different types of texts, have students choose their own books, read aloud, and scaffold skills and strategies in meaningful contexts (Sanacore, 2002). Common among these suggestions based on research findings is the need for children to self-select reading materials, have access to many and varied texts, interact with each other, and see and hear good reading models to cultivate motivation and engagement with texts.

Engagement is a term that has been used by reading researchers and is generally defined as frequent sustained reading (Allen, Michalove, Shockley, & West, 1991). According to Verhoeven and Snow (2001), literacy engagement comes about as a result of having children actively involved in their literacy development, paired with adequate access to books. Guthrie and Knowles (2001) review the literature pertaining to reading motivation and observe classrooms to discover reading engagement variables that relate to motivating students in classrooms. They found motivated and engaged students in classrooms where teachers

- Used conceptual themes to organize instruction (integrate subject matter)
- Allowed students to interact with concrete objects (e.g., watch the metamorphosis of a silk worm to a butterfly)
- Permitted students to self-direct their learning by selecting a topic, book, or tasks about the conceptual theme
- Provided a large variety of books and book types with varying ranges of difficulty
- Allowed peer discussions, practice, and student reflection and served as models or coaches
- Had students work in a variety of grouping formats or social structures
- Let students explain their understandings of books in ways that were personally and culturally appropriate to them

These variables must be working together (rather than in isolation) to be effective since they were not found to be successful in creating motivating and engaging classroom environments alone.

Literacy teaching with a "to, with, and by" approach emphasizes the role of the teacher in fostering learning over teaching (Mooney, 1990). Teacher decision making should be driven by what is needed for children's learning rather than what children need to learn. Using this perception of the learner's role, children are actively involved in and responsible for their learning rather than passive recipients and storage banks of knowledge. Responsive teaching is synonymous with supporting the learner to reach goals and enjoy success in learning and achievements. Mooney states a pattern emerges using this philosophy of teaching that is rhythmic, allowing the student to experience success and move forward with tasks becoming rewarding as achievement is nurtured and familiar.

Conclusion

Neuman, Copple, and Bredekamp (2001) write, "Beginning in infancy and continuing throughout childhood, children may learn from those around them that in language and literacy there is value, enjoyment, and sheer power" (p. 28). Standard 4 highlights the impact of literacy-rich environments on fostering reading and writing skills and helping children develop this powerful experience. For the literacy-rich environment to have the necessary influence on children's literacy development, the teacher needs to design the reading program and lesson with the child in mind, model exemplary reading and literacy behaviors, and motivate students to learn in their classrooms. Teachers have everything to do with developing the affective variables that lead to intrinsic motivation and a love for lifelong reading.

FURTHER READING

Hoffman, J.V., Sailors, M., Duffy, G.R., & Beretvas, N. (2004). The effective elementary classroom literacy environment: Examining the validity of the TEX-IN3 observation system. *Journal of Literacy Research*, 36(3), 289–320.

> This article provides a description of an observation system used to evaluate the literacy environment of elementary classrooms. It includes categories and examples of materials that should be incorporated in a "print rich" environment.

Morrow, L.M. (2004). *Literacy development in the early years: Helping children read and write* (5th ed.). Boston: Allyn & Bacon.

> Chapter 10, specifically, is excellent reading to help teachers prepare the classroom for literacy learning. Morrow includes her own research-based practices to aide in creating an environment that promotes the learning of reading and writing.

Schumm, J.S. (Ed.). (2006). *Reading assessment and instruction for all learners.* New York: Guilford.

> This is a guidebook for differentiated instruction in reading for diverse classrooms. It includes a chapter on organizing the classroom for technology-based reading instruction.

Wolfersberger, M.E., Reutzel, D.R., Sudweeks, R., & Fawson, P.C. (2004). Developing and validating the Classroom Literacy Environmental Profile (CLEP): A tool for examining the "print richness" of early childhood and elementary classrooms. *Journal of Literacy Research*, 36(2), 211–272.

This article discusses the procedures used to develop a reliable and valid measure of the print richness of classrooms for young children. Teacher candidates can use this tool to observe classrooms and to design their own classroom based on research concerning creating literate environments.

The CaseNEX case study selected for Standard 4 addresses Element 4.4. The case study consists of a video clip (transcribed here) of a teacher talking to her students during a writing workshop about their writing. Candidates have the opportunity to earn a high content score of 5 and a low of 0 for writing off topic (see Standard 4 Rubric, Appendix, p. 152).

Case Study for Standard 4: Creating a Literate Environment

Reprinted from CaseNEX LLC, founded at University of Virginia's Curry School of Education. Reprinted with permission.

Case: In the Classroom, Scene: Ms. Rath (Clip 2)

T: And it was just two meals.

T: First you were crazy, waggling all over the place.

T: OK, tell me that part. First, who was crazy? [T hands paper to S in white shirt]

T: He has a great story idea...At first I was crazy, he's going to start that. Ready? At-first-I-was-crazy [T begins counting words on fingers]

T: How many words? Five?

T: What's your first word? *At*?

T: OK, return.

T: I know you are so excited...Conferencing. [T gets up and moves to a new table with S in yellow shirt]

T: Go finish with your problem. Use paper and pencil, you can get started that way. [S in white shirt leans on the table]

S: I want the computer.

T: I know. Start it on paper. [View of computer]

T: You are talking about Bingo Man, right?

T: You know they have [pizza], you know they have [drinks], and you know what they are going to play? Bingo! [T talking with S in yellow shirt]

T: There is your story. I love Bingo.

T: OK, so one day you play Bingo. [T touches arm of S to refocus his thoughts]

T: Wonderful, OK. I am going to help you out with your story. Ready? "One day I played Bingo." Say it with me. "One day I played Bingo." All right, what is your first word?

T: We've got an idea. Let's write that idea; it's a good one. "One day I played Bingo." What is your first word? [T begins counting words on fingers]

T: Wait. "One day I played Bingo." OK, you start it as you want it to start. [S begins to write]

T: What about that part about being crazy at first? "At first I was crazy." This is funny. You think you will like to read this story? I will love to read my story. [T talking to three S's]

[scene of one boy, then one girl, then three students working at computers]

T: This is a published work, you are publishing it? What is it about? This is the Lizard King, the one you were working on before. I love it! Let's see. And you added more to the story? I can't wait to see the published version. [T confers with S's]

T: Read it to me. [S in white shirt begins to read his story] I love it. You know what is so awesome about this story? You use your work and I have a picture in my head. I can picture those sneakers, because they are going to be fast, they are going to be soft, they are going to be [cold]. I love it. Now, are you going to add more to this story?

Question for response: How does Ms. Rath motivate her students to be lifelong writers? Why is it important for this to be done?

Context of Administration

Candidates were provided with the case study and they completed it during a class period using notes and a textbook. After viewing the video clip, transcripts of the video clip were handed out so that candidates could go over the conversations Ms. Rath had with her students. The instructor answered clarifying questions about the process of responding and then allowed 20 minutes for the candidates to discuss the case and share ideas as to how they would respond to the question. During the discussion and writing time, candidates could refer to notes from the class and the required text for the course. Responses were due within 30 minutes following the discussion period. Prior to scoring, the instructor and program advisor met to generate a list of possible response items to help set norms for using the rubric and scoring purposes. The list of items included intrinsic motivation, extrinsic motivation, expectancy x value theory, meaningful writing assignments connecting school work to students' lives, writing conferences, and use of the writing process leading to students' ability to focus on writing ideas rather than emphasizing form or spelling.

Responses

An emerging conceptual understanding is evident in the first response, which clearly provides one strategy (drawing on student interests and backgrounds) for motivating students to become lifelong writers. The response received a content score of 3 and a rationale score of Sufficient.

Ms. Rath actively engages her students by discussing their interests and backgrounds to encourage and stimulate writing. Since her students feel comfortable and enjoy talking about themselves, they are more apt to write. This process promotes an awareness of the importance of writing and contributes to a classroom of eager learners. This is especially helpful for English language learners because it provides opportunities to express themselves through writing, therefore building confidence in their writing abilities.

Using conferences, student interests, and praise were mentioned as ways Ms. Rath motivated her students in the second response; therefore, a content score of 5 was awarded. The rationale was Sufficient because an emerging conceptual understanding is evident. The instructor (Peggy) and advisor who scored the responses felt more could have been written to substantiate the content.

Ms. Rath was conferencing with her 1st grade students during writing. She encouraged her students to use their interest while writing a story. She gave the students positive feedback and was always praising their ideas. Ms. Rath was conferencing with her students about their writing. An example of this in the clip is when a student was writing about playing Bingo. He wanted to write a story about his experience while playing Bingo. Ms. Rath helped him begin his story as he shared his experience with her. She modeled how the story could begin. She was also encouraging another student to use descriptive words in his story because these words help the reader visualize the characters and events in the story. She made sure a student knew that stories can be funny, too. She suggested a student add more to a story. Overall, she showed a lot of interest in what each student had to say about their story.

  Conferencing with young writers helps them understand the stages of the writing process and allows the teacher to give the attention needed to her students. Allowing students to choose a topic can be motivating to them. It is always a good idea to allow students to pick a topic that interests them. Students write much better stories when they choose topics that excite them and that they are familiar with. It is important for the student to first talk about what they are going to write about. The teacher should allow students to talk about their writing and help them recognize the strategies that can improve their writing. Teachers need to ask their students to read their stories and teachers should also ask questions and make suggestions that help the writers by more specific or more organized in what they are saying. Students will develop better writing skills from teacher modeling, questioning, and responding.

The third response was given a content score of 5 and a rationale score of Proficient. The candidate wrote about four valid motivational strategies used by Ms. Rath (i.e., student interests, conferencing, writing process, and technology). The rationale demonstrated a good conceptual understanding of the standard's element.

Ms. Rath uses students' interests as a foundation for her writing program by having them follow the writing process which involves the prewriting, drafting, revising, editing, and publishing stages in order for them to write their stories. The prewriting process was done by having students pair up with a buddy to brainstorm and discuss some topics they were interested in writing about. Students were free to write about whatever they chose, without the teacher assigning a prompt. Some of the topics that students wrote about that were of interest to them were: a time a child acted crazy and wobbled all over the place; the time a boy's dad bought him a new pair of sneakers, or the boy who wrote about bingo night. All these topics were based on students' interests and related to their prior knowledge and life experiences.

The drafting of their work was done in writing centers in which students were equipped with a bin that had the necessary supplies such as paper and pencil. The students completed their drafts and were ready to have their work revised and edited. Ms. Rath met with students individually in writing conferences to discuss their work and to provide feedback and suggestions. Throughout the writing process Ms. Rath continued to build on students' interests by encouraging them to complete their stories by adding more details and incorporating the use of technology in the writing process. Ms. Rath was able to get the students even more interested because she had students at different stages of the writing process work on word processors and computers to publish their stories. As part of the publication process, students were able to use graphics on the computer to design the illustrations of their books.

It is important for Ms. Rath or any teacher to use students' interests as a foundation for a writing program because students will be more successful at their work when there is a connection to their life experiences. When a student is interested in something, they will show more interest and be able to construct meaning from what they are doing as opposed to the teacher assigning the topic and the child having little to no prior knowledge, resulting in disinterest and a lack of motivation to work. Moreover, the students will not put forth their best effort because the child is not being allowed to think creatively by making personal discoveries and developing their own idea. According to cognitive psychologist, Jerome Bruner, he believes that information or knowledge is effectively gained through personal discovery by the child. He further stated that if students were allowed to pursue concepts on their own, they would gain a better understanding. Based on Ms. Rath's approach of allowing students to choose their own topics to write about and just being there to facilitate and guide them along the work through active dialogue (conferencing), Bruner would support her approach because by doing this she is enabling them to progressively build their own knowledge as opposed to specifically being told what to write.

The fourth response is an excellent example of how the content of a response (the how) should be tied into the rationale (the why). In this response, more than three motivating practices are mentioned, earning a content score of 5, with a solid rationale behind each one, warranting a Distinguished response. (References are included and were revised to include correct and complete information.)

Ms. Rath has created a classroom environment that fosters the growth of reading and writing through student interests by displaying student work (motivation to create and do well), having technology available (also motivating to students), teaching the connection between reading and writing, arranging the room into identifiable areas targeting specific objects, providing positive feedback along with enthusiasm and guidance as motivation and validation of thoughts, and finally, allowing for a general atmosphere that is non-threatening and promotes learning.

At the heart of her instruction is using the student's interests and prior knowledge to help build a foundation for writing. Once the students have thought of something that they want to explore, Ms. Rath has them describe to her the events. She then guides them through organizing their thoughts, while emphasizing the fact that words can create pictures in the mind, thus making them aware of the fundamentals of reading and writing. During this initial stage of instruction, Ms. Rath makes it a point to positively affirm student ideas, as well as show enthusiasm and interest in what the student has to say. Next Ms. Rath takes the ideas given by the student and helps them transfer their oral thoughts to paper. She explains that students must use the details of their experiences to enhance their writing.

In addition to the explicit teaching and encouragement, Ms. Rath has made available to the students the use of technology, in the form of computers and Alpha Smarts. The video showed students engaged in assignments on the various forms of technology, while the teacher gave individual help to other students. As a final point, it is evident by watching the two boys in the video, as they observed the writing instruction of a fellow classmate, that Ms. Rath has established an atmosphere that does not lend itself to criticism of individual thoughts; for instead of mocking the thoughts of their peer, they stood by and listened to the dialogue between him and the teacher!

1. Using students' interests to engage them — In their book, Intervention Strategies to Follow Informal Reading Inventory Assessment, Caldwell and Leslie (2004) stress that students must read and write for meaning. They suggest that teachers provide materials that cover a wide range of interests,

while having students read for authentic purposes, to "enjoy and learn." When someone is reading for personal interest, they will acquire information that is meaningful to them, thus engaging them. Calkins in her book, The Art of Teaching Reading (2000) explains, "Although learning about subjects outside our realm of interest is an important part of any person's education, the easiest way to teach reading is first to create opportunities for young children to read within the realm of their interests." She explains how passion for a particular subject leads to engagement and knowledge acquisition. She then stresses the significance of adjusting classroom libraries to support students' interests. To further this point, Blachowicz and Ogle (2001) explain, "Having good models, access to excellent materials, and adequate time for reading is still not enough to get all students into reading, however to have a good 'fit' between students and materials, teachers need to know what their students' interests are, and to create new interests as well as providing for current interests."

2. Allowing students to use prior experiences and observations – In the book Reading and Learning to Read (2005), Vacca, Vacca, Gove, Burkey, Lenhart and Mckeon recommend using students' experiences and interests to guide writing. Students should choose topics in which they have "strong feelings about." In doing this, the teacher relays to the student that their thoughts are valid and that they do indeed have something to write about. They go on to say that children should have numerous occasions to write about things that are important to them; it helps in developing voice. Things like punctuation and mechanics should be addressed later. A strategy that is suggested for the ELL (English Language Learner) is the LEA (Language Experience Approach.) "Through the regular use of LEA, my students are able to take ownership of their writing, truly seeing themselves as real readers and writers." As stated in Teaching Reading– Sourcebook for Kindergarten Through Eighth Grade, Honig, Diamond, and Gutlohn, and Mahler (2007) also highlight the fact that experiences with print (through reading and writing) help children develop an understanding of the conventions, purpose, and function of print. Muschla in his book, Teach Terrific Writing (2006) explains, "To help your students discover ideas for writing, you need to make them realize that they have a reservoir of ideas within themselves. The starting point is personal experience." He goes on to explain how personal experiences generate additional ideas. Giving students the opportunity to recognize the wealth of information within them, helps in giving them the confidence to write. Ruddell, in the book Teaching Children to Read and Write (2005), suggest the Guided Writing strategy for developing expressive writing, simulating visualization, identification, and vicarious experience.

3. The classroom environment/atmosphere as motivation to express thoughts and interests — Muschla (2006) explains, "Perhaps most important, you must establish a classroom atmosphere in which an appreciation of ideas is fostered and supported. Your classroom should be a place where students are comfortable to share their ideas without fear of mockery or sarcasm." Students must feel free to take chances without negative criticism. Criticism should be positive and constructive. In addition, the classroom should be designed to have a center for reading, writing, be print-rich, and a section to display student work (Ruddell, 2005).

4. The use of technology — It is no secret that students nowadays are comfortable on the computer, and are motivated by the alternative to pen and paper. This was recognized by the National Reading Panel (NICHD, 2000), and it is suggested that teachers integrate technology into the classroom. "The use of computers as word processors may be useful given that reading instruction is most effective when combined with writing instruction." "Capitalize on students' love of technology by utilizing technology that can teach" (Blachowicz & Ogle, 2001).

References

Blachowicz, C. & Ogle, D. (2001). Reading comprehension: Strategies for independent learners. New York: Guilford.

Caldwell, J. & Leslie, L. (2004). Intervention strategies to follow informal reading inventory assessment: So what do I do now? Boston: Allyn & Bacon.

Calkins, L.M. (2000). The art of teaching reading. Boston: Allyn & Bacon.

Honig, B., Diamond, L., Gutlohn, L., & Mahler, J. (2007). Teaching reading sourcebook: Sourcebook for Kindergarten through eight grade (Core Literacy Training Series). Novato, CA: High Noon Books.

Muschla, G.R. (2006). Teach terrific writing, grades 4-5. New York: McGraw Hill.

National Institute of Child Health and Human Development. (2000). Report of the National Reading Panel. Teach children to read: An evidence-based assessment of the scientific research literature on reading and its implications for reading instruction (NIH Publication Non. 00-4769). Washington, DC: U.S. Government Printing Office.

Ruddell, R.B. (2005). Teaching children to read and write: Becoming an effective literacy teacher (4th ed). Boston: Allyn & Bacon.

Vacca, J.L., Vacca, R.T., Gove, M.K., Burkey, L.C., Lenhart, L.A., & McKeon, C.A. (2005). Reading and learning to read (6th ed). Boston: Allyn & Bacon.

CHAPTER 5

Learning About and Assessing Standard 5—Professional Development

Effective teachers in 21st century classrooms should have a deep understanding of the knowledge and capabilities of their students. They need to be able to identify the areas of strength and weakness in each student and plan appropriate instruction. Both elementary and secondary teachers must be aware of the content knowledge of the variety of subjects they teach as well as the pedagogical knowledge base for teaching each of those disciplines (Wilson, Schulman, & Richert, 1987). In addition, they must possess the key dispositions of professional educators as outlined by NCATE (2002). Programs for professional development are essential to the creation and development of classrooms where effective teaching is the norm and appropriate strategies and materials are used.

Helping students become proficient readers requires that teachers have not only knowledge of instructional strategies and activities but also the ability to use these to develop skillful instruction that enables students to transfer those strategies and skills to the reading of connected text. The NRP (NICHD, 2000) suggests that teachers must be skillful in instruction and be able to provide individualized instructional feedback to students. In order to accomplish this task, teachers must have a thorough understanding of effective instructional strategies as well as those strategies that enable students to become proficient readers. Once teachers are in the workforce, they must receive well-conceived and implemented inservice education that will build upon the knowledge gained during preservice course work. Funding for teacher professional development programs, which may include signing bonuses or compensation for attendance, is integral to efforts focusing on helping low performing students make substantial gains (Trotter, 2007). In addition to adequate funding, there are many obstacles to the development of effective inservice experiences. Snow and colleagues (1998) acknowledge that programs often flounder because of the following:

- Lack of a strong apprenticeship system
- The highly complex and diverse classroom needs that must be addressed
- The challenge of time to keep abreast of new developments in research and practice
- The complexity of the pedagogical and content area knowledge base
- The difficulty of presenting many of the skills required to enact the knowledge base with children having the most difficulties (p. 279)

Despite these obstacles, Snow and colleagues (1998) believe that continuing to educate teachers through quality professional development programs has netted greater student achievement than any other use of education dollars. Bennett (1987) investigated the effects of theory, demonstration, practice, and feedback on the knowledge and transfer to practice of the content of professional development experiences. Findings demonstrated that combining these components and adding in-class coaching yielded the largest increase in student achievement.

Although content, context, and quality are indicators of successful professional development opportunities, these aspects vary widely from program to program (Snow et al., 1998). Effective efforts should build on the knowledge and skills teachers acquire in their preservice education programs and enable them access to evaluate new knowledge and strategies. This chapter describes successful programs that allow teachers to build on the knowledge and skills of literacy to which they were exposed in preservice education courses. In addition, the issues surrounding the development of these professional development opportunities are discussed.

Darling-Hammond (1997) and Ball and Cohen (1999) indicate that professional development in literacy is constrained by several factors. First is the lack of time most teachers have to devote to anything beyond the tasks of lesson preparation, execution, and assessment, and the endless paper work and meetings required of professionals in 21st century classrooms. In the high-stakes testing atmosphere of today's classrooms, there are few on-the-job opportunities in which teachers can develop and refine new knowledge and skills. There is a lack of support for professional development from both district and state administrators. According to Darling-Hammond, one-shot workshops are the norm and lack the effectiveness of ongoing, longer term events that allow teachers to refine and improve their instructional plans. At the elementary school level, teachers are responsible for so many content areas that there is very little time that can be devoted exclusively to staff development in literacy.

Historically, professional development can be described as a cookbook effort, or one-shot, "here's how to solve your students' reading difficulties" program (Feiman-Nemser, 2001; Gersten & Brengelman, 1996). However, we believe there has been a recent shift to workshops that deepen teachers' understandings of how students learn as well as demonstrations of how these understandings can lead to increased learning on the part of their students. Feiman-Nemser notes that the descriptors "inservice training," which connotes a deficit model, and "staff development," which connotes instruction in new programs, preceded the more recent designation of "professional development." She states, "professional development means transformations in teachers' knowledge, understandings, skills, and commitments, in what they know and what they are able to do in their individual practice as well as in their shared responsibilities" (p. 1038).

According to Schulte, Edick, Edward, and Mackiel (2004), research regarding effective teachers has moved from exclusively studying teachers to studying their effects on students in order to determine which teacher behaviors result in desirable student performance. Teacher dispositions strongly influence the impact teachers will have on student learning and development (Collinson, Killeavy, & Stephenson, 1999). The research demonstrates a complex picture of effective teaching that includes teacher knowledge, pedagogical skills, and dispositions.

Effective teachers understand the progression of learning to read and how to provide instruction to support this development. Inservice opportunities must give teachers the necessary tools to keep abreast of new research findings and analyze the applicability of new instructional strategies to the context in which they teach. The development and revision of standards for literacy professionals at the state and national levels has recently occurred. One of the most widely known of these efforts is the National Board for Professional Teaching Standards (NBPTS, 2007). Although this is a volunteer certification, teachers who successfully work through the process are recognized as accomplished members of the teaching profession in the content areas they select for NBPTS certification. The outcome achievements of NBPTS-certified teachers are a reflection of the effectiveness of their preservice education and inservice professional development opportunities as well as of the teachers' dedication and commitment to their fields.

Snow and colleagues (1998) emphasize that while preservice and inservice professional development experiences for K–12 teachers are abundant and aligned with state performance standards at elementary and secondary levels, not every state has certification requirements for preschool teachers. Even the highly respected NBPTS standards do not sufficiently address all aspects of reading in early childhood. The performance standards for preschool programs generally focus on adult–child ratio, safety, and health. They seldom ensure the quality of the literacy environment. Preschool level teachers are not adequately served with extensive, systematic, quality professional development. Snow and colleagues find this particularly troubling in view of the dearth of high quality programs for initial preparation of teachers at this level.

Teachers of identified special needs students also require professional development opportunities that enable them to successfully work with special education students, ELLs, and students who have reading difficulties. According to Snow and colleagues (1998), professional development for these teachers should include the following:

- Knowledge of ways to access and evaluate ongoing research regarding typical development and the prevention of reading difficulties;
- Knowledge and techniques for helping other professionals (classroom teachers, administrators) learn new skills relevant for preventing or identifying and ameliorating reading difficulties; and
- Knowledge and techniques for promoting home support (by parents and other household members) to encourage emergent and conventional literacy and to prevent or ameliorate reading difficulties. (p. 297)

Standard 5 ensures that "candidates view professional development as a career-long effort and responsibility" (IRA, 2004, p. 18). The elements that make up Standard 5 include the following:

- Positive dispositions
- Pursuit of professional knowledge
- Effectively collaborating with colleagues
- Participating in professional development programs

Element 5.1

Display positive dispositions related to reading and the teaching of reading.

In *Merriam-Webster's Collegiate Dictionary* (2003), *dispositions* is defined as "qualities that characterize a person as an individual: the controlling perceptual (mental, emotional, spiritual) qualities that determine the person's natural or usual ways of thinking and acting" (p. 190). NCATE (2002) defines *dispositions* as,

> The values, commitments and professional ethics that influence behaviors toward students, families, colleagues, and communities and affect student learning, motivation, and development as well as educator's own professional growth. Dispositions are guided by beliefs and attitudes related to values such as caring, fairness, honesty, responsibility, and social justice. For example, they might include a belief that all students can learn, a vision of high and challenging standards, or a commitment to a safe and supportive learning environment. (p. 53)

Effective and ineffective teachers differ significantly in their dispositions toward self, students, and teaching (Freiberg, 1999). With regard to self, effective teachers have positive, realistic self-perceptions and believe that they can help most any student. However, ineffective teachers frequently have doubts about their abilities to reach students and to deal with problems that may occur in the classroom. The effective teachers' disposition toward students is one which creates within the students a feeling of being worthwhile, cared about, and important. Additionally, the effective teacher has high expectations for each student. In contrast, the disposition of the ineffective teacher is characterized by low expectations for students and negative beliefs about student worth. For example, Waiscko (2004) relates an interesting comment of his own fourth-grade teacher who confided to his mother during a parent–teacher conference, "I was really cut out to teach gifted kids, but they keep sending me kids like your son" (p. 41). Concerning effective teachers' dispositions toward teaching, much of their time is spent building relationships and pursuing knowledge that will enhance their teaching. Ineffective teachers focus on the short-range aspects of teaching. Again, Waiscko tells a personal story of a high school math teacher who immediately continued working the daily math problems on the blackboard after an announcement that President Kennedy had been assassinated. Rather than asking the question, "How will my students be better 10 years from now because of what they are learning today?" this teacher did not see the larger implications of his teaching.

Strong (2007) identifies the following as seven indicators of positive qualities or dispositions that characterize effective teachers.

1. Caring—Active listening; concern for students' emotional and physical well-being; shows interest and concern in students' personal lives outside of school; creates a supportive and warm classroom climate.

2. Fairness and respect—Responds to misbehavior on an individual level; treats students equally; creates situations for all children to succeed; is respectful to all students.

3. Interactions with students—Friendly while maintaining professional role; gives students responsibility; knows students' interests in and out of school; values what students say; fun, playful, jokes when appropriate.

4. Enthusiasm—Shows joy in [teaching reading and the language arts]; takes pleasure in teaching and makes the most of "teachable moments"; involved in learning activities outside of school.

5. Motivation—Returns student work in a timely manner with appropriate, meaningful feedback; high quality of work.

6. Dedication to teaching—Possesses a positive attitude about life and teaching; spends time outside of school preparing; participates in collegial activities; accepts responsibility for student outcomes; seeks professional development; finds, implements, and shares new instructional strategies.

7. Reflective practice—Knows areas of personal strengths and weaknesses; uses reflection to improve teaching; has high expectations for personal classroom performance; demonstrates high efficacy.

Schulte and colleagues (2004) assert, "One of the most difficult situations faced by teacher educators is encountering candidates who meet the requirements of content knowledge and pedagogical skills yet lack the dispositions essential to effective teaching" (p. 4). Even with a firm grasp of content and pedagogical knowledge many individuals do not succeed in the role of classroom teacher. Waiscko (2004) believes, "most teachers who do not succeed fail because they do not have the right dispositions" (p. 40).

According to Usher, Usher, and Usher (2003), there are three major issues involved in designing professional development opportunities that foster growth in teachers' dispositions. The first of these issues is creating an atmosphere that makes involvement and participation possible. Activities attuned to the learners' needs and interests, setting clear yet flexible limits, and providing a sense of identification and belonging all contribute to an atmosphere that is challenging yet nonthreatening.

The second issue is the need to provide information and experience that is relevant. Usher and colleagues (2003) believe this can be accomplished by a focus on important principles and structures related to the predetermined needs of the group. Providing information on best practices in a variety of formats and diverse approaches ensures the knowledge communicated within the framework of the workshop will be disseminated in the most effective manner.

The third issue focuses on the necessity of professional development participants to develop personal meaning from the understanding gained from each opportunity. Some approaches to promote the exploration and discovery of personal meaning are reflection, discussion groups, and relaxed structure and timing. These three primary learning conditions may serve as guidelines for the development of effective dispositions in a variety of formats: individual projects, lessons, workshops, courses, units, and entire programs of study as each play a role in the pursuit of professional knowledge.

Element 5.2

Continue to pursue the development of professional knowledge and dispositions.

The importance of pursuing the development of professional knowledge is supported by the findings of *Preventing Reading Difficulties in Young Children* (Snow et al., 1998):

> What needs to be learned cannot be seen as the consummate function of an undergraduate program or a fifth-year credential program.... Instead, teacher preparation must be seen as a long-term developmental process, beginning with undergraduate preparation, continuing with professional schooling in upper-division and fifth-year courses, and field practica and continuing further once teachers are technically credentialed. (p. 284)

Feiman-Nemser (2001) recommends that professional development be a consistent part of every teacher's learning-to-teach continuum. Central to the recommendation is her view of the new reform model of teaching.

> If conventional models emphasize teaching as telling and learning as listening, reform-oriented models call for teachers to do more listening as they elicit student thinking and assess their understanding and for students to do more asking and explaining.... Teachers who embrace this kind of teaching must also be practical intellectuals, curriculum developers, and generators of knowledge in practice. (p. 1015)

The two most common forms of professional development are staff development sponsored by school districts and courses offered as part of a university graduate degree program. Both of these experiences provide knowledge in a form that is decontextualized and disconnected from teachers' classrooms. Often there is little ongoing support to encourage a change in teachers' belief and practice. Darling-Hammond and McLaughlin (1995) and Hawley and Valli (1999) suggest that professional development experiences that build on the needs of teachers can result in a positive and valuable change in beliefs and practice.

McLane and McNamee (1997) describe a Chicago professional development program for participating Head Start teachers that included a 10-month program of seminars and on-site experience. The Erikson Institute provided an introduction to new activities, strategies, and concepts the teachers took into their classrooms. Initially, the institute staff noticed that the information they provided in the professional development workshops was modified in such a way that much of the effect on literacy development was lost. An example of this type of adaptation was the way in which preschool teachers frequently favored oral over written communication. By turning shared storybook reading into storytelling, group writing into storytelling, and dramatic play into an activity that disregarded the influence of the written word, the teachers made modifications that lost the ability to foster the development of both reading *and* writing. Continued communication with the workshop participants, a hallmark of effective professional development, was the key that empowered these teachers to modify their previous beliefs and adaptations, maximizing the effect of this new learning on literacy development for the Head Start children.

The NRP (NICHD, 2000) searched for experimental studies investigating the qualities of teacher preparation programs leading to improvement in students' reading comprehension. The four programs analyzed were inservice professional development opportunities, rather than part of a preservice, undergraduate program. Although the studies differed along parameters such as teacher preparation method, intervention, and type of student, as a whole they indicated that providing teachers with instruction that helps them create lessons with high levels of student involvement had positive effects on reading comprehension. With regard to teacher preparation the studies, examined questions such as these:

- Can teachers learn to be more explicit in explaining the reasoning associated with using basal text skills as strategies? (Duffy et al., 1987)

- Will instruction for teachers in how to gradually release responsibility for active reading (transactional strategy instruction) be effective in helping severely reading-delayed adolescents take a more active approach to understanding informational texts? (Anderson, 1992)

- Will teacher training in direct explanation, modeling, coaching, and scaffolded practice of Transactional Strategy Instruction result in increased comprehension, strategy use, and more personalized understandings of text? (Brown, Pressley, Van Meter, & Schuder, 1996)

The panel concluded that as a result of effective professional development programs, proficiency in teaching comprehension strategies lead to improved performance on the part of their students. However, the panel cautioned that, "Teaching comprehension strategies in the natural setting of the classroom involves a level of proficiency and flexibility that often requires substantial and intensive teacher preparation" (p. 4-126). They suggest further research regarding how much professional development is needed to achieve and maintain proficiency in teaching comprehension strategies.

In addition to these studies, the NRP (NICHD, 2000) analyzed 21 studies investigating the effectiveness of inservice preparation of reading teachers. In order to be included in the analysis, the studies needed to include data on student outcomes as well as data on teacher change. The distribution of studies across the K–12 grade levels revealed a preponderance of studies at the elementary level with only a few studies at the secondary level. The topics investigated in these studies included comprehension and strategy instruction, general methods, classroom management and improving teachers' attitudes. More than half of the studies (16) provided professional development experiences for an entire school year. There were 6 studies that extended over multiple school years. In every study where teacher outcomes showed improvement there was a concomitant gain in student achievement. However, the panel found no relationship between the duration of the professional development program and student outcomes. Due to the divergent content of the programs studied there were few specific conclusions as to the content of the professional development programs. However, some general implications suggested that extensive support, both in time and money, is essential for effective professional development. Since it is difficult to maintain a change in practice without a change in attitude, the panel was heartened to find that teacher attitudes did positively change as a result of the interventions. It would be beneficial if future research focuses on how to sustain this change in teacher attitude and student achievement.

Element 5.3

Work with colleagues to observe, evaluate, and provide feedback on each other's practice.

Collaboration with colleagues in order to improve practice is an essential aspect of effective professional development experiences. According to Snow and colleagues (1998), "Professional development includes not only formal meetings and courses but also opportunities for teachers to work with each other and to visit classrooms" (p. 284). Collaborative discussions regarding planning and implementing instruction and collective assessment of student work enables teachers to learn from others' experiences. Langer, Colton, and Goff (2003) present the *Collaborative Analysis of Student Learning* (CASL) as a framework for this type of conversation. The goal of CASL is to help teachers develop a culture of inquiry to result in a deeper understanding of the link between their instruction and student learning. In order to avoid the pitfall of collaborative conversations degenerating into simply sharing anecdotes, the CASL process does the following:

- Focuses on student work samples relative to a particular content standard
- Engages teachers in a study of selected students' learning over time
- Follows a systematic analysis cycle
- Occurs within a collaborative culture for inquiry
- Provides written documentation of teacher and student learning (p. 3)

In addition, using student work samples in conjunction with descriptions of instruction, perhaps supplemented by classroom videos, moves the discussion out of the anecdotal arena into an area supported by evidence.

The descriptive review (Carini, 1986) is a process by which a presenting teacher requests a review by fellow teachers of an individual student's problem behavior or learning difficulty. After the requesting teacher provides a description of the student's physical characteristics, disposition, relationships with others, interests, activities, and learning, the teacher review group asks questions and provides recommendations for the requesting teacher to consider. Although the discussion that occurs as a result of the descriptive review provides new insights into ways to help the specific student under study, Featherstone (1993) speculates that it may also enrich the knowledge base of all the participating teachers by providing insights on how to help other children as well.

The Community of Learners project (Grossman & Wineburg, 1998; Grossman, Wineburg, & Woolworth, 2001) describes the development of conversations within a group of high school English and history teachers as they participated in a monthly book club discussion group. The discussion provided opportunities to practice evidence-based reactions and interpretations of text, which led to more complex and productive discussions as this group of teacher-learners met later to design an interdisciplinary humanities curriculum. Participation in the group allowed the participants to practice the same type of reading and resultant discussion that they hoped to develop in their own students.

In addition to collaborative conversations among teachers at the same site, frequent and open communication with professionals located on other school campuses, university professors, subject matter organizations, and community resource people are needed to offer teachers a more extensive body of knowledge and support (Lieberman & Grolnick, 1996; Vaishali, 2007).

Element 5.4

Participate in, initiate, and evaluate professional development programs.

Beginning teachers need support provided by well-planned mentorship programs and more experienced teachers must continue to receive effective inservice opportunities. Feiman-Nemser (2001) argues that "learning continues for thoughtful teachers as long as they remain in teaching" (p. 1039). According to the National Commission on Teaching and America's Future (1996), the opportunity to participate in both mentoring and inservice programs is essential to the maintenance of a cadre of professional teachers.

Snow and colleagues (1998) suggest that teachers must be prepared in the following areas in order to provide opportunities for children to become readers:

- Linguistic and psychological studies through which they can understand the distinctive features of oral and written language
- Rhetorical, sociological, sociolinguistic, and anthropological studies through which they can understand genres, registers, and functions of texts as well as social and cultural contexts of texts and literacy activities
- Pedagogy of reading through which they can understand how to use a variety of texts, integrate school experience with written language out of school, develop activities to practice letter-sound association, word identification, and comprehension and

develop activities to encourage the cooperation of families and communities in helping children learn to read

- Psychology of reading through which they can understand oral language, phoneme identity, letter–sound association, working memory, and the ontogeny of alphabetic reading and writing

Can all of this knowledge be assimilated within the one or two courses taken as the reading requirement in most undergraduate, preservice education programs? The likely answer is that teachers must continue to participate in, initiate, and evaluate professional development experiences throughout their careers. Teachers must have ongoing preparation to ensure access to new knowledge in literacy and to provide them with tools to appropriately place this new knowledge into their instructional framework. Schools where teachers have input into the focus and implementation of these efforts result in a healthy workplace culture, empowering educators (Adams, 2007). District professional development programs such as those associated with federal policies (e.g., Put Reading First) should not be undertaken without input from those who will be most affected—the classroom teacher (Jehlen, 2007). Jehlen's study, conducted in North Carolina, surveyed both teachers and administrators. The study revealed that "nearly all principals reported that teachers are central to educational decisions, while only half of teachers felt this to be true" (p. 11). Clearly, this important issue merits further discussion in the context of individual schools.

Effective models for inservice education include modeling, coaching, and explicit feedback for participants (Winn & Mitchell, 1991). Although these are important considerations, Futrell, Holmes, Christie, and Cushman (1995) suggest that teacher involvement in the planning and development of sessions results in experiences that more clearly meet their needs. A preference for professional development delivered on site is also suggested. According to Showers and Joyce (1996), about 10% of workshop participants actually implement the knowledge they receive. Consequently, care in how information is presented is of great importance in planning a professional development experience. Staff development that focuses on working collaboratively with teachers over time have been beneficial in helping to place new instructional methodologies in the classroom (Foegen, Espin, Allinder, & Markell, 2001). Snow and colleagues (1998) posit that when staff development involves teacher discussion groups as well as school–university partnerships and activities associated with NBPTS certification, a positive form of collective responsibility for student learning develops. They believe that these collaborative partnerships can bring about more lasting change than the common one-shot workshops. Rather than simply sharing personal experiences and anecdotes, in collaborative conversations the focus of the discussion should be specific practices and possibilities for improving instruction and student learning. Care should be taken so that collaborative study and inquiry groups do not become simply emotional support groups (Thompson & Zeuli, 1999). Professional development can take place through serious, ongoing discussions teachers have about teaching, learning, subject matter, and students. Ball and Cohen (1999) suggest that teachers can develop a deep sense of efficacy as a result of such conversations.

Teachers can improve their practice when they work together by looking at other students' work and observing in one another's classroom. The objective viewpoint of a fellow professional can enable teachers to see strengths and weaknesses in their instruction and give a new perspective to the work students do as a result of that instruction. This working in community encourages teachers to play a more active role by participating in school-based decision making. From a holistic viewpoint, successful professional development should include the collective wisdom that thoughtful teachers can generate by working together. Action research, projects, teacher study groups, and school improvement initiatives are a few of the formats this collaboration can take. Adams (2007) suggests that collaboration is most likely to happen when it is encouraged by building-level administrators. She states, "Forced collegiality, when the principal requires collaboration on a prescribed agenda, often doesn't work. Learning communities work when teachers have an internal commitment to the group and choose the topics themselves" (p. 48). If our goal for students is that they be able to work cooperatively to construct knowledge, this will best happen when their classroom teachers learn to work together collaboratively to produce the very best in collegial, collaborative communities of practice (Feiman-Nemser, 2001).

Conclusion

We can conclude that professional development supports teachers in enhancing their pedagogical and content expertise: "An important part of learning to teach involves transforming different kinds of knowledge into a flexible, evolving set of commitments, understandings, and skills" (Feiman-Nemser, 2001, p. 1048). The use of terms like *deepening*, *refining*, and *extending* to frame these tasks implies that learning to teach involves continuing growth and development in core aspects of teaching.

FURTHER READING

Allen, J. (2006). *Becoming a literacy leader: Supporting learning and change.* Portland, ME: Stenhouse.

> This resource discusses ideas for the many practical challenges literacy leaders face, including how to organize a literacy room with resources for teachers, possible interventions for struggling readers, coaching teachers, and creating model programs for schoolwide problems (i.e., study groups).

Bean, R. (2004). *The reading specialist: Leadership for the classroom, school, and community.* New York: Guilford.

> This book discusses the many responsibilities of the reading specialist and provides research-based frameworks for working with struggling readers and their teachers, providing professional development and coaching, planning curriculum, assessment

administration, collaborating with parents and other stakeholders, and writing grant proposals.

Kise, J.A. (2004). *Differentiated coaching: A framework for helping teachers change.* Thousand Oaks, CA: Corwin Press.

This book melds the latest research on personality type, multiple intelligences, experiential learning models, and mind styles models to generate a model for staff professional development.

Langer, G.M., Colton, A.B., & Goff, L.S. (2003). *Collaborative analysis of student work: Improving teaching and learning.* Baltimore: Association for Supervision and Curriculum Development.

This text offers a structured framework for working with teachers in collaboratively examining and reflecting upon student work to ultimately affect student achievement.

Robb, L. (2000). *Redefining staff development: A collaborative model for teachers and administrators.* Portsmouth, NH: Heinemann.

Using activities that all educators should be involved with (reading, self-evaluating, discussing, kid and colleague watching, peer mentoring, and collaborating), this book describes how to go about making meaningful changes for teachers and administrators.

Vogt, M.E., & Shearer, B.A. (2006). *Reading specialists and literacy coaches in the real world* (2nd ed.). Boston: Allyn & Bacon.

Designed to assist reading specialists and literacy coaches implement reading programs at the school and district levels, this text includes both theoretical and practical information to implement, coordinate, and evaluate reading/language arts programs.

The CaseNEX case study selected for Standard 5 addresses Element 5.3, working collaboratively with colleagues. The content rubric for Element 5.3 allows a high score of 7 and a low score of 0 (see Standard 5 Rubric, Appendix, p. 155).

Case Study for Standard 5: Professional Development

Reprinted from CaseNEX LLC, founded at University of Virginia's Curry School of Education. Reprinted with permission.

Pandora's Box, Scene 3

"Mrs. Ferndon," Alexandria smiled at me both shyly and mischievously. "Read the dinosaur book?" She was one of my favorites this year, not only because I was touched by the story of her adoption and prior life as an orphan in Russia, but because I loved to see her sparkle when she opened up a bit. Although she was still hesitant to speak in front of the class or even in small groups of native speakers, one-on-one she was much more conversational, so I usually found time throughout the day to help her individually and regularly paired her with just one peer. Between my class, her parents, and daily time in Judith's class, her English was developing quickly and I knew she could understand most of what went on. I was fairly certain she'd place out of ESOL by the end of second grade.

Alexandria went to the side book shelf, returning with *The Big Book of Dinosaurs* and the plastic baggie of felt dinosaurs that went with it. She had read this book a number of times and had most of the information memorized. I'd shown her a few websites about dinosaurs, and she clearly had prior experience with a mouse, as she negotiated the screen quite nimbly. She was most concerned with how each dinosaur escaped from danger, and after reading the book, she'd quietly stage various predator and prey scenarios with the felt dinosaurs. I sometimes followed up with writing activities and the sentences she was constructing were quite impressive. Last week I transcribed, "I ride *ornithomimus*," one of the fastest dinosaurs, "to escape if *T. rex* come after me."

I must say her parents followed up on whatever we did in class, in this instance, taking her to a natural history museum and buying dinosaur books.

But I still didn't have a SMART Board like Judith.

At parent conferences, we'd talked about ways to help Alexandria, and I'd hinted heavily about how effective technology was at enhancing lessons and providing individualized instructional support. Their response had both puzzled and irritated me.

"Have you used the SMART Board we donated yet?" Her father, Colby, had asked.

"Well, no, it's in Mrs. Shearborn's classroom."

"Can't you move it to your classroom for part of the day? We really want Alexandria to have access to lessons using it as much as possible. That's why we gave it to the school." He sounded a bit exasperated with me.

The thought of disconnecting all those cords, transporting the behemoth across the hall, reconnecting everything, and then doing the same process in reverse, all while monitoring students, sent a shudder down my spine. Did he really think Judith and I should and could share?

But he was serious and he obviously had clout. He'd gone to Helen Washington, Director of Curriculum and Instruction for the county, who had sent me yet another email regarding the collaboration Judith and I were supposed to be working on, along with a copy of our technology standards for K–2 students and teachers. Helen had even gone ahead and hired a sub for the past two Wednesday afternoons so that I could observe Judith working with Alexandria and her classmates. Our follow-up meeting was scheduled for this Wednesday, when we were supposed to develop a more integrated unit than our usual slapdash "plan."

It had been an interesting experience sitting in Judith's room as students I normally saw as shy and silent waved hands excitedly and eagerly participated. But, to be honest, it was the SMART Board that held my attention and not what the students were doing. It was just so *cool*! With its large illuminated screen, it compelled not just my focus, but that of the students as well.

Judith Shearborn's Reading Lesson (video transcript)

Judith: OK, so today I made some pictures [Pointing to a row of pictures at the bottom of a SMART Board], and we're going to sort the pictures. [Judith holds up two books, *Arrow to the Sun* and *Moon Rope*.] We're going to put each picture under the title it goes with and when we're finished we're going to talk about characters, setting, problem, and solution. Who remembers what those words mean? Who remembers what *characters* mean?

Student: The people in the book.

Judith: Very good, the people in the book. Who remembers what the setting is. Jose?

Jose: Where it happens.

Judith: Where it happens, excellent. Every book has a problem. Who remembers what that word *problem* means? Nina?

Nina: What is going on wrong in the story.

Judith:	What is going on wrong in that story. And what about *solution*? Alexandra?
Alexandra:	How do you solve the problem.
Judith:	How do you solve the problem, how do you fix it and make it right. This person is a character. Which book do you think that person is from? What do you think Christian?
Christian:	Um, *Arrow to the Sun*.
Judith:	OK, let's come over here and see if we can move it over there. And if we're having… [Christian walks to the board, selects a picture, and moves it to a location underneath the title, *Arrow to the Sun.*] that's good, good job Christian, nice. So there we have a character for *Arrow to the Sun*. Now, did *Moon Rope* have people in it?
Students:	No.
Judith:	No.
Students:	Animals.
Judith:	Animals. Can you see one of the animals that's in *Moon Rope*. Tara?
Tara:	A fox.
Judith:	A fox. Can you put the fox over to *Moon Rope*? [Tara moves the picture of the fox to a location under the title *Moon Rope*] Nice job. There was another animal in *Moon Rope* but it was a funny animal that dug tunnels. Do you remember what that was called? Do you remember Julio?
Julio:	A mole.
Judith:	A mole. Is there a picture of a mole there? Where is he? There he is. [Julio moves the picture of the mole under *Moon Rope*] Good job. I'm going to move this over just a little so he doesn't cover Mr. Fox there. [Julio places the picture of the mole too close to the fox so Judith moves it over a bit] So what do I have here? These are the what?
Students:	Characters.
Judith:	So I'm going to spell characters. [Judith writes the word *characters* on the SMART Board] Good. Now what is the next thing we talked about after characters? Yes?
Student:	Where...
Judith:	Where... [Leading student]
Student:	Where it happens.
Judith:	Where it happens. And who remembers what that word is? Nina?
Nina:	The setting.
Judith:	The setting, excellent. Emmanuel, what's the setting for *Arrow to the Sun*?

Emmanuel:	The Hopi Indians.
Judith:	The Hopi Indians; very good. Why don't we put him down because we're going to write something next to him? [Judith takes the picture of the Hopi Indians from the bottom of the board and places it under *Arrow to the Sun*] Now the other one, we talked about it took place in a country. You remember? What country are you studying right now in social studies? Zachary?
Zachary:	Mexico.
Judith:	Mexico. Do you see a map of Mexico up there? [Judith points to the pictures at the bottom of the SMART Board] [Zachary points to Mexico] Good job. They're kind of together. Nice job, Zachary. Why don't we put it down here, right across from this setting so then I can write next to it? [Zachary places the picture under the title *Arrow to the Sun* across from the word *setting*] All right. Good. So we have the characters for both stories, and now we have the setting for both stories. Can someone help me spell *setting*? Who can help me spell *setting*? What's the copy cat letter for "c", the other letter that makes that /sss/?
Students:	S.
Judith:	S, you got it. S, now what. Set, Set...there's a T but there's a missing letter. Do you know what it is Julio, I mean Christian? Se..e...e...e...
Christian:	Y?
Judith:	No, but close. Nina?
Nina:	E.
Judith:	Everybody knew that didn't they. Set...
Students:	T, T.
Judith:	Good for you, and then, ing...
Students:	I, N, G.
Judith:	Oh you're such super spellers. Setting, OK.

I left Judith's room abuzz with ideas and full of enthusiasm. If only I had a SMART Board in my room! It just didn't seem fair that she had the only one.

I slipped back into my classroom to jot down ideas while the sub attempted to finish up the lesson and end the day. Settling into my desk in the back of the room, I opened my notebook and began chewing on my pen as I mulled over what I'd seen. Glancing around the room, I saw that Alexandria had slipped away from the group and was surreptitiously playing with the felt dinosaurs in another corner. As I watched her maneuver the figures, I began to wonder about Judith's lesson. It was great to see the kids becoming more comfortable with the literacy terms we'd been studying and being able to correctly sort the characters from the two stories. But was the lesson really that revolutionary?

Judith and I were supposed to meet next week. I was sure Judith expected the rave reviews and positive feedback she usually got. I didn't want her to get defensive, but I was feeling the pressure from both Helen Washington [the director of Curriculum and Instruction for the county] and Colby Martin [a parent who donated the SMART Board to the school.]. If we really were going to integrate both our curriculums and our technology according to the standards Helen sent me, we would have to do things differently.

As I struggled to muster enthusiasm for working with Judith, I thought back to the arrival of the big box last summer. How little I realized then the problems it would create.

Question for response: As a reading coach, how would you respond to Judith's lesson with the Smart Board? How would you assist Maxie in working with Judith to ensure collaboration and equality in using technology? Be sure to include a rationale for your response.

Context of Administration

The sample responses were elicited as a part of a take-home final exam in a reading seminar course toward the end of a graduate program in reading. The course included several weeks on the topic of leadership and professionalism in reading education as well as the role of a reading specialist in schools. Candidates were provided the case and allowed to read it over to ask any clarifying questions they may have had at the end of class. The responses were due within seven days to be uploaded to the candidates' electronic portfolios for review by the instructor. Collaboration was not allowed and candidates signed an honor statement to verify that their responses were their own work. Before scoring the responses, the instructor and candidates' advisor met to create a list of possible responses based on course objectives and readings to set minimum, but not exclusive, criteria for scoring. The list included addressing the use (low level) of technology and how that might be expanded, practical issues of sharing the SMART Board (an interactive whiteboard), and ways and reasons to effectively foster collaboration to enhance learning for all students.

Responses

The first response mentions positive aspects of the case's lesson, as well as the need to collaborate. There is no mention of the possibility of using a higher level of technology with students (see, for reference, Chapter 2, Element 2.2's literature review regarding this topic) or how to approach both teachers with feedback on how to improve the lesson or foster collaboration; rather, the focus is on how to work around practical issues. Although practical issues are regarded as important, based on the content of the course experienced by the candidates, more could have been written to demonstrate stronger leadership skills, a better understanding of technology use, and how to approach teachers with collaboration strategies. An emerging conceptual understanding is evident in the rationale. (Note that the first response was edited to fit a content score of 3 and a Novice rationale.)

Judith's lesson with the SMART Board was great! It caught the student's attention from the very beginning and for the most part it kept their attention until the end of the lesson. The SMART Board provided the teacher and the students with so many advantages. The students were able to show mastery during the lesson, visual learning students were able to keep up with the lesson with ease, ESOL [English for Speakers of Other Languages] students were able to see different examples on the board that would help them translate in English, the teacher provided a lesson that included technology and was hands on, along with enabling the students to participate in a nontraditional lesson. Judith's lesson showed enthusiasm—the students were eager to learn and eager to answer questions. Using the SMART Board gave the students a lot of motivation—the students wanted to show what they knew.

In speaking with both teachers, I would mention the importance of team work and remembering that the students are our priority. I'd suggest to the teachers that maybe they could move the students and not move the SMART Board as that may be easier than reconnecting the cords each time—that could be very time consuming. The main idea is to help the teachers realize that the SMART Board should be shared and used to the utmost.

The second response scored at the Proficient level. The reasoning behind the response demonstrates a good conceptual understanding of the issues raised, although not all possible issues are mentioned (i.e., the level of technology use), thus the content score awarded was 4. In addition, professional development pertaining to collaboration is suggested, but we (Mary, as the instructor, as well as the remaining authors) would have liked to see more specific suggestions as to actual activities or strategies that might be implemented by the reading coach to resolve the dilemma of sharing the SMART Board and at the same time, move the teachers to a true spirit of collaboration (i.e., team building activities, Collaborative Analysis of Student Learning, learning communities, and so forth).

As a reading coach I would say that this lesson has been taught using effective instructional strategies, it has been designed paying attention to the students' instructional needs and levels of language development. The lesson keeps the students engaged at all times, the teacher provides opportunities for all students to participate. She uses technology to make her lesson creative and motivates the students to learn. She also uses technology to support learner-centered strategies addressing the students' diverse needs, and she applies technology to develop students' creativity. She uses a variety of effective ESOL strategies that help the students to understand and apply grade level material.

In a situation like this the leadership role of the reading coach needs to motivate others to work together to improve students' learning. The reading coach may ask Judith to lead the team as she is the experienced teacher, but at the same time the reading coach should also encourage Maxie to actively participate by providing feedback and new ideas. As the reading coach, it is very important to establish a clear understanding of the goal to be achieved and a commitment to achieving that goal (Bean, 2004).

Judith seems to be a very good and experienced classroom teacher, but she needs the support of the reading coach in knowing how to collaborate with Maxie. The lesson is effective for meeting Judith's lesson objectives, but the way they are "collaborating" is neither effective nor efficient. Dieker (2005) lists barriers teachers face when collaborating, including shortage of time, grading, student readiness, and teacher readiness. Considering these barriers, it would be effective if the reading coach, in this particular situation, could provide professional development on collaboration and cooperative teaching for these two teachers that would address the barriers mentioned by Dieker. It would also be very helpful to model the process to make sure it is carried out in a smooth and professional way to avoid personal conflicts and to ensure effectiveness. The reading coach has a determinant role in assisting teachers in how to carry out collaboration. This needs to be addressed at school sites to improve student learning and avoid possible professional conflict.

References

Bean, R. (2004). *The reading specialist: Leadership for the classroom, school, and community.* New York: Guilford.

Dieker, L. (2005). *An introduction to cooperative teaching.* Retrieved April 28, 2007, from www.specialconnections.ku.edu/cgi-bin/cgiwrap/specconn/main.php?cat=collaboration&ion=coteaching/main

The third response indicates a deep conceptual understanding of the issues raised and provides specific examples of how the reading coach would work with the teachers to facilitate collaboration and expand the use of the SMART Board with students. The response shows continual questioning of practice and student outcomes, pointing to modeling and scaffolding by the reading coach to initiate teacher reflection and discussion. The response received a content score of 7 with a Distinguished rationale because strong and appropriate leadership skills are evident.

As the reading coach at Gloucester Elementary School, I have various responsibilities to the school and the staff. Among my assignments, I work with teachers on a one to one basis to help assist them by providing them with additional support in their classrooms. This year, one of our student's parents donated a SMART Board to our school to facilitate their daughter's learning. The board is being used by Judith, the ESL teacher. However, the parents would like for their daughter to have as much access to the SMART Board as possible. This means that Maxie, her first grade teacher, and Judith need to develop a way to collaborate on their lessons and use the technology together.

While observing Judith's lesson, I noticed that there were many positive aspects of using the SMART Board in the classroom. It allows the students to participate actively in the lesson and work with technology. During the lesson, Judith incorporated many useful strategies to teach her ESL students. She is careful to use repetition of vocabulary and key terms. She also incorporates phonics instruction to help the students develop their spelling and decoding skill. The classroom also appears to be a safe learning environment. The students are obviously very comfortable with Judith and their lesson. Judith is very supportive and is consistently praising the students for their answers and participation.

After the observation, I would arrange to meet with Judith to discuss her lesson and additional suggestions for using the SMART Board. I would ask her some questions for reflection and to see how content she is with her lesson. Also, I would like for her decide in which areas she may need added support from me. Some of the questions that come to mind are:

· Are your students demonstrating growth in the use of oral language?
· Are they stating their ideas orally in complete sentences?
· Do they have an appropriate grasp of vocabulary?
· Are they capable of following oral instructions?
· Do they participate actively during instruction?
· Are they differentiating and using phonemes appropriately?
· Can they identify parts of the plot?
· Do they have strong decoding and spelling skills?

As Judith reflects and responds to questions about her lesson, we can talk about specific aspects of the lesson and brainstorm strategies that can complement her instruction. We should also discuss the students' progress and how the SMART Board impacted their progression. Following reflection, we need to discuss how to use class time more effectively and develop appropriate instructional activities to fit the need of the ESL students.

The SMART Board needs to enhance the students' lessons. Judith needs to develop lessons that use the board at a higher technological level. The lessons must facilitate the students' ability to interact with technology, while providing the students with opportunities to learn and discover new ideas. Examples of suggestions include the use of the SMART Board for interactive writing, language experience approach, or accessing the Internet to take a shared Google Lit Trip (a virtual field trip based on a book or novel).

Judith's job is directly related with the general classroom teacher, Maxie. Judith and Maxie share the same students and should collaborate for more effective instruction. Until now, there has been very little collaboration between the two teachers. However, with the addition of the SMART Board, they need to find a way to plan their lessons more carefully and share the new technology.

First of all, I would recommend that Judith and Maxie attend professional development workshops together. They need to make sure to make the most of their time planning together and attend technology workshops to facilitate their use of the SMART Board.

As the reading coach, I would meet with each teacher individually and establish the goals and objectives that each teacher would like to achieve. Then I would hold a group meeting with Judith and Maxie, after they have attended their collaboration workshop, to help them with their joint lessons and provide them with support. In a sense, I would become a mediator between the two in an attempt to help them begin working together comfortably.

During the group meeting, Maxie and Judith should use any skills or strategies that they acquired during the teacher collaboration workshop. I would encourage the teachers to work on certain areas that may help them improve their planning time and lessons. I would suggest that they develop a schedule that is convenient for both of them to share the SMART Board. They can set aside time for Maxie to bring her class into Judith's room so that she too can use the SMART Board. I would also provide some suggestions on how they can develop lessons across the curriculum. They can complement each other's math, science, language arts, and social studies lessons to enhance student learning.

Both Judith and Maxie need to observe each other teaching. They should be aware of their teaching styles, the materials they are using, and the lessons being taught. Once both teachers have had an opportunity to work with the SMART Board they can meet to reflect on their experiences. The SMART Board has a very useful function, in that you can print all the lessons that are written on the board. Judith and Maxie can bring their print out and review the information that was taught, the strategies used, and develop ways to enhance their work. They can also reflect on each other's lessons and provide positive feedback for planning future lessons. In this case, I would continue meeting with Judith and Maxie during their planning time, but begin taking a more passive role. I would offer them any assistance they may need and gradually decrease my involvement in their collaboration.

Standards-Based Rubrics

Standard 1 Rubric: Foundational Knowledge

Candidates have knowledge of the foundations of reading and writing processes and instruction. As a result, candidates:

Element	Distinguished	Proficient	Sufficient	Novice	Unacceptable
	Rationale is expanded—Uses explicit, in-depth statements referring to case study information, as well as other sources (i.e., theory, research, experience, etc.) *throughout* the response. A deep conceptual understanding is evident.	Rationale is focused—Uses explicit statements referring to case study information and is clearly written. A good conceptual understanding is evident.	Rationale is adequate—Uses more specific statements referring to case study, but reader must infer at times while reading. An emergent conceptual understanding is evident.	Rationale is limited—Uses broad, general statements (i.e., "to improve reading...") or generic statements that could apply to almost any reader. There is little evidence of conceptual understanding.	Rationale did not address standard element.
1.1 Demonstrate knowledge of psychological, sociological, and linguistic foundations of reading and writing processes and instruction.	11 = Demonstrates knowledge of a wide range of theories and how they relate to classroom practices and materials, specifically linking reading and writing processes and instruction. 10 = Demonstrates knowledge of a wide range of theories and how they relate to classroom practices and materials; other more contemporary learning theories may be present.	9 = Demonstrates essential knowledge and application of more than two foundational theories and how they relate to classroom practices and materials; other more contemporary learning theories may be present. 8 = Demonstrates essential knowledge and application of two foundational theories related to practices and materials; other more contemporary learning theories may be present. 7 = Demonstrates essential knowledge and application of one foundational theory related to practices and materials; other more contemporary learning theories may be present.	6 = Demonstrates knowledge of most elements from foundational theory, but evidence of application is minimal. 5 = Demonstrates knowledge of two to three elements from theory, but evidence of application is minimal or not present. 4 = Demonstrates knowledge of one element from theory, but evidence of application is minimal or not present.	3 = Minimal evidence of theoretical foundational knowledge found in response. 2 = Evidence of inappropriate or incorrect foundational knowledge found in response. 1 = No evidence of foundational knowledge found in response.	0 = Response did not address standard element or question from case study.

Element	Distinguished	Proficient	Sufficient	Novice	Unacceptable
1.2 Demonstrate knowledge of reading research and histories of reading.	10 = Demonstrates knowledge and application of more than two research studies or periods of reading history. 9 = Demonstrates knowledge and application of one to two research studies or one to two periods of reading history.	8 = Demonstrates knowledge and application of two periods of reading history. 7 = Demonstrates knowledge and application of two reading research studies. 6 = Demonstrates knowledge and application of one reading research study and one period of reading history.	5 = Demonstrates knowledge and application of one period of reading history. 4 = Demonstrates knowledge and application of one reading research study.	3 = Evidence of appropriate reading research or history knowledge found in response, but misapplied for the case study's context. 2 = Evidence of inappropriate or incorrect reading research or history knowledge found in response. 1 = No evidence of reading research or histories knowledge found in response.	0 = Response did not address standard element or question from case study.

(continued)

Standard 1 Rubric: Foundational Knowledge (continued)

Candidates have knowledge of the foundations of reading and writing processes and instruction. As a result, candidates:

Element	Distinguished	Proficient	Sufficient	Novice	Unacceptable
1.3 Demonstrate knowledge of language development and reading acquisition and the variations related to cultural and linguistic diversity (CLD).	9 = Demonstrates extensive knowledge and application of language development and reading acquisition or variations related to CLD. 8 = Demonstrates extensive knowledge of language development and reading acquisition or variations related to CLD.	7 = Demonstrates significant knowledge and application of language development and reading acquisition or variations related to CLD. 6 = Demonstrates significant knowledge of language development and reading acquisition or variations related to CLD.	5 = Demonstrates some knowledge and application of language development and reading acquisition or variations related to CLD. 4 = Demonstrates some knowledge of language development and reading acquisition or variations related to CLD.	3 = Evidence of appropriate knowledge concerning language development and reading acquisition or variations related to CLD found in response, but misapplied for the case study's context. 2 = Evidence of inappropriate/incorrect knowledge concerning language development and reading acquisition or variations related to CLD found in response. 1 = No evidence of knowledge concerning language development and reading acquisition or variations related to CLD found in response.	0 = Response did not address standard element or question from case study.

Element	Distinguished	Proficient	Sufficient	Novice	Unacceptable
1.4 Demonstrate knowledge of the major components of reading (phonemic awareness, word identification and phonics, vocabulary and background knowledge, fluency, comprehension strategies, and motivation) and how they are integrated in fluent reading.	9 = Demonstrates knowledge of four or more of the major components of reading and how they are integrated in fluent reading.	8 = Demonstrates knowledge of three to four of the major components of reading and how they are integrated in fluent reading.	7 = Demonstrates knowledge of two of the major components of reading and how they are integrated in fluent reading. 6 = Demonstrates knowledge of two or more of the major components of reading, but not how they are integrated in fluent reading. 5 = Demonstrates knowledge of one of the major components of reading and how it is integrated in fluent reading. 4 = Demonstrates knowledge of one of the major components of reading, but not how it is integrated in fluent reading.	3 = Evidence of appropriate knowledge concerning how the major components of reading are integrated in fluent reading, but misapplied for the case study's context. 2 = Evidence of inappropriate or incorrect knowledge concerning the major components of reading and how they are integrated in fluent reading. 1 = No evidence of how the major components of reading are integrated in fluent reading.	0 = Response did not address standard element or question from case study.

Standard 2 Rubric: Instructional Strategies and Curriculum Materials

Candidates use a wide range of instructional practices, approaches, methods, and curriculum materials to support reading and writing instruction. As a result, they:

Element	Distinguished	Proficient	Sufficient	Novice
	Rationale is expanded—Uses explicit, in-depth statements referring to case study information, as well as other sources (i.e., theory, research, experience, etc.) *throughout* the response. A deep conceptual understanding is evident.	Rationale is focused—Uses explicit statements referring to case study information and is clearly written. A good conceptual understanding is evident.	Rationale is adequate—Uses more specific statements referring to case study, but reader must infer at times while reading. An emergent conceptual understanding is evident.	Rationale is limited—Uses broad, general statements (i.e., "to improve reading...") or generic statements that could apply to almost any reader. There is little evidence of conceptual understanding.
2.1 Use instructional grouping options (individual, small-group, whole-class, and computer-based) as appropriate for accomplishing given purposes.	8 = Identifies four or more instructional grouping options appropriate for the purpose.	7 = Identifies three instructional grouping options appropriate for the purpose. 6 = Identifies two instructional grouping options appropriate for the purpose.	5 = Identifies one valid instructional grouping option appropriate for the purpose. 4 = Identifies two or more valid instructional grouping options *along with* invalid options.	3 = Identifies one valid instructional grouping option *with* invalid grouping options. 2 = Identifies invalid grouping options only and includes other information that does not qualify as a grouping option (i.e., provides strategy suggestions). 1 = No instructional grouping suggestions identified. 0 = Response did not address standard element or question from case study.

Element	Distinguished	Proficient	Sufficient	Novice
2.2 Use a wide range of instructional practices, approaches, and methods, including technology-based practices for learners at differing stages of development and from differing cultural and linguistic backgrounds.	9 = Identifies three or more instructional practices, approaches, or methods addressing two or more of the element's variables, *along with* other valid instructional approaches that may or may not address these variables.	8 = Identifies two instructional practices, approaches, or methods addressing two of the element's variables, *along with* other valid instructional approaches that may or may not address these variables. 7 = Identifies one instructional practice, approach, or method addressing two of the element's variables, *along with* other valid instructional approaches that may or may not address these variables.	6 = Identifies three or more instructional practices, approaches, or methods addressing one of the element's variables, *along with* other valid instructional approaches that may or may not address these variables. 5 = Identifies two instructional practices, approaches, or methods addressing one of the element's variables, *along with* other valid instructional approaches that may or may not address these variables. 4 = Identifies one instructional practice, approach, or method addressing one of the element's variables, *along with* other valid instructional approaches that may or may not address these variables.	3 = Identifies one or more valid instructional practice, approach, or method, but does not address the bolded variables in this element. 2 = Identifies invalid or inappropriate instructional practices, approaches, or methods only and includes information that does not address instruction (i.e., provides generic grouping suggestion such as "cooperative learning" without instructional approach). 1 = Invalid or inappropriate instructional practices, approaches, or methods suggested. 0 = Response did not address standard element or question from case study.

(continued)

Standard 2 Rubric: Instructional Strategies and Curriculum Materials (*continued*)

Candidates use a wide range of instructional practices, approaches, methods, and curriculum materials to support reading and writing instruction. As a result they:

Element	Distinguished	Proficient	Sufficient	Novice
2.3 Use a wide range of curriculum materials in effective reading instruction for learners at different stages of reading and writing development and from different cultural and linguistic backgrounds.	9 = Identifies three or more appropriate curriculum materials addressing *all* of the variables	8 = Identifies two appropriate curriculum materials addressing *all* of the element's variables, *perhaps* with other appropriate suggestions. 7 = Identifies one appropriate curriculum material addressing *all* of the element's variables, *perhaps* with other valid suggestions.	6 = Identifies three or more appropriate curriculum materials addressing one of the element's variables, *perhaps* with other valid suggestions. 5 = Identifies two appropriate curriculum materials addressing one of the element's variables, *perhaps* with other valid suggestions. 4 = Identifies one appropriate curriculum material addressing one of the element's variables, *perhaps* with other valid suggestions.	3 = Identifies two appropriate curriculum materials that do not address the bolded variables of this element, *perhaps* with inappropriate curriculum suggestions. 2 = Identifies one appropriate curriculum material that does not address the bolded variables of this element, *perhaps* with inappropriate curriculum suggestions. 1 = Inappropriate curriculum materials suggested. 0 = Response did not address standard element or question from case study.

Standard 3 Rubric: Assessment, Diagnosis, and Evaluation

Candidates use a variety of assessment tools and practices to plan and evaluate effective reading instruction. As result, candidates:

Element	Distinguished	Proficient	Sufficient	Novice	Unacceptable
	Rationale is expanded— Uses explicit, in-depth statements referring to case study information, as well as another source or sources (i.e., theory, research, experience, etc.) *throughout* the response. A deep conceptual understanding is evident.	Rationale is focused— Uses explicit statements referring to case study information and is clearly written. A good conceptual understanding is evident.	Rationale is adequate— Uses more specific statements referring to case study, but reader must infer at times while reading. An emergent conceptual understanding is evident.	Rationale is limited— Uses broad, general statements (i.e., "to improve reading...") or generic statements that could apply to almost any reader. There is little evidence of conceptual understanding.	Rationale did not address standard element or question from case study.
3.1 Use a wide range of assessment tools and practices that range from individual and group standardized tests to individuals and group informal classroom assessment strategies, including technology-based assessment tools.	7 = More than one informal *and* formal assessment is suggested for appropriate audiences and purposes, including at least one technology-based assessment tool.	6 = One informal *and* formal assessment is suggested for appropriate audience and purpose, with at least one technology-based assessment tool.	5 = More than one informal *or* formal assessment is suggested for appropriate audiences and purposes.	4 = One informal *and* formal assessment is suggested for appropriate audiences and purposes. 3 = At least one appropriate informal or formal assessment is suggested for audience or purpose. 2 = At least one appropriate informal or formal assessment is suggested, along with other inappropriate assessments.	1 = All assessments suggested are inappropriate (for audience or purpose). 0 = Response did not address standard element or question from case study.

(continued)

Ready for the Classroom? Preparing Reading Teachers With Authentic Assessments by Mary A. Avalos, Ana Maria Pazos-Rego, Peggy D. Cuevas, Susan R. Massey, and Jeanne Shay Schumm. ©2009 International Reading Association. May be copied for classroom use.

Standard 3 Rubric: Assessment, Diagnosis, and Evaluation (continued)

Candidates use a variety of assessment tools and practices to plan and evaluate effective reading instruction. As result, candidates:

Element	Distinguished	Proficient	Sufficient	Novice	Unacceptable
3.2 Place students along a developmental continuum and identify students' proficiencies and difficulties.	7 = Accurate identification of proficiencies *and* difficulties with developmental continuum.	6 = Accurate identification of at least one proficiency *and* difficulty with developmental continuum.	5 = Accurate identification of at least one proficiency or difficulty with developmental continuum. 4 = Accurate identification of at least one proficiency or difficulty without mention of a developmental continuum.	3 = Accurate identification of at least one proficiency or difficulty along with inaccurate identification of proficiencies or difficulties without mention of developmental continuum.	2 = Inaccurate identification of all proficiencies or difficulties without developmental continuum. 1 = Inaccurate identification of proficiencies *and* difficulties. 0 = Response did not address standard element or question from case study.

Ready for the Classroom? Preparing Reading Teachers With Authentic Assessments by Mary A. Avalos, Ana Maria Pazos-Rego, Peggy D. Cuevas, Susan R. Massey, and Jeanne Shay Schumm. ©2009 International Reading Association. May be copied for classroom use.

Element	Distinguished	Proficient	Sufficient	Novice	Unacceptable
3.3 Use assessment information to plan, evaluate, and revise effective instruction that meets the needs of all students, including those at different developmental stages and those from different cultural and linguistic backgrounds.	8 = Evidence of consistent use of an assessment/diagnosis cycle driving instruction for all students.	7 = Evidence of appropriate planning *and* evaluation *and* revision of instruction based on more than one assessment.	6 = Evidence of appropriate use of two or three goals of assessment based on the results of more than one assessment. 5 = Evidence of appropriate use of planning *or* evaluating *or* revising instruction based on more than one assessment. 4 = Evidence of appropriate planning *and* evaluating *and* revision of instruction based on a single assessment.	3 = Evidence of appropriate use of two of three goals of assessment (planning, evaluating, or revising instruction). 2 = Evidence of appropriate use of one goal (planning *or* evaluating, *or* revising instruction) based on assessment.	1 = No evidence of planning, evaluating, or revising instruction based on assessment. 0 = Response did not address standard element or question from case study.
3.4 Communicate results of assessment to specific individuals (student, parents, caregivers, colleagues, administrators, policymakers, policy officials, community, etc.)		4 = Evidence of correct selection, interpretation, and communication of assessment information based on the needs of the specific stakeholder.	3 = Evidence of correct use of assessment information for two of the three categories of selection, interpretation, and communication.	2 = Evidence of appropriate levels of assessment information for *one* of the following: specific individuals, interpretation, or communication of assessment information based on the specific stakeholder.	1 = No evidence of appropriate interpretation or communication of assessment information to stakeholders. 0 = Response did not address standard element or question from case study.

Standard 4 Rubric: Creating a Literate Environment

Candidates create a literate environment that fosters reading and writing by integrating foundational knowledge, use of instructional practices, approaches and methods, curriculum materials, and the appropriate use of assessments. As a result, candidates:

Element	Distinguished	Proficient	Sufficient	Novice	Unacceptable
	Rationale is expanded— Uses explicit, in-depth statements referring to case study information, as well as other source(s) (i.e., theory, research, experience, etc.) *throughout* the response. A deep conceptual understanding is evident.	Rationale is focused— Uses explicit statements referring to case study information and is clearly written. A good conceptual understanding is evident.	Rationale is adequate— Uses more specific statements referring to case study, but reader must infer at times while reading. An emergent conceptual understanding is evident.	Rationale is limited— Uses broad, general statements (i.e., "to improve reading...") or generic statements that could apply to almost any reader. There is little evidence of conceptual understanding.	Rationale did not address standard element or question from case study.
4.1 Use students' interests, reading abilities, and backgrounds as foundations for the reading and writing program.	7 = Identifies and builds the reading and writing program based on the students' interests, reading abilities, and backgrounds and builds the reading and writing program to each of these areas.	6 = Identifies and builds the reading and writing program based on the students' interests, reading abilities, and backgrounds and links the reading and writing program to two of these areas. 5 = Identifies and builds the reading and writing program based on the students' interests, reading abilities, and backgrounds and links the reading and writing program to one of these areas.	4 = Identifies the students' interests, or reading abilities, or backgrounds and builds the reading and writing program based on two of these areas. 3 = Identifies the students' interests, or reading abilities, or backgrounds and builds the reading and writing program based on one of these areas.	2 = Identifies either students' interests, or reading abilities, or backgrounds, but no evidence of these areas as foundation for the reading and writing program.	1 = Provides no evidence of identification of any of the specific areas of need (students' interests, reading abilities, or backgrounds) or provides no evidence of designing an appropriate reading and writing program. 0 = Response did not address standard element or question from case study.

Element	Distinguished	Proficient	Sufficient	Novice	Unacceptable
4.2 Uses a large supply of books, technology-based information, and nonprint materials representing multiple levels, broad interests, and cultural and linguistic backgrounds.	5 = Is able to identify books, sources of technology-based information, or different nonprint materials representing all three of the following categories: multiple levels, broad interests, and cultural and linguistic backgrounds appropriate for the student.	4 = Is able to identify books, technology-based resources, and types of nonprint materials representing at least two of the following categories: multiple levels, broad interests, or cultural/linguistic backgrounds.	3 = Is able to identify one of the following: books, technology-based resource, or type of nonprint material representing one of the following: multiple levels, broad interests, or cultural and linguistic backgrounds.	2 = Is able to identify one of the following: books, technology-based resource, or type of nonprint material, but may be inappropriate to address the needs of the student because the material does not represent multiple levels, broad interests, or cultural and linguistic backgrounds.	1 = Provides no evidence of identifying any of the following: books, technology-based resource, or type of nonprint material. 0 = Response did not address standard element or question from case study.
4.3 Models reading and writing enthusiastically as a valued lifelong activity.		4 = Describes three or more effective ways to model reading and writing enthusiastically as a valued lifelong activity.	3 = Describes at least two effective ways to model reading and writing enthusiastically as a valued lifelong activity.	2 = Describes at least one effective way to model reading and writing enthusiastically as a valued lifelong activity.	1 = Shows no evidence of describing any effective way to model reading and writing enthusiastically. 0 = Response did not address standard element or question from case study.

(continued)

Standard 4 Rubric: Creating a Literate Environment (continued)

Candidates create a literate environment that fosters reading and writing by integrating foundational knowledge, use of instructional practices, approaches and methods, curriculum materials, and the appropriate use of assessments. As a result, candidates:

Element	Distinguished	Proficient	Sufficient	Novice	Unacceptable
4.4 Motivates learners to be lifelong readers.	6 = Describes three or more effective strategies that motivate readers intrinsically and extrinsically to become lifelong readers.	5 = Describes two effective strategies that motivate readers intrinsically and extrinsically to become lifelong readers.	4 = Describes one effective strategy that will motivate readers intrinsically and extrinsically to become lifelong readers. 3 = Describes valid and invalid strategies that will motivate readers intrinsically and extrinsically to become lifelong readers.	2 = Describes invalid strategies to motivate readers intrinsically and extrinsically to become lifelong readers.	1 = Does not describe strategies or understand the importance of motivating students to become lifelong readers. 0 = Response did not address standard element or question from case study.

Standard 5 Rubric: Professional Development

Candidates view professional development as a career-long effort and responsibility. As a result, candidates:

Element	Distinguished	Proficient	Sufficient	Novice
	Rationale is expanded—Uses explicit, in-depth statements referring to case study information, as well as other sources (i.e., theory, research, experience, etc.) *throughout* the response. A deep conceptual understanding is evident.	Rationale is focused—Uses explicit statements referring to case study information and is clearly written. A good conceptual understanding is evident.	Rationale is adequate—Uses more specific statements referring to case study, but reader must infer at times while reading. An emergent conceptual understanding is evident.	Rationale is limited—Uses broad, general statements (i.e., "to improve reading...") or generic statements that could apply to almost any reader. There is little evidence of conceptual understanding.
5.1 Display positive dispositions related to reading and the teaching of reading.	4 = Five or more positive dispositions evident.	3 = Three or four positive dispositions evident.	2 = One or two positive dispositions evident, although not necessarily from the list.	1 = Inappropriate dispositions evident in response (e.g, sarcasm, disrespect). 0 = Response did not address standard element or question from case study.
5.2 Continue to pursue the development of professional knowledge and dispositions.	4 = Recognized or awarded honors, has pursued and is currently pursuing the development of professional knowledge and dispositions in a high-quality program.	3 = In the past has pursued, and is currently pursuing, development of professional knowledge and dispositions in a high-quality professional development program.	2 = Currently pursuing development of professional knowledge and dispositions in a high-quality professional development program.	1 = No evidence of pursuing development of professional knowledge and dispositions. 0 = Response did not address standard element or question from case study.

(continued)

Standard 5 Rubric: Professional Development (continued)

Candidates view professional development as a career-long effort and responsibility. As a result, candidates:

Element	Distinguished	Proficient	Sufficient	Novice
5.3 Work with colleagues to observe, evaluate, and provide feedback on each other's practice.	7 = Works with colleagues to observe *and* evaluate *and* provide feedback on each other's practice, communicating in a positive manner and reflecting on feedback to implement changes; continually questions practice and discusses these questions with colleagues using appropriate leadership techniques.	6 = Works with colleagues to observe *and* evaluate *and* provide feedback on each other's practice, communicating in a positive manner and reflecting on feedback to implement changes using appropriate leadership techniques. 5 = Works with colleagues to observe *and* evaluate *and* provide feedback on each other's practice, using appropriate leadership techniques; response addresses important issues of the case.	4 = Works with colleagues to observe *and* evaluate *and* provide feedback on each other's practice, using appropriate leadership techniques; response does not address all important issues. 3 = Works with colleagues to observe *and* evaluate *and* provide feedback on each other's practice, using weak or questionable leadership techniques (e.g., condescending, controlling, authoritarian, or demeaning tone).	2 = Appears to work with colleagues in a limited way observing or evaluating or providing feedback on each other's practice. Some or most content of response may lack relevancy to the question. 1 = Does not appear to work with colleagues to observe, evaluate, and provide feedback on each other's practice or content of response does not address question. 0 = Response did not address standard element or question from case study.
5.4 Participate in, initiate, and evaluate professional development programs.	4 = Presents at and attends professional conferences, courses, or other high-quality professional development based on learners' needs and effectively evaluates professional development programs.	3 = Attends professional conferences, courses, or other high-quality professional development based on learners' needs and effectively evaluates professional development programs.	2 = Able to recognize areas where professional development is needed, participates in, initiates, and evaluates professional development programs.	1 = Does not participate in, initiate, or evaluate professional development programs. 0 = Response did not address standard element or question from case study.

"Positive dispositions" include the following (adapted from Stronge, 2007): Caring, fairness and respect, interactions with students, enthusiasm, motivation, dedication to teaching, reflective practice

REFERENCES

Abedi, J. (2001, Summer). Assessment and accommodations for English language learners. *CRESST Policy Brief 4*. Retrieved March 2, 2007, from www.cse.ucla.edu/products/policy/cresst_policy4_ref.pdf

Abedi, J. (2006). Language issues in item development. In S.M. Downing & T.M. Haladyna (Eds.), *Handbook of test development* (pp. 377–398). Mahwah, NJ: Erlbaum.

Abu-Alhija, F.N. (2007). Large-scale testing: Benefits and pitfalls. *Studies in Educational Evaluation, 33*(1), 50–68. doi:10.1016/j.stueduc.2007.01.005

Achilles, C.M. (1999). *Let's put kids first, finally: Getting class size right*. Thousand Oaks, CA: Corwin.

Adams, C. (2007, May/June). Not getting along? *Instructor, 116*(7), 47–50.

Adams, M.J. (1990). *Beginning to read: Thinking and learning about print*. Cambridge, MA: MIT Press.

Afflerbach, P. (2005). National Reading Conference Policy Brief: High stakes testing and reading assessment. *Journal of Literacy Research, 37*(2), 151–162. doi:10.1207/s15548430jlr3702_2

Afflerbach, P. (2007). *Understanding and using reading assessment, K–12*. Newark, DE: International Reading Association.

Alexander, P.A., & Fox, E. (2004). A historical perspective on reading research and practice. In R.B. Ruddell & N.J. Unrau (Eds.), *Theoretical models and processes of reading* (5th ed., pp. 33–68). Newark, DE: International Reading Association.

Allen, J.B., Michalove, B., Shockley, B., & West, M. (1991). "I'm really worried about Joseph": Reducing the risks of literacy learning. *The Reading Teacher, 44*(7), 458–467.

Allen, V.G. (1994). Selecting materials for the reading instruction of ESL children. In K. Spangenberg-Urbschat & R. Pritchard (Eds.), *Kids come in all languages: Reading instruction for ESL students* (pp. 108–131). Newark, DE: International Reading Association.

Allinder, R.M., Dunse, L., Brunken, C.D., & Obermiller-Krolikowski, H.J. (2001). Improving fluency in at-risk readers and students with learning disabilities. *Remedial and Special Education, 22*(1), 48–54. doi:10.1177/074193250102200106

Allington, R.L. (1983). The reading instruction provided readers of differing reading ability. *The Elementary School Journal, 83*(5), 548–559. doi:10.1086/461333

Allington, R.L. (2001). *What really matters for struggling readers: Designing research-based programs*. New York: Longman.

Allington, R.L. (2002a). *Big brother and the national reading curriculum: How ideology trumped evidence*. Portsmouth, NH: Heinemann.

Allington, R.L. (2002b). Research on reading/learning disability interventions. In A.E. Farstrup & S.J. Samuels (Eds.), *What research has to say about reading instruction* (3rd ed., pp. 261–290). Newark, DE: International Reading Association.

Allington, R.L. (2006). *What really matters for struggling readers* (2nd ed.). Boston: Allyn & Bacon.

American Educational Research Association. (2000). *AERA position statements on high-stakes testing in PreK–12 education*. Retrieved March 2, 2007, from www.aera.net/policyandprograms/?id=378

American Institutes for Research. (2007). *Literacy-rich environments*. Retrieved October 1, 2008, from www.k8accesscenter.org/training_resources/literacy-richenvironments.asp

American Psychological Association. (1998). *Rights and responsibilities of test takers: Guidelines and expectations*. Retrieved March 2, 2007, from www.apa.org/science/ttrr.html

Amrein, A.L., & Berliner, D.C. (2002, March 28). High-stakes testing, uncertainty, and student learning, *Education Policy Analysis Archives, 10*(18). Retrieved September 4, 2007, from epaa.asu.edu/epaa/v10n18/

Anderson, R.C., & Freebody, P. (1981). Vocabulary knowledge. In J. Guthrie (Ed.), *Comprehension and teaching: Research reviews* (pp. 77–117). Newark, DE: International Reading Association.

Anderson, R.C., Hiebert, E.H., Scott, J.A., & Wilkinson, I.A.G. (1985). *Becoming a nation of readers: The report of the Commission on Reading*. Washington, DC: National Academy of Education.

Anderson, R.C., Reynolds, R.E., Schallert, D.L., & Goetz, E.T. (1977). Frameworks for comprehending discourse. *American Educational Research Journal, 14*(4), 367–381.

Anderson, V. (1992). A teacher development project in transactional strategy instruction for teachers of severely reading-disabled adolescents. *Teaching and Teacher Education, 8*(4), 391–403. doi:10.1016/0742-051X(92)90064-A

Anderson-Inmann, L., & Horney, M.A. (1998). Transforming text for at-risk readers. In D. Reinking, M.C. McKenna, L.D. Labbo, & R.D. Kieffer (Eds.), *Handbook of literacy and technology: Transformations in a post-typographic world* (pp. 15–44). Mahwah, NJ: Erlbaum.

Andrews, K.R. (Ed.). (1953). *The case method of teaching human relations and administration: An interim statement.* Cambridge, MA: Harvard University Press.

Applebee, A.N., Langer, J.A., Nysstrand, M., & Gamoran, A. (2003). Discussion-based approaches to developing understanding: Classroom instruction and student performance in middle and high school English. *American Educational Research Journal, 40*(3), 685–730. doi:10.3102/00028312040003685

Armbruster, B.B., Lehr, F., & Osborn, J. (2001). *Put reading first: The research building blocks of teaching children to read.* Jessup, MD: National Institute for Literacy/U.S. Department of Education.

Artiles, A.J., & Klingner, J.K. (2006). Forging a knowledge base on English language learners with special needs: Theoretical, population, and technical issues. *Teachers College Record, 108*(11), 2187–2194. doi:10.1111/j.1467-9620.2006.00778.x

Au, K.H. (1995). Multicultural perspectives on literacy research. *JRB: A Journal of Literacy, 27*(1), 85–100.

Au, K.H. (2000). A multicultural perspective on policies for improving literacy achievement: Equity and excellence. In M.L. Kamil, P.B. Mosenthal, P.D. Pearson, & R. Barr (Eds.), *Handbook of reading research* (Vol. 3, pp. 835–851). Mahwah, NJ: Erlbaum.

August, D., & Hakuta, K. (1997). *Improving schooling for language-minority children.* Washington, DC: National Academies Press.

August, D., & Shanahan, T. (Eds.). (2006). *Developing literacy in second-language learners: Report of the National Literacy Panel on language-minority children and youth.* Mahwah, NJ: Erlbaum/Center for Applied Linguistics.

Avalos, M.A. (2006). No two learners are alike: Readers with linguistic and cultural differences. In J.S. Schumm (Ed.), *Reading assessment and instruction for all learners: A comprehensive guide for classroom and resource settings* (pp. 59–86). New York: Guilford.

Avalos, M.A., & Pazos-Rego, A.M. (September, 2006). *University-district partnerships: Merging graduate education and professional development.* Paper presented at the Florida Association of Teacher Educators Annual Conference, Orlando, FL.

Avalos, M.A., Pazos-Rego, A.M., Cuevas, P.D., & Massey, S.R. (2006, January). *Practicing what we preach: An authentic, standards-based assessment model for teacher education.* Paper presented at the 58th American Association of Colleges for Teacher Education (AACTE) Annual Meeting and Exhibits, San Diego, CA.

Avalos, M.A., Plasencia, A., Chavez, C., & Rascón, J. (2007). Modified guided reading: Gateway to English as a second language and literacy learning. *The Reading Teacher, 61*(4), 318–329. doi:10.1598/RT.61.4.4

Baker, L., & Wigfield, A. (1999). Dimensions of children's motivation for reading and their relations to reading activity and reading achievement. *Reading Research Quarterly, 34*(4), 452–477.

Ball, D.L., & Cohen, D.K. (1999). Developing practice, developing practitioners: Toward a practiced based theory of professional education. In G. Sykes & L. Darling-Hammond (Eds.), *Teaching as the Learning Profession: Handbook of Policy and Practice* (pp. 3–32). San Francisco: Jossey Bass.

Bandura, A. (1969). *Principles of behavior modification.* New York: Holt Rinehart & Winston.

Barker, P.G. (1978). *Habitats, environments, and human behavior. Studies in ecological psychology and eco-behavioral science from the Midwest Psychological Field Station, 1947–1972.* San Francisco: Jossey-Bass.

Barone, D., Hardman, D., & Taylor, J. (2006). *Reading first in the classroom.* Boston: Allyn & Bacon.

Barr, R. (1995). What research says about grouping in the past and present and what it suggests about the future. In M. Radencich & L. McKay (Eds.), *Flexible grouping for literacy in the elementary grades.* (pp. 1–24). Boston: Allyn & Bacon.

Barr, R., Kamil, M.L., Mosenthal, P.B., & Pearson, P.D. (Eds.). (1991). *Handbook of reading research* (Vol. 2). White Plains, NY: Longman.

Barrows, H.S., & Tamblyn, R.M. (1980). *Problem-based learning: An approach to medical education*. New York: Springer.

Barton, J., & Collins, A. (1993). Portfolios in teacher education. *Journal of Teacher Education, 44*(3), 200–210. doi:10.1177/002248719304400307

Baumann, J.F., & Ivey, G. (1997). Delicate balances: Striving for curricular and instructional equilibrium in a second-grade, literature/strategy-based classroom. *Reading Research Quarterly, 32*(3), 244–275. doi:10.1598/RRQ.32.3.2

Baumann, J.F., & Kame'enui, E.J. (1991). Research on vocabulary instruction: Ode to Voltaire. In J. Flood, J.M. Jensen, D. Lapp, & J.R. Squire (Eds.), *Handbook of research on teaching the English language arts* (pp. 604–632). New York: Macmillan.

Baumann, J.F., Kame'enui, E.J., & Ash, G.E. (2003). Research on vocabulary instruction: Voltaire redux. In J. Flood, D. Lapp, J.R. Squire, & J.M. Jensen (Eds.), *Handbook on research on teaching the English language arts* (2nd ed., pp. 752–785). Mahwah, NJ: Erlbaum.

Baume, D., Yorke, M., & Coffey, M. (2004). What is happening when we assess, and how can we use our understanding of this to improve assessment? *Assessment & Evaluation in Higher Education, 29*(4), 451–477. doi:10.1080/02602930310001689037

Bean, R. (2004). *The reading specialist: Leadership for the classroom, school, and community*. New York: Guilford.

Bear, D.R., Invernizzi, M.A., Templeton, S., & Johnston, F. (1996). *Words their way*. Des Moines, IA: Merrill.

Bear, D.R., Invernizzi, M.A., Templeton, S., & Johnston, F. (2008). *Words their way: Word study for phonics, vocabulary, and spelling instruction* (4th ed.). Boston: Prentice Hall.

Beck, I.L., & McKeown, M.G. (1991). Conditions of vocabulary acquisition. In R. Barr, M. Kamil, P. Mosenthal, & P.D. Pearson (Eds.), *Handbook of reading research* (Vol. 2, pp. 789–814). New York: Longman.

Beck, I.L., McKeown, M.G., & Kucan, L. (2002). *Bringing words to life: Robust vocabulary instruction*. New York: Guilford.

Beck, I.L., McKeown, M.G., & Omanson, R.C. (1987). The effects and uses of diverse vocabulary instruction techniques. In M.G. McKeown & M.E. Curtis (Eds.), *The nature of vocabulary acquisition* (pp. 147–163). Hillsdale, NJ: Erlbaum.

Beers, K. (2003). *When kids can't read: What teachers can do: A guide for teachers 6–12*. Portsmouth, NH: Heinemann.

Biemiller, A. (2003). Vocabulary: Needed if more children are to read well. *Reading Psychology, 24*(3-4), 323–336. doi:10.1080/02702710390227297

Bender, L. (1957). Specific reading disability as maturation lag. *Bulletin of the Orton Society, 7*, 9–18.

Bennett, B.B. (1987). *The effectiveness of staff development training practice: A meta analysis*. Unpublished doctoral dissertation, University of Oregon.

Berliner, D.C. (1992). Telling the stories of educational psychology. *Educational Psychologist, 27*(2), 143–161.

Bernhardt, E. (2000). Second-language reading as a case study of reading scholarship in the 20th century. In M.L. Kamil, P.B. Mosenthal, P.D. Pearson, & R. Barr (Eds.), *Handbook of reading research* (Vol. 3, pp. 793–811). Mahwah, NJ: Erlbaum.

Betts, E.A. (1946). *Foundations of reading instruction*. New York: American Book.

Birenbaum, M. (2007). Evaluating the assessment: Sources of evidence for quality assurance. *Studies in Educational Evaluation, 33*(1), 29–49. doi:10.1016/j.stueduc.2007.01.004

Blackwell, P.J., & Diez, M.E. (1998). *Toward a new vision of master's education for teachers*. Washington, DC: National Council for Accreditation of Teacher Education.

Blanton, W.E., & Menendez, R.M. (2006). The digital connection: An exploration of computer-mediated reading instruction. In J.S. Schumm (Ed.), *Reading assessment and instruction for all learners* (pp. 433–459). New York: Guilford.

Blevins, W. (1998). *Phonics from A to Z: A practical guide*. New York: Scholastic.

Block, C.C., & Pressley, M. (2002). Introduction. In C.C. Block & M. Pressley (Eds.), *Comprehension instruction: Research-based best practices* (pp. 1–7). New York: Guilford.

Bloome, D., & Green, J. (1984). Directions in the sociolinguistic study of reading. In P.D. Pearson, R. Barr, M.L. Kamil, & P. Mosenthal (Eds.), *Handbook of reading research* (pp. 394–421). New York: Longman.

Boardman, A.G., Arguelles, M.E., Vaughn, S., Hughes, M.T., & Klingner, J.K. (2005). Special education teachers' views of research-based practices. *The Journal of Special Education, 39*(3), 168–180. doi:10.11 77/00224669050390030401

Bond, G.L., & Dykstra, R. (1997). The cooperative research program in first-grade reading instruction. *Reading Research Quarterly, 32*(4), 348–427. (Reprinted from *Reading Research Quarterly, 2*(4), 5–142, 1967) doi:10.2307/746948

Bower, G.H., & Hilgard, E.R. (1981). *Theories of learning.* Englewood Cliffs, NJ: Prentice Hall.

Bransford, J.D., & Johnson, M.K. (1972). Contextual prerequisites for understanding: Some investigations of comprehension and recall. *Journal of Verbal Learning and Verbal Behavior, 11*(6), 717–726. doi:10.1016/S0022-5371(72)80006-9

Braunger, J., & Lewis, J.P. (2006). *Building a knowledge base in reading* (2nd ed.). Newark, DE: International Reading Association.

Brent, R., & Anderson, P. (1993). Developing children's classroom listening strategies. *The Reading Teacher, 47*(2), 122–126.

Brophy, J. (2004). *Motivating students to learn.* London: Erlbaum.

Brown, A.L. (1985). Metacognition: The development of selective attention strategies for learning from texts. In H. Singer & R.B. Ruddell (Eds.), *Theoretical models and processes of reading* (3rd ed., pp. 501–526). Newark, DE: International Reading Association.

Brown, R., Pressley, M., Van Meter, P., & Schuder, J. (1996). A quasi-experimental validation of transactional strategies instruction with low-achieving second grade-readers. *Journal of Educational Psychology, 88*(1), 18–37. doi:10.1037/0022-0663.88.1.18

Bruner, J.S. (1986). *Actual minds, possible worlds.* Cambridge, MA: Harvard University Press.

Burnett, J. (1999). Student groupings for reading instruction. *OSEP Digest,* E579. Retrieved August 30, 2006, from www.ericdigests.org/2000-2/groupings.htm

Bus, A.G. (2001). Parent–child book reading through the lens of attachment theory. In L. Verhoeven & C. Snow (Eds.), *Literacy and motivation: Reading engagement in individuals and groups* (pp. 39–53). Mahwah, NJ: Erlbaum.

Byrnes, M.A. (2004). Alternate assessment FAQs (and answers). *Teaching Exceptional Children, 36*(6), 58–63.

Caldwell, J.S., & Leslie, L. (2005). *Intervention strategies to follow informal reading: So what do I do now?* Boston: Allyn & Bacon.

Calfee, R.C., Lindamood, P., & Lindamood, C. (1973, June). Acoustic-phonetic skills and reading: Kindergarten through twelfth grade. *Journal of Educational Psychology, 64*(3), 293–298. doi:10.1037/h0034586

Cambourne, B. (1988). *The whole story: Natural learning and the acquisition of literacy in the classroom.* New York: Scholastic.

Campbell, C., & Collins, V.L. (2007, Spring). Identifying essential topics in general and special education introductory assessment textbooks. *Educational measurement: Issues and practices,* 9–18.

Carini, P.F. (1986). Building from children's strengths. *Journal of Education, 168*(3), 13–24.

Chall, J.S. (1967). *Learning to read: The great debate.* New York: McGraw-Hill.

Chall, J.S. (1983). *Stages of reading development.* New York: McGraw-Hill.

Chard, D.J., Vaughn, S., & Tyler, B. (2002). A synthesis of research on effective interventions for building reading fluency with elementary students with learning disabilities. *Journal of Learning Disabilities, 35*(5), 386–406. doi:10.1177/00222194020350050101

Chomsky, C. (1968). *Language and mind.* New York: Harcourt.

Chomsky, C. (1972). Stages in language development and reading exposure. *Harvard Educational Review, 42*(1), 1–33.

Chomsky, N. (1957). *Syntactic structures.* The Hauge: Mouton.

Chomsky, N. (1959). A review of B.F. Skinner's *Verbal Behavior. Language, 35*(1), 26–58. doi:10.2307/411334

Chomsky, N. (1965). *Aspects of the theory of syntax.* Cambridge, MA: MIT Press.

Chomsky, N. (1967). The general properties of language. In F.L. Darley (Ed.), *Brain mechanism underlying speech and language* (pp. 73–88). New York: Grune and Stratton.

Cimbricz, S. (2002, January 9). State-mandated testing and teachers' beliefs and practice. *Education Policy Analysis Archives, 10.* Retrieved June 4, 2004, from epaa.asu.edu/epaa/v10n2.html

Cisneros, S. (April, 1993). Keynote address. TESOL Conference, Atlanta, GA.

Cizek, G. (2001). More intended consequences of high-stakes testing. *Educational Measurement: Issues and Practice, 20*(4), 19–27. doi:10.1111/j.1745-3992.2001.tb00072.x

Clark, H.H., & Clark, E.V. (1977). *Psychology and language: An introduction to psycholinguistics.* New York: Harcourt.

Clark, P., & Kragler, S. (2005, May). The impact of including writing materials in early childhood classrooms on the early literacy development of children from low-income families. *Early Child Development and Care, 175*(4), 285–301. doi:10.1080/0300443042000266295

Clay, M.M. (1991). *Becoming literate: The construction of inner control.* Portsmouth, NH: Heinemann.

Clay, M.M. (1993). *Reading recovery: A guidebook for teachers in training.* Portsmouth, NH: Heinemann.

Cohen, D.K. (1987). Behaviorism. In R.L. Gregory (Ed.), *The Oxford companion to the mind* (pp. 71–74). New York: Oxford University Press.

Cohen, V.L., & Cowen, J.E. (2007). *Literacy for children in an information age: Teaching reading, writing, and thinking.* Belmont, CA: Thomson.

Collinson, V., Killeavy, M., & Stephenson, H. (1999). Exemplary teachers: Practicing an ethic of care in England, Ireland, and the United States. *Journal for a Just and Caring Education, 5*(4), 349–366.

Compton, D.L., Fuchs, D., Fuchs, L.S., & Bryant, J.D. (2006). Selecting at-risk readers in first grade for early intervention: A two-year longitudinal study of decision rules and procedures. *Journal of Educational Psychology, 98*(2), 394–409. doi:10.1037/0022-0663.98.2.394

Conley, M.W. (2005). *Connecting standards and assessment through literacy.* Boston: Allyn & Bacon.

Conley, M.W., & Hinchman, K.A. (2004). No Child Left Behind: What it means for U.S. adolescents and what we can do about it. *Journal of Adolescent & Adult Literacy, 48*(1), 42–51. doi:10.1598/JAAL.48.1.4

Cooper, J.D., & Kiger, N.D. (2008). *Literacy assessment: Helping teachers plan instruction* (3rd ed.). Boston: Houghton Mifflin.

Cox, C. (2005). *Teaching language arts: A student- and response-centered classroom.* Boston: Allyn & Bacon.

Cramer, E.H., & Castle, M. (1994). Developing lifelong readers. In E.H. Cramer & M. Castle (Eds.), *Fostering the love of reading: The affective domain in reading education* (pp. 3–9). Newark, DE: International Reading Association.

Cranney, A.G. (1989). Why study the history of reading? *History of Reading News, 12*(4), 5.

Cubberley, E.P. (1919). *Public education in the United States.* Cambridge, MA: Riverside.

Cuevas, P.D., Schumm, J.S., Mits Cash, M., & Pilonieta, P. (2006). Reading clinics in the U.S.: A national survey of present practice. *Journal of Teacher Education in Reading, 31*(2), 5–12.

Cunningham, P.M., Hall, D.P., & Sigmon, C.M. (2000). *The teacher's guide to the Four Blocks.* Greensboro, NC: Carson-Dellosa.

Daane, M.C., Campbell, J.R., Grigg, W.S., Goodman, M.J., & Oranje. A. (2005). *Fourth-grade students reading aloud: NAEP 2002 special study of oral reading (NCES 2006-469).* Washington, DC: U.S. Department of Education, Institute of Education Sciences.

Damico, J.S. (2005, April). Multiple dimensions of literacy and conceptions of readers: Toward a more expansive view of accountability. *The Reading Teacher, 58*(7), 644–652. doi:10.1598/RT.58.7.5

Darling-Hammond, L. (1997). The quality of teaching matters the most. *Journal of Staff Development, 18*(1), 38–41.

Darling-Hammond, L. (1999). *Teacher quality and student achievement: A review of state policy evidence.* Seattle: University of Washington, Center for the Study of Teaching and Policy.

Darling-Hammond, L., Bransford, J.D., LePage, P., Hammerness, K., & Duffy, H. (2005). *Preparing teachers for a changing world: What teachers should learn and be able to do.* Boston: Jossey-Bass.

Darling-Hammond, L., & McLaughlin, M.W. (1995). Policies that support professional development in an era of reform. *Phi Delta Kappan, 76*(8), 597–604.

Darling-Hammond, L., & Snyder, J. (2000). Authentic assessment of teaching in context. *Teaching and Teacher Education, 16*(5–6), 523–545. doi:10.1016/S0742-051X(00)00015-9

Davis, F.B. (1942). Two new measures of reading ability. *Journal of Educational Psychology, 33*(5), 365–372. doi:10.1037/h0053582

De Temple, J., & Snow, C.E. (2003). Learning words from books. In A. van Kleeck, S.A. Stahl, & E.B. Bauer (Eds.), *On reading books to children: Parents and teachers* (pp. 16–36). Mahwah, NJ: Erlbaum.

Debes, J.L. (1969). The loom of visual literacy. *Audiovisual Instruction, 14*(8), 25–27.

DeFord, D.E. (1985). Validating the construct of theoretical orientation in reading instruction. *Reading Research and Instruction, 20*(3), 351–367.

Devine, T.G. (1978). Listening: What do we know after fifty years of research and theorizing? *Journal of Reading, 21*(4), 296–304.

Diez, M.E., & Blackwell, P.J. (2001). *Quality assessment for quality outcomes: Implications for the design and implementation of advanced master's programs.* Washington, DC: National Council for Accreditation of Teacher Education.

Donovan, M.S., & Cross, C.T. (2002). *Minority students in special and gifted education.* Washington, DC: National Academies Press.

Dowhower, S.L. (1994). Repeated reading revisited: Research into practice. *Reading & Writing Quarterly, 10*(4), 343–358. doi:10.1080/1057356940100406

Duffy, G.G., Roehler, L.R., Sivan, E., Rackliffe, G., Book, C., Meloth, M.S., et al. (1987). Effects of explaining the reasoning associated with using reading strategies. *Reading Research Quarterly, 22*(3), 347–368. doi:10.2307/747973

Durkin, D. (1978/1979). What classroom observations reveal about reading comprehension instruction. *Reading Research Quarterly, 14*(4), 481–538. doi:10.1598/RRQ.14.4.2

Dyson, A.H. (1994). *Social worlds of children learning to write in an urban primary school.* New York: Teachers College Press.

Edelsky, C. (2006). *With literacy and justice for all: Rethinking the social in language and education* (3rd ed.). Mahwah, NJ: Erlbaum.

Education Development Center. (2004). *Technology and teaching children to read.* Retrieved December 15, 2007, from www.neirtec.org/reading_report

Edwards, P.A. (2004). *Children's literacy development: Making it happen through school, family, and community involvement.* Boston: Allyn & Bacon.

Edwards, P.A. (2005). Introduction: Right 7. In P.A. Mason & J.S. Schumm (Eds.), *Promising practices for urban reading instruction* (pp. 308–318). Newark, DE: International Reading Association.

Ehri, L.C. (1994). Development of the ability to read words: Update. In R.B. Ruddell, M.R. Ruddell, & H. Singer (Eds.), *Theoretical models and processes of reading* (4th ed., pp. 323–358). Newark, DE: International Reading Association.

Ehri, L.C. (1995). Phases of development in learning to read words by sight. *Journal of Research in Reading, 18*(2), 116–125. doi:10.1111/j.1467-9817.1995.tb00077.x

Ehri, L.C. (1997). Learning to read and learning to spell are one and the same, almost. In C.A. Perfetti, L. Rieben, & M. Fayol (Eds.), *Learning to spell: Research, theory, and practice across languages* (pp. 237–269). Mahwah, NJ: Erlbaum.

Ehri, L.C. (1998). Grapheme-phoneme knowledge is essential for learning to read words in English. In J. Metsala & L.C. Ehri (Eds.), *Word recognition in beginning literacy* (pp. 3–40). Mahwah, NJ: Erlbaum.

Ehri, L.C. (2004). Teaching phonemic awareness and phonics: An explanation of the National Reading Panel meta-analyses. In P. McCardle & V. Chhabra (Eds.), *The voice of evidence: Bringing research to the classroom* (pp. 153–186). Baltimore: Paul H. Brookes.

Ehri, L.C., & Wilce, L.S. (1980). The influence of orthography on readers' conceptualization of the phonemic structure of words. *Applied Psycholinguistics, 1*(4), 371–385.

Ehri, L.C., & Wilce, L.S. (1985). Movement into reading: Is the first stage of printed word learning visual or phonetic? *Reading Research Quarterly, 20*(2), 163–179. doi:10.2307/747753

Elbaum, B.E., Schumm, J.S., & Vaughn, S. (1997). Urban middle elementary students' perception of grouping formats for reading instruction. *The Elementary School Journal, 97*(5), 475–500. doi:10.1086/461877

Elliott, E.J. (2003). *Assessing education candidate performance: A look at changing practices.* Washington, DC: National Council for Accreditation of Teacher Education.

Everts Danielson, K., & Everts Rogers, S. (2000). You can't pass it on if you don't have it: Encouraging lifelong reading. *Reading Horizons, 41*(1), 35–45.

Fallon, M.A., & Watts, E. (2001). Portfolio assessment and use: Navigating uncharted territory. *Teacher Education and Special Education, 24*(1), 50–57.

Fang, Z. (Ed.). (2005). *Literacy teaching and learning: Current issues and trends.* Upper Saddle River, NJ: Pearson/Merrill/Prentice Hall.

Farstrup, A.E. (2004, April/May). Reading is hot, and so is IRA. *Reading Today, 21*(5), p. 8.

Featherstone, H. (1993). Learning from the first years of classroom teaching: The journey in, the journey out. *Teachers College Record, 95*(1), 93–112.

Feiman-Nemser, S. (2001). From preparation to practice: Designing a continuum to strengthen and sustain teaching. *Teachers College Record, 103*(6), 1013–1055. doi:10.1111/0161-4681.00141

Fink, R., & Samuels, S.J. (Eds.). (2008). *Inspiring reading success: Interest and motivation in an age of high-stakes testing.* Newark, DE: International Reading Association.

Fischer, K.W. (1980). A theory of cognitive development: The control and construction of hierarchies of skills. *Psychological Review, 87*(6), 477–531. doi:10.1037/0033-295X.87.6.477

Fischer, K.W., & Knight, C.C. (1990). Cognitive development in real children: Levels and variations. In B. Presseisen (Ed.), *Styles of learning and thinking: Interactions in the classroom* (pp. 43–67). Washington, DC: National Education Association.

Fisher, D., Flood, J., Lapp, D., & Frey, N. (2004). Interactive read-alouds: Is there a common set of implementation practices? *The Reading Teacher, 58*(1), 8–17. doi:10.1598/RT.58.1.1

Fitzgerald, J. (1999). What is this thing called "balance?" *The Reading Teacher, 53*(2), 100–107.

Flesch, R. (1955). *Why Johnny can't read and what you can do about it.* New York: Harper & Row.

Fletcher, J.M., Francis, D.J., Shaywitz, S.E., Lyon, G.R., Foorman, B.R., Steubing, K.K., et al. (1998). Intelligence testing and the discrepancy model for children with learning disabilities. *Learning Disabilities Research & Practice, 13*(4), 186–203.

Flood, J., & Lapp, D. (1989). Reporting reading progress: A comparison portfolio for parents. *The Reading Teacher, 42*(7), 508–514.

Flood, J., Lapp, D., Squire, J.R., & Jensen J.M. (Eds.). (2002). *Handbook of research on the teaching of the English language arts* (2nd ed.). Mahwah, NJ: Erlbaum.

Foegen, A., Espin, C.A., Allinder, R.M., & Markell, M.A. (2001). Translating research into practice: Preservice teachers' beliefs bout curriculum-based measurement. *The Journal of Special Education, 34*(4), 226–236. doi:10.1177/002246690103400405

Fountas, I.C., & Pinnell, G.S. (1996). *Guided reading: Good first reading for all children.* Portsmouth, NH: Heinemann.

Fountas, I.C., & Pinnell, G.S. (2001). *Guiding readers and writers (Grades 3–6): Teaching comprehension, genre, and content literacy.* Portsmouth, NH: Heinemann.

Freiberg, J. (1999). *Perceiving, behaving, becoming, and the schools we need.* Alexandria, VA: Association for Supervision and Curriculum Development.

Fresch, M.J. (Ed.). (2008). *An essential history of current reading practices.* Newark, DE: International Reading Association.

Fries, C.C. (1963). *Linguistics and reading.* New York: Holt, Rinehart and Winston.

Frith, U. (1985). Beneath the surface of developmental dyslexia. In K. Patterson, J. Marshall, & M. Coltheart (Eds.), *Surface dyslexia: Neuropsychological and cognitive studies of phonological reading* (pp. 301–330). London: Erlbaum.

Fry, E.B. (1971). The orangoutang score. *The Reading Teacher, 24*(4), 360–362.

Fuchs, L.S., Fuchs, D., Hosp, M.K., & Jenkins, J.R. (2001). Oral reading fluency as an indicator of reading competence: A theoretical, empirical and historical analysis. *Scientific Studies of Reading, 5*(3), 239–258. doi:10.1207/S1532799XSSR0503_3

Funk, H.D., & Funk, G.D. (1989). Guidelines for developing listening skills. *The Reading Teacher, 42*(9), 660–663.

Futrell, M.H., Holmes, D.H., Christie, J.L., & Cushman, E.J. (1995). *Linking education reform and teachers' professional development: The efforts of nine school districts.* Washington, DC: The George Washington

University, Graduate School of Education and Human Development, Center for Policy Studies, Institute for Curriculum, Standards, and Technology.

Gambrell, L.B. (1996). Creating classroom cultures that foster reading motivation. *The Reading Teacher, 50*(1), 14–25.

Garcia, E.E., & Cuellar, D. (2006). Who are these linguistically and culturally diverse students? *Teachers College Record, 108*(11), 2220–2246. doi:10.1111/j.1467-9620.2006.00780.x

Garcia, G.E. (2000). Bilingual children's reading. In M.L. Kamil, P.B. Mosenthal, P.D. Pearson, & R. Barr (Eds.), *Handbook of reading research* (Vol. 3, pp. 813–834). Mahwah, NJ: Erlbaum.

Gentry, J.R., & Gillet, J.W. (1993). *Teaching kids to spell*. Portsmouth, NH: Heinemann.

Gersten, R., & Brengelman, S. (1996). The quest to translate research into classroom practice: The emerging knowledge base. *Remedial and Special Education, 17*(2), 67–74.

Gersten, R., & Dimino, J. (2001). The realities of translating research into classroom practice. *Learning Disabilities Research & Practice, 16*(2), 120–130. doi:10.1111/0938-8982.00013

Gersten, R., Vaughn, S., Deshler, D., & Schiller, E. (1997). What we know about using research findings: Implications for improving special education practice. *Journal of Learning Disabilities, 30*(5), 466–476.

Gersten, R., & Woodward, J. (1992). Refining the working knowledge of experienced teachers. *Educational Leadership, 49*(7), 34–38.

Glazer, S.M. (1989). Oral language and literacy development. In D.S. Strickland & L.M. Morrow (Eds.), *Emerging literacy: Young children learn to read and write* (pp. 16–26). Newark, DE: International Reading Association.

Good, R.H., Kaminski, R.A., Smith, S., Laimon, D., & Dill, D. (2001). *Dynamic indicators of basic early literacy skills* (5th ed.). Eugene: University of Oregon, Institute for Development of Educational Achievement.

Goodman, K.S. (1965, October). A linguistic study of cues and miscues in reading. *Elementary English, 42*, 639–643.

Goodman, K.S. (1967). Reading: A psycholinguistic guessing game. *Journal of the Reading Specialist, 6*(1), 126–135.

Goodman, K.S. (1985). Unity in reading. In H. Singer & R.B. Ruddell (Eds.), *Theoretical models and processes of reading* (pp. 813–840). Newark, DE: International Reading Association.

Goodman, K.S. (2006). *The truth about DIBELS: What it is, what it does*. Portsmouth, NH: Heinemann.

Gough, P.B. (1972). One second of reading. In J.F. Kavanagh & I.G. Mattingly (Eds.), *Language by ear and by eye: The relationship between speech and reading* (pp. 331–358). Cambridge, MA: MIT Press.

Grant, R.A., & Wong, S.D. (2003). Barriers to literacy for language-minority learners: An argument for change in the literacy education profession. *Journal of Adolescent & Adult Literacy, 46*(5), 386–394. doi:10.1598/JAAL.46.5.2

Greene Brabham, E.., & Lynch-Brown, C. (2002). Effects of teachers' reading-aloud styles on vocabulary acquisition and comprehension of students in early elementary grades. *Journal of Educational Psychology, 94*(3), 465–473. doi:10.1037/0022-0663.94.3.465

Greenleaf, C.L., & Schoenbach, R. (2001, January). *Close readings: A study of key issues in the use of literacy learning cases for the professional development of secondary teachers*. Report to the Spencer Foundation. San Francisco: Strategic Literacy Initiative, WestEd.

Grossman, P., & Wineburg, S. (1998). Creating a community of learners among high school teachers. *Phi Delta Kappan, 79*(5), 350–353.

Grossman, P., Wineburg, S., & Woolworth, S. (2001). Toward a theory of teacher community. *Teachers College Record, 103*(6), 942–1012. doi:10.1111/0161-4681.00140

Guskey, T.R. (2007). Multiple sources of evidence: An analysis of stakeholders' perceptions of various indicators of student learning. *Educational Measurement: Issues and Practice, 26*(1), 19–27. doi:10.1111/j.1745-3992.2007.00085.x

Guthrie, J.T., & Knowles, K.T. (2001). Promoting reading motivation. In L. Verhoeven & C. Snow (Eds.), *Literacy and motivation: Reading engagement in individuals and groups* (pp. 159–176). Mahwah, NJ: Erlbaum.

Guthrie, J.T., & Wigfield, A. (1999). How motivation fits into a science of reading. *Scientific Studies of Reading, 3*(3), 199–206. doi:10.1207/s1532799xssr0303_1

Guthrie, J.T., & Wigfield, A. (2000). Engagement and motivation in reading. In M.L. Kamil, P.B. Mosenthal, P.D. Pearson, & R. Barr (Eds.), *Handbook of reading research* (Vol. 3, pp. 403–422). New York: Erlbaum.

Haager, D., Klingner, J.K., & Vaughn, S. (2007). *Evidence-based reading practices for response to intervention.* Baltimore: Paul H. Brookes.

Hakuta, K. (1997). *Memorandum on READ Institute press release on NRC Report.* Retrieved June 15, 2007, from ourworld.compuserve.com/homepages/JWCRAWFORD/hakuta.htm

Hall, T. (2002). *NCAC differentiated instruction: Effective classroom practices report.* Wakefield, MA: National Center on Assessing the General Curriculum. Retrieved September 20, 2007, from www.cast.org/ncac/index.cfm?i=2876

Harp, B. (2006). *The handbook of literacy assessment and evaluation* (3rd ed.). Norwood, MA: Christopher-Gordon.

Harp, B., & Brewer, J. (2005). *The informed reading teacher: Research-based practice.* Upper Saddle River, NJ: Pearson Education.

Harris, T.L., & Hodges, R.E. (Eds.). (1981). *A dictionary of reading and related terms.* Newark, DE: International Reading Association.

Harris, T.L., & Hodges, R.E. (Eds.). (1999). *The literacy dictionary: The vocabulary of reading and writing.* Newark, DE: International Reading Association.

Harry, B., & Klingner, J.K. (2005). *Why are so many minority students in special education: Understanding race and disability in school.* New York: Teachers College Press.

Havighurst, R.J. (1952). *Developmental tasks and education.* New York: David McKay.

Hawley, W.D., & Valli, L. (1999). The essentials of effective professional development: A new consensus. In L. Darling-Hammond & G. Sykes (Eds.), *Teaching as the learning profession: Handbook of policy and practice* (pp. 127–150). San Francisco: Jossey-Bass.

Hayes, L.L., & Robnolt, V.J. (2007). Data-driven professional development: The professional development plan for a Reading Excellence Act school. *Reading Research and Instruction, 46*(2), 95–120.

Heacox, D. (2002). *Differentiating instruction in the regular classroom: How to reach and teach all learners, grades 3–12.* Minneapolis, MN: Free Spirit Publishing.

Heath, S.B. (1982). What no bedtime story means: Narrative skills at home and school. *Language in Society, 11*(1), 49–76.

Heath, S.B. (1993). The madness(es) of reading and writing ethnography. *Anthropology & Education Quarterly, 24*(3), 256–268. doi:10.1525/aeq.1993.24.3.05x0971i

Hefflin, B.R., & Barksdale-Ladd, M.A. (2003). African American children's literature that helps students find themselves: Selection guidelines for grades K–3. In P.A. Mason & J.S. Schumm (Eds.), *Promising practices for urban reading instruction* (pp. 203–219). Newark, DE: International Reading Association.

Heller, R.S. (1990). The role of hypermedia in education: A look at the research issues. *Journal of Research on Computing in Education, 22*(4), 431–441.

Herman, J.L. (1997). Large-scale assessment in support of school reform: Lessons in the search for alternative measures. *International Journal of Educational Research, 27*(5), 395–413.

Hewett, G. (1995). *A portfolio primer: Teaching, collecting, and assessing student writing.* Portsmouth, NH: Heinemann.

Hewitt, M.A., & Homan, S.P. (2004). Readability level of standardized test items and student performance: The forgotten validity variable. *Reading Research and Instruction, 43*(2), 1–16.

Hidi, S., & Harackiewicz, J. (2000). Motivating the academically unmotivated: A critical issue for the 21st century. *Review of Educational Research, 70*(2), 151–179.

Hiebert, E.H. (2005). In pursuit of an effective, efficient vocabulary curriculum for elementary students. In E.H. Hiebert & M.L. Kamil (Eds.), *Teaching and learning vocabulary: Bringing research to practice* (pp. 243–263). Mahwah, NJ: Erlbaum.

Hiebert, E.H., & Calfee, R.C. (1989). Advancing academic literacy through teachers' assessments. *Educational Leadership, 46*(7), 50–54.

Hill, J.D., & Flynn, K.M. (2006). *Classroom instruction that works with English language learners.* Alexandria, VA: Association for Supervision and Curriculum Development.

Hoffman, J.V., Sailors, M., Duffy, G.R., & Beretvas, N. (2004). The effective elementary classroom literacy environment: Examining the validity of the TEX-IN3 observation system. *Journal of Literacy Research*, 36(3), 289–320. doi:10.1207/s15548430jlr3603_3

Huerta, G.C. (2009). *Educational foundations: Diverse histories, diverse perspectives.* Florence, KY: Wadsworth, Cengage Learning.

Huey, E.B. (1908). *The psychology and pedagogy of reading.* New York: Macmillan.

International Reading Association. (1994). Who is teaching our children? Implications of the use of aids in Chapter 1. *ERS Spectrum*, 12(2), 28–34.

International Reading Association. (1999). *High-stakes assessments in reading* (Position statement). Newark, DE: Author.

International Reading Association. (2000a). *Excellent reading teachers* (Position statement). Newark, DE: Author.

International Reading Association. (2000b). *Making a difference means making it different: Honoring children's rights to excellent reading instruction* (Position statement). Newark, DE: Author.

International Reading Association. (2002a). *Evidence-based reading instruction: Putting the National Reading Panel Report into practice.* Newark, DE: Author.

International Reading Association. (2002b). *Resolution: On buyer be wary.* Retrieved November 3, 2006, from www.reading.org/downloads/resolutions/resolution02_buyer_be_wary.pdf#search='reading%20 program%20evaluations%20from%20publishers

International Reading Association. (2002c). *What is evidence-based reading instruction?* (Position statement). Newark, DE: Author.

International Reading Association. (2004). *Standards for reading professionals—Revised 2003.* Newark, DE: Author.

International Reading Association. (2007). *Teaching reading well: A synthesis of the International Reading Association's research on teacher preparation for reading instruction.* Newark, DE: Author. Retrieved May 30, 2008, from www.reading.org/resources/issues/reports/teacher_education.html

International Reading Association. (2008). *Code of ethics.* Newark, DE: Author. Retrieved August 6, 2008, from www.reading.org/association/about/code.html

Invernizzi, M.A., Landrum, T.J., Howell, J.L., & Warley, H.P. (2005). Toward the peaceful coexistence of test developers, policymakers, and teachers in an era of accountability. *The Reading Teacher*, 58(7), 610–618. doi:10.1598/RT.58.7.2

Irwin, J.W. (2006). *Teaching reading comprehension processes* (3rd ed.). Boston: Allyn & Bacon.

Ivey, G. (1999). A multicase study in the middle school: Complexities among young adolescent readers. *Reading Research Quarterly*, 34(2), 172–192. doi:10.1598/RRQ.34.2.3

Jehlen, A. (2007). Don't be left behind. *NEA Today*, 25(8), 19.

Johns, J.L., & VanLeirsburg, P. (1994). Promoting the reading habit: Considerations and strategies. In E.H. Cramer & M. Castle (Eds.), *Fostering the love of reading: The affective domain in reading education* (pp. 91–103). Newark, DE: International Reading Association.

Johnston, P. (1985). Understanding reading disability: A case study approach. *Harvard Educational Review*, 55(2), 153–177.

Johnston, P. (2005). Literacy assessment and the future. *The Reading Teacher*, 58(7), 684–686. doi:10.1598/RT.58.7.9

Joint Committee on Testing Practices. (2004). *Code of fair testing practices in education.* Retrieved May 31, 2007, from www.apa.org/science/FinalCode.pdf

Jongsma, K.S. (1989). Portfolio assessment. *The Reading Teacher*, 43(3), 264–265.

Juel, C. (1988). Learning to read and write: A longitudinal study of 54 children from first through fourth grade. *Journal of Educational Psychology*, 80(4), 437–447. doi:10.1037/0022-0663.80.4.437

Juel, C. (1991). Beginning reading. In R. Barr, M.L. Kamil, P.B. Mosenthal, & P.D. Pearson (Eds.), *Handbook of reading research* (Vol. 2, pp. 759–788). White Plains, NY: Longman.

Kame'enui, E.J. (2002, May). *Final report on the analysis of reading assessment instruments for K–3.* Eugene: University of Oregon, Institute for the Development of Educational Achievement.

Kamil, M.L., Intrator, S., & Kim, H. (2000). The effects of other technologies on literacy and literacy learning. In M.L. Kamil, P.B. Mosenthal, P.D. Pearson, & R. Barr (Eds.), *Handbook of research on teaching the English language arts* (pp. 771–790). Mahwah, NJ: Erlbaum.

Kamil, M.L., Mosenthal, P.B., Pearson, P.D., & Barr R. (Eds.). (2000). *Handbook of reading research* (Vol. 3). Mahwah, NJ: Erlbaum.

Katz, A. (1988). The academic context. In P. Lowe, Jr., & C.W. Stansfield (Eds.), *Second language proficiency assessment: Current issues* (pp. 178–201). Englewood Cliffs, NJ: Prentice Hall Regents.

Kaufman, P., & Alt, M.N. (2004). *Dropout rates in the United States: 2001*. Washington, DC: U.S. Department of Education.

Kintsch, W. (1977). *Memory and cognition*. New York: Wiley.

Kintsch, W., & Kintsch, E. (2005). Comprehension. In S.G. Paris & S.A. Stahl (Eds.), *Current issues in reading comprehension and assessment* (pp. 71–92). Mahwah, NJ: Erlbaum.

Kinzer, C.K., & Risko, V.J. (1998). Multimedia and enhanced learning: Transforming preservice education. In D. Reinking, M. McKenna, L. Labbo, & R. Kieffer (Eds.), *Handbook of technology and literacy: Transformations in a post-typographic world* (pp. 185–202). Hillsdale, NJ: Erlbaum.

Kinzer, C.K., Singer Gabella, M., & Rieth, H. (1994). An argument for using multimedia and anchored instruction to facilitate mildly disabled students' learning of literacy and social studies. *Technology and Disability Quarterly, 3*(2), 117–128.

Klenowski, V. (2000). Portfolios: Promoting teaching. *Assessment in Education: Principles, Policies, and Practice, 7*(2), 215–236. doi:10.1080/713613329

Klingner, J.K., & Edwards, P.A. (2006). Cultural considerations with response to intervention models. *Reading Research Quarterly, 41*(1), 108–117. doi:10.1598/RRQ.41.1.6

Klingner, J.K., & Vaughn, S. (1999). Promoting reading comprehension, content learning, and English acquisition through Collaborative Strategic Reading (CSR). *The Reading Teacher, 52*(7), 738–747.

Kohn, A. (2000). *The case against standardized testing: Raising the scores, ruining the schools*. Portsmouth, NH: Heinemann.

Krashen, S. (2001). More smoke and mirrors: A critique of the National Reading Panel Report on fluency. *Phi Delta Kappan, 83*(2), 119–123.

Krashen, S. (2002). The NRP comparison of whole language and phonics: Ignoring the crucial variable in reading. *Talking Points, 13*(3), 22–28.

Kristeva, J. (1984). *Revolution in poetic language*. New York: Columbia University Press.

Kuhn, M.R., & Stahl, S.A. (2003). Fluency: A review of developmental and remedial practices. *Journal of Educational Psychology, 95*(1), 3–21. doi:10.1037/0022-0663.95.1.3

Kulik, J. (2003). *Effects of using instructional technology in elementary and secondary schools: What controlled evaluation studies say*. Retrieved August 12, 2007, from www.sri.com/policy/csted/reports/sandt/it/Kulik_ITinK-12_Main_Report.pdf

LaBerge, D., & Samuels, S.J. (1974). Toward a theory of automatic information processing in reading. *Cognitive Psychology, 6*(2), 293–323. doi:10.1016/0010-0285(74)90015-2

Langer, G.M., Colton, A.B., & Goff, L.S. (2003). *Collaborative analysis of student work: Improving teaching and learning*. Baltimore: Association for Supervision and Curriculum Development.

Langer, J.A. (1991). Literacy and schooling: A sociocognitive perspective. In E. Hiebert (Ed.), *Literacy for a diverse society* (pp. 9–27). New York: Teachers College Press.

Langer, J.A. (2002). *Effective literacy instruction: Building successful reading and writing programs*. Urbana, IL: National Council of Teachers of English.

Lesaux, N., & Geva, E. (2006). Synthesis: Development of literacy in language-minority students. In D. August & T. Shanahan (Eds.), *Developing literacy in second-language learners. Report of the National Literacy Panel on language-minority children and youth* (pp. 53–74). Mahwah, NJ: Erlbaum.

Leu, D.J., Jr. (2002). The new literacies: Research on reading instruction with the Internet. In A.E. Farstrup & S.J. Samuels (Eds.), *What research has to say about reading instruction* (3rd ed., pp. 310–336). Newark, DE: International Reading Association.

Leu, D.J., Jr. & Kinzer, C.K. (1991). *Effective reading instruction in the elementary grades* (2nd ed.). Columbus, OH: Merrill.

Lewis, J., Jongsma, K.S., & Berger, A. (2005). *Educators on the frontline: Advocacy strategies for your classroom, your school, and your profession*. Newark, DE: International Reading Association.

Liberman, I.Y., Shankweiler, D., Fischer, F.W., & Carter, B. (1974). Explicit syllable and phoneme segmentation in the young child. *Journal of Experimental Child Psychology, 18*(2), 201–212. doi:10.1016/0022-0965(74)90101-5

Liebars, C.S. (1999). Journals and portfolios: Alternative assessment for preservice teachers. *Teaching Children Mathematics, 6*(3), 164–169.

Lieberman, A., & Grolnick, M. (1996). Networks and reform in American education. *Teachers College Record, 98*(1), 7–45.

Linn, R.L. (2001). A century of standardized testing: Controversies and pendulum swings. *Educational Assessment, 7*(1), 29–38. doi:10.1207/S15326977EA0701_4

Lukin, L.E., Bandalos, D.L., Eckhout, T.J., & Mickelson, K. (2004). Facilitating the development of assessment literacy. *Educational Measurement: Issues and Practice, 23*(2), 26–32. doi:10.1111/j.1745-3992.2004.tb00156.x

Maclellan, E. (2004). Authenticity in assessment tasks: A heuristic exploration of academics' perceptions. *Higher Education Research & Development, 23*(1), 19–33. doi:10.1080/0729436032000168478

Mann, D., Shakeshaft, C., Becker, J., & Kottkamp, R. (1999). *West Virginia story: Achievement gains from a statewide comprehensive instructional technology program*. Retrieved October 31, 2006, from www.mff.org/publications/publications.taf?page=155

Manson, T.J. (1999). *Cross-ethnic, cross-racial dynamics of instruction: Implication for teacher education*. (Report No. UD032861). Clarksville, TN: Austin Peay State University. (ERIC Document Reproduction Service No. ED429141)

Martin, L.M. (2003). Web reading: Linking text and technology. *The Reading Teacher, 56*(8), 735–737.

Martinez, M.G., & Teale, W.H. (1993). Teaching storybook reading style: A comparison of six teachers. *Research in the Teaching of English, 27*(2), 175–199.

Marzano, R.J., Pickering, D.J., & Pollock, J.E. (2001). *Classroom instruction that works: Research-based strategies for increasing student achievement* Alexandria, VA: Association for Supervision and Curriculum Development.

Massey, S.R. (2007). *Effects of variations of text previews on the oral reading fluency of second grade students*. Unpublished dissertation proposal, University of Miami, Coral Gables, Florida.

Mastropieri, M.A., & Scruggs, T.E. (2007). *The inclusive classroom: Strategies for effective instruction* (3rd ed.). Upper Saddle River, NJ: Pearson Merrill/Prentice Hall.

Mastropieri, M.A., Scruggs, T.E., Bakken, J.P., & Whedon, C. (1996). Reading comprehension: A synthesis of research in learning disabilities. In T.E. Scruggs & M.A. Mastropieri (Eds.), *Advances in learning and behavioral disabilities* (Vol. 10, pp. 201–227). Greenwich, CT: JAI Press.

McCaster, J.C. (1998). "Doing" literature: Using drama to build literacy classrooms: The segue for a few struggling readers. *The Reading Teacher, 51*(7), 574–584.

McCormick, L., & Schiefelbusch, R.L. (1984). *Early language intervention: An introduction*. Columbus, OH: Merrill.

McGee, L.M., & Richgels, D.J. (2004). *Literacy's beginnings: Supporting young readers and writers* (4th ed.). Boston: Allyn & Bacon.

McGee, L.M., & Richgels, D.J. (2007). *Literacy's beginnings: Supporting young readers and writers* (5th ed.). Boston: Allyn & Bacon.

McGill-Franzen, A., & Allington, R.L. (1991). The gridlock of low reading achievement: Perspectives on practice and policy. *Remedial and Special Education, 12*(3), 20–30.

McGill-Franzen, A., Allington, R.L., Yokoi, L., & Brooks, G. (1999). Putting books in the classroom seems necessary but not sufficient. *The Journal of Educational Research, 93*(2), 67–74.

McGuinness, D. (2004). *Early reading instruction: What science really tells us about how to teach reading*. Cambridge, MA: MIT Press.

McKenna, M.C. (1998). Electronic text and the transformation of beginning reading. In D. Reinking, M.C. McKenna, L.D. Labbo, & R.D. Keiffer (Eds.), *Handbook of literacy and technology: Transformations in a post-typographic world* (pp. 45–59). Mahwah, NJ: Erlbaum.

McKenna, M.C., & Kear, D.J. (1990). Measuring attitude toward reading: A new tool for teachers. *The Reading Teacher, 43*(8), 626–639. doi:10.1598/RT.43.8.3

McLane, J.B., & McNamee, G.D. (1997, March). *Cultural transformation and ownership in literacy development: Moving from community to school discourse patterns.* Paper presented at the meeting of the American Educational Research Association, Chicago, IL.

McLaughlin, M., & Kennedy, A. (1993). *A classroom teacher's guide to performance-based assessment.* Boston: Houghton Mifflin.

McLaughlin, M., & Vogt, M.E. (1997). *Portfolios in teacher education.* Newark, DE: International Reading Association.

McMillan, J.H. (2001). *Classroom assessment: Principles and practice for effective instruction* (2nd ed.). Boston: Allyn & Bacon.

McMillan, J.H. (2003). Understanding and improving teachers' classroom assessment decision making: Implications for theory and practice. *Educational Measurement: Issues and Practice, 22*(4), 34–43. doi:10.1111/j.1745-3992.2003.tb00142.x

McNabb, M.L. (2005). Raising the bar on technology research in English language arts. *Journal of Research on Technology in Education, 38*(1), 113–119.

McNabb, M.L., Hassel, B., & Steiner, L. (2002). Literacy learning on the Net: An exploratory study. *Reading Online, 5*(10). Retrieved October 27, 2006, from www.readingonline.org/articles/art_index .asp?HREF=/articles/mcnabb/index.html

Meadows, R.B., Dyal, A.B., & Wright, J.V. (1998). Preparing educational leaders through the use of portfolio assessment: An alternative comprehensive examination. *Journal of Instructional Psychology, 25*(2), 94–99.

Meier, T. (2003). "Why can't she remember that?" The importance of storybook reading in multilingual, multicultural classrooms. *The Reading Teacher, 57*(3), 242–252.

Merriam-Webster, Inc. (2003). *Merriam-Webster's collegiate dictionary* (11th ed.). New York: Author.

Miller, G.A. (1956). The magical number seven, plus or minus two: Some limits on our capacity for processing information. *Psychological Review, 63*(2), 81–97. doi:10.1037/h0043158

Moats, L.C. (1994). The missing foundation in teacher education: Knowledge about the structure of language. *Annals of Dyslexia, 44*(1), 81–102. doi:10.1007/BF02648156

Moats, L.C. (1999). *Teaching reading is rocket science: What expert teachers of reading should know and be able to do.* Washington, DC: American Federation of Teachers.

Moll, L.C., & Gonzalez, N. (1994). Critical issues: Lessons from research with language-minority children. *Journal of Reading Behavior, 26*(4), 439–456.

Monaghan, E.J. (1989). Why study the history of reading? *History of Reading News, 12*(4), 5–6.

Monaghan, E.J., & Hartman, D.K. (2000). Undertaking historical research in literacy. In R. Barr, M.L. Kamil, P.B. Mosenthal, & P.D. Pearson (Eds.), *Handbook of reading research* (Vol. 3, pp. 109–121). White Plains, NY: Longman.

Montgomery, D.J., & Marks, L.J. (2006). Using technology to build independence in writing for students with disabilities. *Preventing School Failure, 50*(3), 33–38. doi:10.3200/PSFL.50.3.33-38

Mooney, M.E. (1990). *Reading to, with, and by children.* Katonah, NY: Richard C. Owen.

Morris, D. (1999). Preventing reading failure in the primary grades. In T. Shanahan & F. Rodriquez-Brown (Eds.), *National Reading Conference Yearbook, 48,* 17–38.

Morrow, L.M. (1993). *Literacy development in the early years: Helping children read and write* (2nd ed.). Boston: Allyn & Bacon.

Morrow, L.M. (2003). Motivating lifelong voluntary readers. In J. Flood, D. Lapp, J.R. Squire, & J.M. Jensen (Eds.), *Handbook of research on teaching the English language arts* (2nd ed., pp. 857–867). Mahwah, NJ: Erlbaum.

Morrow, L.M. (2005). *Literacy development in the early years: Helping children read and write.* Boston: Pearson, Allyn & Bacon.

Morrow, L.M. (2007). *Developing literacy in preschool. Tools for teaching literacy.* New York: Guilford.

Morrow, L.M., & Gambrell, L.B. (2002). Literature-based instruction in the early years. In S.B. Neuman & D.K. Dickinson (Eds.), *Handbook of early literacy research* (pp. 348–360). New York: Guilford.

Morrow, L.M., Tracy, D.H., Woo, D.G., & Pressley, M. (1999). Characteristics of exemplary first-grade literacy instruction. *The Reading Teacher, 52*(5), 462–476.

Morrow, L.M., & Weinstein, C.S. (1982). Increasing children's use of literature through program and physical design changes. *The Elementary School Journal, 85*(2), 133–137.

Murphy, S., Shannon, P., Johnston, P., & Hansen, J. (1998). *Fragile evidence: A critique of reading assessment.* Mahwah, NJ: Erlbaum.

Nagy, W.E., & Herman, P.A. (1987). Breadth and depth of vocabulary knowledge: Implications for acquisition and instruction. In M. McKeown & M. Curtis (Eds.), *The nature of vocabulary acquisition* (pp. 19–35). Hillsdale, NJ: Erlbaum.

Nagy, W.E., & Scott, J.A. (2000). Vocabulary processes. In M.L. Kamil, P.B. Mosenthal, P.D. Pearson, & R. Barr (Eds.), *Handbook of reading research* (Vol. 3, pp. 269–284). Mahwah, NJ: Erlbaum.

Nathan, R.G., & Stanovich, K.E. (1991). The causes and consequences of differences in reading fluency. *Theory Into Practice, 30*(3), 176–184.

National Board for Professional Teaching Standards. (2007). *Welcome to the national board certification process.* Retrieved June 27, 2007, from www.nbpts.org/for_candidates

National Center for Education Statistics. (2003). *The nation's report card: Reading highlights 2003.* Retrieved September 20, 2006, from nces.ed.gov/nationsreportcard/pdf/main2003/2004452.pdf

National Commission on Teaching and America's Future. (1996). *What matters most: Teaching for America's future.* Woodbridge, VA: Author.

National Council for Accreditation of Teacher Education. (2002). *Professional standards for the accreditation of schools, colleges, and departments of education.* Washington, DC: Author. Retrieved December 29, 2004, from www.ncate.org/documents/unit_stnds_2002.pdf

National Council of Teachers of English. (1997). *On the importance of a print-rich classroom environment.* Retrieved June 28, 2007, from www.ncte.org/about/over/positions/category/literacy/107510.htm

National Council of Teachers of English. (2004). *On reading, learning to read, and effective reading instruction: An overview of what we know and how we know it.* Retrieved August 15, 2007, from www.ncte.org/about/policy/guidelines/118620.htm

National Institute of Child Health and Human Development. (2000). *Report of the National Reading Panel. Teaching children to read: An evidence-based assessment of the scientific research literature on reading and its implications for reading instruction (NIH Publication No. 00-4769).* Washington, DC: U.S. Government Printing Office.

National Reading Council. (2001). *Knowing what students know: The science and design of educational assessment.* Washington, DC: National Academy Press.

Neill, D.M., & Medina, N.J. (1989). Standardized testing: Harmful to educational health. *Phi Delta Kappan, 70*(9), 688–697.

Neuman, S.B., Copple, C., Bredekamp, S. (2001). *El aprendizaje de la lectura y la escritura: Practicas apropiadas para el desarrollo infantil (Learning to read and write: developmentally appropriate practices for young children).* Report: ED464330. Washington, DC: National Association for the Education of Young Children.

Nicholson, J.M. (2000). *Examining evidence of the consequential aspects of validity in a curriculum-embedded performance assessment.* Unpublished doctoral dissertation, University of Michigan, Ann Arbor.

No Child Left Behind Act of 2001, Pub L. No. 107–110, 115 Stat. 1425. (2002).

Noyes, D. (2000, November 5–7). Developing the disposition to be a reader: The educator's role. In *Issues in early childhood education: Curriculum, teacher education, & dissemination of information.* Proceedings of the Lilian Katz Symposium, Champaign, IL. (ERIC Document Reproduction Service No. ED470902)

Nye, B., Konstantopoulos, S., & Hedges, L.V. (2004). How large are teacher effects? *Educational Evaluation and Policy Analysis, 26*(3), 237–257.

Opitz, M.F., & Ford, M.P. (2006). Assessment can be friendly! *The Reading Teacher, 59*(8), 814–816. doi:10.1598/RT.59.8.10

Orlich, D.C., Harder, R.J., Callahan, R.C., Trevisan, M.S., & Brown, A.H. (2004). *Teaching strategies: A guide to effective instruction* (7th ed.). Boston: Houghton Mifflin.

Ortiz, A.A., & Yates, J.R. (2001). A framework for serving English language learners with disabilities. *Journal of Special Education Leadership, 14*(2), 72–80.

Padak, N., & Rasinski, T.V. (2008). *Evidence-based instruction in reading: A professional development guide to fluency.* Boston: Allyn & Bacon.

Pang, V., Colvin, C., Tran, M., & Barbra, R. (1992). Beyond chopsticks and dragons: Selecting Asian-American literature for children. *The Reading Teacher, 46*(3), 216–224.

Paris, S.G., & Carpenter, R.D. (2003). FAQs about IRIs. *The Reading Teacher, 56*(6), 578–580.

Partridge, H., Invernizzi, M., Meier, J., & Sullivan, A. (2003). Linking assessment and instruction via web-based technology: A case study of a statewide early literacy initiative. *Reading Online, 7*(3), Retrieved October 7, 2008, from www.readingonline.org/articles/art_index.asp?HREF=partridge/index.html

Paterson, W.A., Henry, J.J., O'Quin, K., Ceprano, M.A., & Blue, E.V. (2003). Investigating the effectiveness of an integrated learning system on early emergent readers. *Reading Research Quarterly, 38*(2), 172–207. doi:10.1598/RRQ.38.2.2

Paul, D.G. (2004). The train has left: The No Child Left Behind Act leaves black and Latino literacy learners waiting at the station. *Journal of Adolescent & Adult Literacy, 47*(8), 648–657.

Pavlov, I.P. (1928). *Lectures on conditioned reflexes.* New York: International.

Pearson, P.D., Barr, R., Kamil, M.L., & Mosenthal, P.B. (1984). *Handbook of reading research.* New York: Longman.

Pearson, P.D., Roehler, L.R., Dole, J.A., & Duffy, G.G. (1992). Developing expertise in reading comprehension. In S.J. Samuels & A.E. Farstrup (Eds.), *What research has to say about reading instruction* (2nd ed., pp. 145–199). Newark, DE: International Reading Association.

Pearson, P.D., & Stephens, D. (1994). Learning about literacy: A 30-year journey. In R.B. Ruddell, M.R. Ruddell, & H. Singer (Eds.), *Theoretical models and processes of reading* (4th ed., pp. 22–42). Newark, DE: International Reading Association.

Perfetti, C.A., Beck, I.L., Bell, L., & Hughes, C. (1987). Phonemic knowledge and learning to read are reciprocal: A longitudinal study of first grade children. *Merrill-Palmer Quarterly, 33*(3), 283–319.

Phillips, L.M., & Walker, L. (1987). Three views of language and their influence on instruction in reading and writing. *Educational Theory, 37*(2), 135–144. doi:10.1111/j.1741-5446.1987.00135.x

Piaget, J. (1969). *The mechanisms of perception.* New York: Basic.

Pinnell, G.S., & Jaggar, A.M. (2003). Oral language: Speaking and listening in elementary classrooms. In J. Flood, D. Lapp, J.R. Squire, & J.M. Jensen (Eds.), *Handbook of research on teaching the English language arts* (2nd ed., pp. 881–913). Mahwah, NJ: Erlbaum.

Pinnell, G.S., Lyons, C.A., DeFord, D.E., Bryk, A., & Seltzer, M. (1994). Comparing instructional models for the literacy education of high-risk first graders. *Reading Research Quarterly, 29*(1), 8–39. doi:10.2307/747736

Pinnell, G.S., Pikulski, J.J., Wixson, K.K., Campbell, J.R., Gough, P.B., & Beatty, A.S. (1995). *Listening to children read aloud.* Washington, DC: Office of Educational Research and Improvement, U.S. Department of Education.

Plotnik, R. (1999). *Introduction to psychology* (5th ed.). Belmont, CA: Wadsworth.

Popham, W.J. (1997). What's wrong—and what's right—with rubrics. *Educational Leadership, 55*(2), 72–75.

Popham, W.J. (2006). Content standards: The unindicted co-conspirator. *Educational Leadership, 64*(1), 87–88.

Pressley, M. (1998). *Reading instruction that works: The case for balanced teaching.* New York: Guilford.

Pressley, M. (2000). What should comprehension instruction be the instruction of? In M.L. Kamil, P.B. Mosenthal, P.D. Pearson, & R. Barr (Eds.), *Handbook of reading research* (Vol. 3, pp. 545–561). Mahwah, NJ: Erlbaum.

Pressley, M. (2002). *Reading instruction that works: The case for balanced teaching.* New York: Guilford.

Pressley, M. (2003). A few things reading educators should know about instructional experiments. *The Reading Teacher, 57*(1), 64–71.

Pressley, M., & Afflerbach, P. (1995). *Verbal protocols of reading: The nature of constructively responsive reading.* Hillsdale, NJ: Erlbaum.

Pressley, M., Allington, R.L., Wharton-McDonald, R., Block, C.C., & Morrow, L.M. (2001). *Learning to read: Lessons from exemplary first-grade classrooms.* New York: Guilford.

Pressley, M., & Block, C.C. (2002). Summing up: What comprehension instruction could be. In C.C. Block & M. Pressley (Eds.), *Comprehension instruction: Research-based best practices* (pp. 383–392). New York: Guilford

Pressley, M., Johnson, C.J., Symons, S., McGoldrick, J.A., & Kurita, J.A. (1989). Strategies that improve children's memory and comprehension of text. *The Elementary School Journal, 90*(1), 3–32.

Pressley, M., & Wharton-McDonald, R. (1997). Skilled comprehension and its development through instruction. *School Psychology Review, 26*(3), 448–466.

Pressley, M., Rankin, J., & Yokoi, L. (1996). A survey of instructional practices of primary teachers nominated as effective in promoting literacy. *The Elementary School Journal, 96*(4), 363–384. doi:10.1086/461834

Proctor, C.P., Carlo, M.S., August, D., & Snow, C.E. (2005). Native Spanish-speaking children reading in English: Toward a model of comprehension. *Journal of Educational Psychology, 97*(2), 246–256. doi:10.1037/0022-0663.97.2.246

Putnam, L.R., & Reutzel, R. (1997). Beginning reading methods: A review of the past. In W.M. Linek & E.G. Sturtevant (Eds.), *Exploring literacy* (19th yearbook of the College Reading Association, pp. 51–55). Carrollton, GA: College Reading Association.

Rankin, P.T. (1928). The importance of listening ability. *English Journal, 17*(8), 623–630. doi:10.2307/803100

Rasinski, T.V., & Hoffman, J.V. (2003). Oral reading in the school literacy curriculum. *Reading Research Quarterly, 38*(4), 510–522. doi:10.1598/RRQ.38.4.5

Rayner, K., Foorman, B.R., Perfetti, C.A., Pesetsky, D., & Seidenberg, M.S. (2001). How psychological science informs the teaching of reading. *Psychological Science in the Public Interest, 2*, 31–74.

Rayner, K., & Pollatsek, A. (1989). *The psychology of reading.* Hillsdale, NJ. Erlbaum.

Reinking, D. (1997). Me and my hypertext:) A multiple digression analysis of technology and literacy (sic). *The Reading Teacher, 50*(8), 626–643.

Reutzel, D.R., & Cooter, R.B. (2005). *The essentials of teaching children to read: What every teacher needs to know.* Upper Saddle River, NJ: Merrill/Prentice-Hall.

Reutzel, D.R., & Mitchell, J. (2005). High-stakes accountability themed issue: How did we get here from there? *The Reading Teacher, 58*(7), 606–609. doi:10.1598/RT.58.7.1

Riddle Buly, M., & Valencia, S.W. (2003). *Meeting the needs of failing readers: Cautions and considerations for state policy: An occasional paper.* Olympia: University of Washington Center for the Study of Teaching and Policy.

Robinson, R.D. (2005). *Readings in reading instruction: Its history, theory, and development.* Boston: Allyn & Bacon.

Roeber, E.D. (1995). *Critical issue: Reporting assessment results.* North Central Regional Educational Laboratory. Retrieved May 24, 2007, from www.ncrel.org/sdrs/areas/issues/methods/assment/as600.htm

Rosemary, C.A., Roskos, K.A., & Landreth, L.K. (2007). *Designing professional development in literacy: A framework for effective instruction.* New York: Guilford.

Rosenblatt, L.M. (1969). Towards a transactional theory of reading. *Journal of Reading Behavior, 1*(1), 31–51.

Routman, R. (2003). *Reading essentials: The specifics you need to teach reading well.* Portsmouth, NH: Heinemann.

Ruddell, R.B., & Haggard, M.R. (1985). Oral and written language acquisition and the reading process. In H. Singer & R.B. Ruddell (Eds.), *Theoretical models and processes of reading* (3rd ed., pp. 63–80). Newark, DE: International Reading Association.

Ruddell, R.B., & Ruddell, M.R. (1994). Preface. In R.B. Ruddell, M.R. Ruddell, & H. Singer (Eds.), *Theoretical models and processes of reading* (4th ed., pp. xiv–xvi). Newark, DE: International Reading Association.

Ruddell, R.B., Ruddell, M.R., & Singer, H. (Eds.). (1994). *Theoretical models and processes of reading* (4th ed.). Newark, DE: International Reading Association.

Ruddell, R.B., & Unrau, N.J. (1994). Reading as a meaning-construction process: The reader, the text, and the teacher. In R.B. Ruddell, M.R. Ruddell, & H. Singer (Eds.), *Theoretical models and processes of reading* (4th ed., pp. 996–1056). Newark, DE: International Reading Association.

Ruddell, R.B., & Unrau, N.J. (Eds.). (2004). *Theoretical models and processes of reading* (5th ed.). Newark, DE: International Reading Association.

Rumelhart, D.E. (1985). Toward an interactive model of reading. In H. Singer & R.B. Ruddell (Eds.), *Theoretical models and processes of reading* (3rd ed., pp. 722–750). Newark, DE: International Reading Association.

Russell, D.H. (1961). Reading research that makes a difference. *Elementary English, 38*, 74–78.

Salerno, C. (1995). The effect of time on computer-assisted instruction for at-risk students. *Journal of Research on Computing in Education, 28*(1), 85–97.

Samuels, S.J. (1985). Automaticity and repeated reading. In J. Osborn, P.T. Wilson, & R.C. Anderson (Eds.), *Reading education: Foundations for a literate America* (pp. 215–230). Lexington, MA: Lexington Books.

Sanacore, J. (2002). Struggling literacy learners benefit from lifetime literacy efforts. *Reading Psychology, 23*(2), 67–86. doi:10.1080/027027102760351007

Sanders, W.L., & Rivers, J.C. (1996). *Cumulative and residual effects of teachers on future student academic achievement: Research progress report.* Knoxville, TN: University of Tennessee, Value-Added Research and Assessment Center. Retrieved August 5, 2008, from www.heartland.org/pdf/21803a.pdf

Saville-Troike, M. (1978). *A guide to culture in the classroom.* Arlington, VA: National Clearinghouse for Bilingual Education.

Sawyer, D.J. (1992). Language abilities, reading acquisition, and developmental dyslexia: A discussion of hypothetical and observed relationships. *Journal of Learning Disabilities, 25*(2), 82–95.

Schrum, L. (Ed.). (2005). Editor's introduction. *Journal of Research on Technology in Education, 38*(1), 113.

Schulte, L., Edick, N., Edwards, S., & Mackiel, D. (2004, Winter). The development and validation of the Teacher Disposition Index. *Essays in Education, 12.* Retrieved May 11, 2006, from www.usca.edu/essays/vol122004/schulte.pdf

Schumm, J.S. (Ed.). (2006). *Reading assessment and instruction for all learners.* New York: Guilford.

Schumm, J.S., & Arguelles, M.E. (2006). No two learners are alike: The importance of assessment and differentiated instruction. In Schumm, J.S. (Ed.), *Reading assessment and instruction for all learners* (pp. 27–59). New York: Guilford.

Schunk, D.H. (2003). Self-efficacy for reading and writing: Influence of modeling, goal setting, and self-evaluation. *Reading & Writing Quarterly, 19*(2), 159–172. doi:10.1080/10573560308219

Scribner, S., & Cole, M. (1978). Literacy without schooling: Testing for intellectual effects. *Harvard Educational Review, 48*(4), 448–461.

Serafini, F. (2000/2001). Three paradigms of assessment: Measurement, procedure, and inquiry. *The Reading Teacher, 54*(4), 384–393.

Shah, N., & deLuzuriaga, T. (2007, May 25). Despite mistakes, FCAT not going away. *The Miami Herald,* pp. 1B, 2B.

Shanahan, T. (2000). Research synthesis: Making sense of the accumulation of knowledge in reading. In M.L. Kamil, P.B. Mosenthal, P.D. Pearson, & R. Barr (Eds.), *Handbook of reading research* (Vol. 3, pp. 209–226). Mahwah, NJ: Erlbaum.

Shanahan, T. (2003). Research-based reading instruction: Myths about the National Reading Panel report. *The Reading Teacher, 56*(7), 646–654.

Shanahan, T., & Neuman, S.B. (1997). Literacy research that makes a difference. *Reading Research Quarterly, 32*(2), 202–210.

Share, D., Jorm, A., Maclean, R., & Matthews, R. (1984). Sources of individual differences in reading acquisition. *Journal of Educational Psychology, 76*(6), 1309–1324. doi:10.1037/0022-0663.76.6.1309

Sharif, I., Ozuah, P.O., Dinkevich, E.I., & Mulvihill, M. (2003, March). Impact of a brief literacy intervention on urban preschoolers. *Early Childhood Education Journal, 30*(3), 177–180. doi:10.1023/A:1022018006701

Shavelson, R.J., & Towne, L. (Eds.). (2002). *Scientific research in education.* Washington, DC: National Academies Press.

Shea, M., Murray, R., & Harlin, R. (2005). *Drowing in data? How to collect, organize, and document student performance.* Portsmouth, NH: Heinemann.

Shepard, L.A. (1989). Why we need better assessments. *Educational Leadership, 46*(7), 4–9.

Shepard, L.A. (2001). The role of classroom assessment in teaching and learning. In V. Richardson (Ed.), *Handbook of research on teaching* (4th ed., pp. 1066–1101). Washington, DC: American Educational Research Association.

Showers, B., & Joyce, B. (1996). The evolution of peer coaching. *Educational Leadership, 53*(6), 5–9.

Shulman, J.H. (1992). *Case methods in teacher education.* New York: Teachers College Press.

Shulman, J.H. (2000). *Case methods as a bridge between standards and classroom practice.* Washington, DC: National Partnership for Excellence and Accountability in Teaching. (ERIC Document Reproduction Service No. 452188)

Shulman, L.S. (1988). A union of insufficiencies: Strategies for teacher assessment in a period of educational reform. *Educational Leadership, 46*(3), 36–43.

Siegel, L.S. (1989). Why we do not need intelligence scores in the definition and analysis of learning disabilities. *Journal of Learning Disabilities, 22*(8), 514–518.

Silverman, R., & Welty, W.M. (1994). *Case studies in diversity for university faculty development.* New York: Pace University Center for Case Studies in Education.

Singer, H. (1970). Research that should have made a difference. *Elementary English, 47*(1), 27–34.

Singer, H. (1978). Research in reading that should make a difference in classroom instruction. In S.J. Samuels (Ed.), *What research has to say about reading instruction* (pp. 55–71). Newark, DE: International Reading Association.

Singer, H., & Ruddell, R.B. (Eds.). (1985). *Theoretical models and processes of reading* (3rd ed.). Newark, DE: International Reading Association.

Sipe, L.R. (2000). The construction of literary understanding by first and second graders in oral response to picture storybook read-alouds. *Reading Research Quarterly, 35*(2), 252–275. doi:10.1598/RRQ.35.2.4

Skinner, B.F. (1957). *Verbal behavior.* Acton, MA: Copley.

Skinner, B.F. (1976). *About behaviorism.* New York: Vintage.

Slavin, R.E., Madden, N.A., Karweit, N.L., Dolan, L.J., & Wasik, B.A. (1994). Success for all: Getting reading right the first time. In E.H. Hiebert & B.M. Taylor (Eds.), *Getting reading right from the start: Effective early literacy interventions* (pp. 125–148). Boston: Allyn & Bacon.

Slavin, R.E. (2002). Evidence-based education policies: Transforming educational practice and research. *Educational Researcher, 31*(7), 15–21. doi:10.3102/0013189X031007015

Smith, F. (1971). *Understanding reading.* New York: Holt, Rinehart and Winston.

Smith, F. (1994). *Understanding reading* (5th ed.). Hillsdale, NJ: Erlbaum.

Smith, J.A. (2000). Singing and songwriting support early literacy instruction. *The Reading Teacher, 53*(8), 646–651.

Smith, N.B. (2002). *American reading instruction* (Special ed.). Newark, DE: International Reading Association. (Original work published 1934)

Smolin, L.I., & Lawless, K.A. (2003). Becoming literate in the technological age: New responsibilities and tools for teachers. *The Reading Teacher, 56*(6), 570–577.

Snow, C.E. (2002). *Reading for understanding: Toward an R & D program in reading comprehension.* Santa Monica, CA: RAND.

Snow, C.E. (2004). Foreword. In P. McCardle & V. Chhabra (Eds.), *The voice of evidence in reading research* (pp. xix–xxv). Baltimore: Paul H. Brookes.

Snow, C.E., Barnes, W.S., Chandler, J., Goodman, I.F., & Hemphill, L. (1991). *Unfulfilled expectation: Home and school influences on literacy.* Cambridge, MA: Harvard University Press.

Snow, C.E., Burns, M.S., & Griffin, P. (Eds.). (1998). *Preventing reading difficulties in young children.* Washington, DC: National Academies Press.

Snow, C.E., Griffin, P., & Burns M.S. (Eds.). (2005). *Knowledge to support the teaching of reading.* San Francisco: Jossey-Bass.

Sonnenschein, S., Brody, G., & Munsterman, K. (1996). The influence of family beliefs and practices on children's early reading development. In L. Baker, P. Afflerbach, & D. Reinking (Eds.), *Developing engaged readers in school and home communities* (pp. 3–20). Mahwah, NJ: Erlbaum.

Sparapani, E.F., Abel, F.J., Edwards, P.A., Herbster, D.L., & Easton, S.E. (1997, February). *Portfolios: Authentically assessing the diversity of instructional practices*. Paper presented at the 77th Annual Meeting of the Association of Teacher Educators, Washington, DC. (ERIC Document Reproduction Service No. ED406337)

Spear-Swerling, L., & Sternberg, R.J. (1997). *Off track: When poor readers become "learning disabled."* Boulder, CO: Westview.

Spear-Swerling, L., & Sternberg, R.J. (2001). What science offers teachers of reading. *Learning Disabilities Research & Practice, 16*(1), 51–57. doi:10.1111/0938-8982.00006

Spiegel, D.L. (1994). A portrait of parents of successful readers. In E.H. Cramer & M. Castle (Eds.), *Fostering the love of reading: The affective domain in reading education* (pp. 74–87). Newark, DE: International Reading Association.

Spiegel, D.L. (1999). Meeting each child's literacy needs. In L. Gambrell, L. Morrow, S. Neuman, & M. Pressley (Eds.), *Best practices for literacy instruction* (pp. 245–257). New York: Guilford.

Spradley, J.P. (1980). *Participant observation*. New York: Holt, Rinehart and Winston.

Stage, S.A., Abbott, R.D., Jenkins, J.R., & Berninger, V.W. (2003). Predicting response to early reading intervention from verbal IQ, reading-related language abilities, attention ratings, and verbal IQ-word reading discrepancy: Failure to validate discrepancy method. *Journal of Learning Disabilities, 36*(1), 24–33. doi:10.1177/00222194030360010401

Stahl, N.A., King, J.R., Dillon, D., & Walker, J.R. (1994). The roots of reading: Preserving the heritage of a profession through oral history projects. In E.G. Sturtevant & W.M. Linek (Eds.), *Pathways for literacy: Learners teach and teachers learn* (16th yearbook of the College Reading Association, pp. 15–24). Commerce, TX: College Reading Association.

Stahl, S.A. (2003). What do we expect storybook reading to do? How storybook reading impacts word recognition. In A. van Kleeck, S.A. Stahl, & E.B. Bauer (Eds.), *On reading books to children: Parents and teachers* (pp. 363–383). Mahwah, NJ: Erlbaum.

Stahl, S.A., Duffy-Hester, A.M., & Stahl, K.A.D. (1998). Everything you wanted to know about phonics (but were afraid to ask). *Reading Research Quarterly, 33*(3), 338–355. doi:10.1598/RRQ.33.3.5

Stahl, S.A., & Fairbanks, M.M. (1986). The effects of vocabulary instruction: A model-based meta-analysis. *Review of Educational Research, 56*(1), 72–110.

Staiger, R.C. (1985). Foreword. In H. Singer & R.B. Ruddell (Eds.), *Theoretical models and processes of reading* (3rd ed., p. vi). Newark, DE: International Reading Association.

Stanford, M.J., Crookston, R.K., Davis, D.W., & Simmons, S.R. (1992). *Decision cases for agriculture*. St. Paul: University of Minnesota College of Agriculture.

Stanovich, K.E. (1980). Towards an interactive-compensatory model of individual differences in the development of reading fluency. *Reading Research Quarterly, 16*(1), 32–71. doi:10.2307/747348

Stanovich, K.E. (1986). Matthew effects in reading: Some consequences of individual differences in the acquisition of literacy. *Reading Research Quarterly, 21*(4), 360–407. doi:10.1598/RRQ.21.4.1

Stanovich, K.E. (1991). Conceptual and empirical problems with discrepancy definitions of reading disability. *Learning Disability Quarterly, 14*(4), 269–280. doi:10.2307/1510663

Stanovich, K.E. (2000). *Progress in understanding reading: Scientific foundations and new frontiers*. New York: Guilford.

Stanovich, K.E., Cunningham, A.E., & West, R.F. (1998). Literacy experiences and the shaping of cognition. In S.G. Paris & H.M. Wellman (Eds.), *Global prospects for education: Development, culture, and schooling* (pp. 253–288). Washington, DC: American Psychological Association.

Stanovich, P.J., & Stanovich, K.E. (2003). *Using research and reason in education: How teachers can use scientifically based research to make curricular & instructional decisions*. Washington, DC: U.S. Department of Education.

Staples, A., Pugach, M.C., & Himes, D. (2005). Rethinking the technology integration challenge: Cases from three urban elementary schools. *Journal of Research on Technology in Education, 37*(3), 285–312.

Stoicheva, M. (1999). Balanced reading instruction. *Eric Digest* (DE 0-CS-99-05). Retrieved October 14, 2006, from www.indiana.edu/~reading/ieo/digests/d144.html

Strecker, S.K., Roser, N.L., & Martinez, M.G. (1998). *Toward understanding oral reading fluency* (47th yearbook of the National Reading Conference, pp. 295–310). Chicago: National Reading Conference.

Stronge, J.H. (2007). *Qualities of effective teachers* (2nd ed.). Alexandria, VA: Association for Supervision and Curriculum Development.

Swanson, H.L., & Hoskyn, M. (1998). Experimental intervention research on students with learning disabilities: A meta-analysis of treatment outcomes. *Review of Educational Research, 68*(3), 277–321.

Swanson, H.L., Hoskyn, M., & Lee, C. (1999). *Interventions for students with learning disabilities: A meta-analysis of treatment outcomes.* New York: Guilford.

Taberski, S. (2000). *On solid ground: Strategies for teaching reading K–3.* Portsmouth, NH: Heinemann.

Talbott, E., Lloyd, J.W., & Tankersley, M. (1994). Effects of reading comprehension interventions for students with learning disabilities. *Learning Disability Quarterly, 17*(3), 223–232. doi:10.2307/1511075

Taylor, B.M., Pearson, P.D., Clark, K.F., & Walpole, S. (1999a). Effective schools/accomplished teachers. *The Reading Teacher, 53*(2), 156–159.

Taylor, B.M., Pearson, P.D., Clark, K.F., & Walpole, S. (1999b). *Beating the odds in teaching all children to read* (Report #2–006). Ann Arbor: Center for the Improvement of Early Reading Achievement, University of Michigan.

Taylor, N.E., Blum, I., & Logsdon, D.M. (1986). The development of written language awareness: Environmental aspects and program characteristics. *Reading Research Quarterly, 21*(2), 132–149. doi:10.2307/747841

Teale, W.H. (1986). Home background and young children's literacy development. In W.H. Teale & E. Sulzby (Eds.), *Emergent literacy: Writing and reading* (pp. 173–206). Norwood, NJ: Ablex.

Teale, W.H. (2003). Reading aloud to young children as a classroom instructional activity: Insights from research and practice. In A. van Kleeck, S.A. Stahl, & E.B. Bauer (Eds.), *On reading books to children: Parents and teachers* (pp. 114–139). Mahwah, NJ: Erlbaum.

Teale, W.H., Leu, D.J., Jr., Labbo, L.D., & Kinzer, C.K. (2002). The CTELL project: New ways technology can help educate tomorrow's teachers of reading. *The Reading Teacher, 55*(7), 654–659.

Tellez, K. (1996). Authentic assessment. In J. Sikula (Ed.), *Handbook of research on teacher education* (pp. 704–721). New York: Macmillan.

Temple, C., Ogle, D., Crawford, A., & Freppon, P. (2005). *All children read: Teaching for literacy in today's diverse classrooms.* Boston: Pearson Education.

Thomas, C. (2000). From engagement to celebration: A framework for passionate reading. *Voices From the Middle, 8*(2), 16–25.

Thomas, R.M. (2005). *High-stakes testing: Coping with collateral damage.* Mahwah, NJ: Erlbaum.

Thompson, C.L., & Zeuli, J.S. (1999). The frame and tapestry: Standards-based reform and professional development. In L. Darling-Hammond & G. Sykes (Eds.), *Teaching as the learning profession: Handbook of policy and practice* (pp. 341–375). San Francisco: Jossey-Bass.

Thurlow, M.L., Elliott, J.L., & Ysseldyke, J.E. (2003). *Testing students with disabilities: Practical strategies for complying with district and state requirements* (2nd ed.). Thousand Oaks, CA: Corwin.

Tierney, R.J., Carter, M.A., & Desai, L.E. (1991). *Portfolio assessment in the reading/writing classroom.* Norwood, MA: Christopher-Gordon.

Tomlinson, C.A. (2003). *How to differentiate instruction in mixed ability classrooms* (3rd ed.). Alexandria, VA: Association for Supervision and Curriculum Development.

Trabasso, T., & Bouchard, E. (2002). Teaching readers how to comprehend text strategically. In C.C. Block & M. Pressley (Eds.), *Comprehension instruction: Research-based best practices* (pp. 176–200). New York: Guilford.

Trelease, J. (1995). *The read-aloud handbook.* New York: Penguin.

Trotter, A. (2007). Funding level divides legislature and districts. *Education Week, 26*(41), 21–26.

Tunnell, M.O., & Jacobs, J.S. (2007). *Children's literature, briefly* (4th ed.). Upper Saddle River, NJ: Pearson Merrill Prentice Hall.

Turbill, J. (2002). The four ages of reading philosophy and pedagogy: A framework for examining theory and practice. *Reading Online.* Retrieved June 15, 2007, from www.readingonline.org/international/inter_index.asp?HREF=turbill4/index.html

U.S. Department of Education. (2000). *To assure the free appropriate public education of all children with disabilities* (Individuals with Disabilities Education Act, Section 618). *The twenty-fourth annual report to*

Congress on the implementation of the Individuals with Disabilities Education Act, 2002. Washington DC: U.S. Government Printing Office.

U.S. Department of Education. (2003). *Guidance on constitutionally protected prayer in public elementary and secondary schools.* Retrieved November 11, 2007, from www.ed.gov/policy/gen/guid/religionandschools/prayer_guidance.html

Usher, L., Usher, M., & Usher, D. (2003, November). *Nurturing five dispositions of effective teachers.* Paper presented at the Second Annual National Symposium on Educator Dispositions, Richmond, KY.

Vacca, J.L., Vacca, R.T., Gove, M.K., Burkey, L.C., Lenhart, L.A., & McKeon, C.A. (2005). *Reading and learning to read* (6th ed.). Boston: Allyn & Bacon.

Vaishali, H. (2007). Accords designed to turn around troubled schools. *Education Week, 26*(41), 1–15.

Valencia, R.R., & Villarreal, B.J. (2003). Improving students' reading performance via standards-based school reform: A critique. *The Reading Teacher, 56*(7), 612–621.

Valencia, S.W. (1990). Alternative assessment: Separating the wheat from the chaff. *The Reading Teacher, 44*(1), 60–61.

Valencia, S.W., & Riddle Buly, M. (2004). Behind test scores: What struggling readers *really* need. *The Reading Teacher, 57*(6), 520–531.

Vaughn, S., Bos, C.S., & Schumm, J.S. (2007). *Teaching exceptional, diverse, and at-risk learners in the general education classroom* (4th ed.). Boston: Allyn & Bacon.

Vaughn, S., & Dammann, J.E. (2001). Science and sanity in special education. *Behavioral Disorders, 27*(1), 21–29.

Vaughn, S., Hughes, M.T., Moody, S.W., & Elbaum, B.E. (2001). Instructional grouping for reading for students with LD: Implications for practice. *Intervention in School and Clinic, 36*(3), 131–137. doi:10.1177/105345120103600301

Vellutino, F.R., Scanlon, D.M., & Lyon, R.G. (2000). Differentiating between difficult-to-remediate and readily remediated poor readers: more evidence against the IQ-achievement discrepancy definition of reading disability. *Journal of Learning Disabilities, 33*(3), 223–238. doi:10.1177/002221940003300302

Vellutino, F.R., Scanlon, D.M., Sipay, E.R., Small, S.G., Pratt, A., Chen, R., et al. (1996). Cognitive profiles of difficult-to-remediate and readily remediated poor readers: Early intervention as a vehicle for distinguishing between cognitive and experiential deficits as basic causes of specific reading disability. *Journal of Educational Psychology, 88*(4), 601–638. doi:10.1037/0022-0663.88.4.601

Venezky, R.L. (1984). The history of reading research. In P.D. Pearson, R. Barr, M.L. Kamil, & P.B. Mosenthal (Eds.), *Handbook of reading research* (pp. 3–38). New York: Longman.

Verhoeven, L., & Snow, C. (2001). Introduction: Literacy and motivation. In L. Verhoeven & C. Snow (Eds.), *Literacy and motivation: Reading engagement in individuals and groups* (pp. 1–20). Mahwah, NJ: Erlbaum.

Vygotsky, L.S. (1978). *Mind in society: The development of higher psychological processes* (M. Cole, V. John-Steiner, S. Scribner, & E. Souberman, Eds. & Trans.). Cambridge, MA: Harvard University Press.

Waiscko, M. (2004). The 20-minute hiring assessment. *School Administrator, 61*(9), 40–42.

Walpole, S., & McKenna, M.C. (2004). *The literacy coach's handbook: A guide to research-based practice.* New York: Guilford.

Walpole, S., & McKenna, M.C. (2007). *Differentiated reading instruction: Strategies for the primary grades.* New York: Guilford.

Walsh, K., Glaser, D., & Dunne Wilcox, D. (2006). *What education schools aren't teaching about reading and what elementary teachers aren't learning.* Washington, DC: National Council on Teacher Quality. Retrieved August 6, 2008, from www.readingrockets.org/article/12625

Wardhaugh, R. (1969). *Reading: A linguistic perspective.* New York: Harcourt, Brace and World.

Watson, J.B. (1913). Psychology as the behaviourist views it. *Psychological Review, 20*(2), 158–177. doi:10.1037/h0074428

Watson, P.A., & Lacina, J.G. (2004). Lessons learned from integrating technology in a writer's workshop. *Voices From the Middle, 11*(3), 38–44.

Weber, R. (2000). Linguistic diversity and reading in American society. In R. Barr, M.L. Kamil, P.B. Mosenthal, & P.D. Pearson (Eds.), *Handbook of reading research* (Vol. 2, pp. 97–119). New York: Longman.

Wharton-McDonald, R., Pressley, M., Rankin, J., Mistretta, J., & Ettenberger, S. (1997). Effective primary-grades literacy instruction = Balanced literacy instruction. *The Reading Teacher, 50*(6), 518–521.

Whipple, G.M. (Ed.). (1925). *Report of the National Comittee on Reading* (24th yearbook of the National Society for the Study of Education). Bloomington, IL: Public School Publishing.

Wiggins, G. (1989). Teaching to the (authentic) test. *Educational Leadership, 46*(7), 41–47.

Wiggins, G. (1998). *Educative assessment: Designing assessments to inform and improve student performance.* San Francisco: Jossey-Bass.

Wilson, P., Martens, P., & Arya, P. (2005). Accountability for reading and readers: What the numbers don't tell. *The Reading Teacher, 58*(7), 622–631. doi:10.1598/RT.58.7.3

Wilson, R.M., & Hall, M.A. (1972). *Reading and the elementary school child; Theory and practice for teachers* New York: Van Nostrand Reinhold.

Wilson, S., Schulman, L., & Richert, P. (1987). "150 different ways" of knowing: Representations of knowledge in teaching. In J. Calderhead (Ed.), *Exploring teachers' thinking* (pp. 104–124). London: Cassell.

Winn, D. (1988). Develop listening skills as a part of the curriculum. *The Reading Teacher, 42*(2), 144–146.

Winn, D., & Mitchell, J. (1991). Improving reading instruction through staff development. *Reading Improvement, 28*(2), 82–88.

Wolf, D.P. (1989). Portfolio assessment: Sampling student work. *Educational Leadership, 46*(7), 35–39.

Wolf, M., & Katzir-Cohen, T. (2001). Reading fluency and its intervention. *Scientific Studies of Reading, 5*(3), 211–238. doi:10.1207/S1532799XSSR0503_2

Wolfersberger, M.E., Reutzel, D.R., Sudweeks, R., & Fawson, P.C. (2004). Developing and validating the classroom literacy environmental profile (CLEP): A tool for examining the "print richness" of early childhood and elementary classrooms. *Journal of Literacy Research, 36*(2), 211–272.

Womble, S.N. (2006). The leadership role of administrators in the era of No Child Left Behind. In C. Cummins (Ed.), *Understanding and implementing Reading First initiatives: The changing role of administrators* (pp. 7–17). Newark, DE: International Reading Association.

Wood, D.E. (2006). Modeling the relationship between oral reading fluency and performance on a statewide reading test. *Educational Assessment, 11*(2), 85–104. doi:10.1207/s15326977ea1102_1

Wood, J.W. (2006). *Teaching students in inclusive settings: Adapting and accommodating instruction* (5th ed.) Upper Saddle River, NJ: Pearson Merrill Prentice Hall.

Wormeli, R. (2006). *Fair isn't always equal: Assessing and grading in the differentiated classroom.* Portland, ME: Stenhouse.

Ysseldyke, J.E., & Olsen, K. (1997). *Putting alternate assessments into practice: What to measure and possible sources of data* (Synthesis Report 28). Minneapolis: University of Minnesota, National Center on Educational Outcomes.

INDEX

Note. Page numbers followed by *f* or *t* indicate figures or tables, respectively.